Day 1 of the 107 Days.

KAMALA

107 DAYS

HARRIS

SIMON & SCHUSTER

* * *

New York Amsterdam/Antwerp London
Toronto Sydney/Melbourne New Delhi

Simon & Schuster
1230 Avenue of the Americas
New York, NY 10020

First Simon & Schuster hardcover edition September 2025

SIMON & SCHUSTER and colophon are registered trademarks of Simon & Schuster, LLC

Interior design by Lewelin Polanco

Manufactured in the United States of America

1 3 5 7 9 10 8 6 4 2

Library of Congress Control Number has been applied for.

ISBN 978-1-6682-1165-6
ISBN 978-1-6682-1167-0 (ebook)

PHOTO INSERT CREDITS
1, 2: Courtesy of Kamala Harris; 3–50: Official White House Photo

To my team.
From the beginning, and through the joy, pain,
and personal sacrifice, you left it all on the field.
I am forever grateful.

The amount of energy necessary to refute bullshit is an order of magnitude bigger than to produce it.

I got loyalty, got royalty inside my DNA

. . . .

I was born like this.

—KENDRICK LAMAR, "DNA"

107 DAYS

107 Days to the Election

* * *

"Auntie! Auntie!"

A small fist rapped gently on my bedroom door.

I rolled over and reached for my phone. Amara had kept to our deal. It was exactly 7:30 a.m., and my grandniece had waited patiently to wake me at the agreed hour for our promised Sunday pancakes.

I'd flown in late the night before from a campaign event of a thousand people at a packed hall in Provincetown, Massachusetts. Organizers had made a huge-lettered, rainbow-colored sign, VPTOWN, for my event, but there was both energy and tension in the crowd. Joe Biden's debate with Donald Trump, three weeks earlier, had thrown the campaign into chaos, and I'd had to fend off supporters' anxious questions.

I threw on sweatpants and an old Howard University sweatshirt and pulled up my hair in a ponytail. I'd promised bacon and sausage with the pancakes, but before that I needed my half hour on the elliptical.

I'd stopped watching the Sunday-morning shows: no more endless rhetoric about the president's capability. I turned on the cooking channel. The chef was making an elaborate dessert, which captivated Amara, eight, and her sister, Leela, six.

The girls had spent the week with me at the vice president's residence—the sprawling Queen Anne–style house on the grounds of Washington's Naval Observatory. They'd be leaving that afternoon, heading back to Palo Alto, California, ahead of the new school year. After breakfast and a wash of greasy hands, we sat on the rug by the coffee table to do a big jigsaw puzzle together while their mom, my niece, and their dad went upstairs to pack.

And that's where I was when my secure phone rang, at eleven minutes past one.

I glanced at the screen. Caller ID blocked. Only about a dozen people had my secure number. Of those few, only one came up blocked. I unfolded my legs, stood up, and walked around the corner to my office.

"Hi, Joe," I said.

"I need to talk to you." He was calling from his home in Rehoboth Beach, Delaware, where he'd gone to isolate after testing positive for Covid four days earlier. His voice sounded hoarse, exhausted. "I've decided I'm dropping out."

"Are you sure?"

"I'm sure. I'm going to announce in a few minutes."

"Why today?"

"It's the only thing anyone is talking about. And it's too much. There's going to be another letter from Democratic members of Congress on Monday. It's too much."

Really? Give me a bit more time. The whole world is about to change. I'm here in sweatpants, and the two people staffing me right now are under four feet tall.

I put the phone on mute and went back to Amara and Leela. Eyes wide, eyebrows raised, voice urgent: "Go get your parents!"

My husband, Doug, was in Los Angeles, trapped by the global CrowdStrike software glitch that had grounded many flights. My sister, Maya, was in New York. I needed to start alerting the family before this story broke.

The president was still talking. "I want you to do this." He would endorse me, he said, but not for a day, maybe two, when he would make an address to the nation.

That would be ruinous, and I said so.

"Joe, I'm honored, but we live in a twenty-four-hour news cycle, and if you wait that long, the airwaves will be full of nothing but questions: 'Why has he not supported his VP?' If you want to put me in the strongest position, you have to endorse me now." I urged him to reconsider the timing. "What we do, right now, is so important," I said. "People will look at how this moment occurred for decades. There's no reason to rush this. Can we slow it down so I can prepare? And you need to endorse me at the same time. Any gap between the announcement and the endorsement will lead to the same kind of chaos we've had for the last three weeks."

The public statements, the whispering campaigns, and the speculation had done a world of damage. I knew I was the candidate in the strongest position to win. The most qualified and ready. The highest name recognition. A powerful donor base. And I also knew, as he did, that I was the only person who would preserve his legacy. At this point, anyone else was bound to throw him—and all the good he had achieved—right under the bus.

Joe's two closest aides, Steve Ricchetti and Mike Donilon, were in the room with him in Rehoboth. He put Ricchetti on the phone. "We were always going to support you. We just want to do this announcement first and leave a little bit of time."

"Steve, you know that's not going to work," I said. "There needs to be no daylight between the announcements."

"That's a fair point," Steve conceded. He gave the phone back to the president.

Joe said, "Let me call you back."

I waited, hoping I'd convinced them to avoid more turmoil and speculation. He'd resisted this decision for weeks, adamantly ignoring a drumbeat that had ranged from solicitous advice to intense condemnation.

Amid all that cacophony, Joe had said nothing to me about this, until July 15. It was two days after the first assassination attempt on Donald Trump. We were in the Situation Room, at a briefing on the investigation into the shooting. Joe was at the head of the table, as always. I sat to his right. As the meeting concluded, the president thanked everyone and rose to leave. I'm a stickler for protocol, as I believe everyone at the White House should be. I sit only after the president sits, stand when he stands. As everyone else began to file out, Joe turned to me. "Do you have a minute, can you stay?"

Soon we were alone, dwarfed by the long table at which so many momentous decisions had been made. The screens on the walls had all gone dark, except for the red digital clocks showing the time in current conflict zones.

"If for any reason I had to drop out, I would support you, but only if that's what you want. It's occurred to me I haven't asked you." He'd clearly rehearsed this speech, it wasn't a spontaneous thought, and it was the first time I knew he was seriously considering it.

The calls for him to drop out, he said, would probably continue. People were throwing his own words back at him, that he had said he would be a transitional leader.

"I'm fully behind you, Joe," I told him. "But if you decide not to run, I'm ready. And I would give it all I've got, because Trump has to be beaten."

There had been no follow-up discussion. In our relationship, it was common for him to test out ideas on me, and until he decided, I had no reason to believe it would actually happen. All his public statements remained defiant declarations that only "the Lord Almighty" could make him drop out. Then he came down with Covid.

But still, no word. As nearly a week passed, I had come to accept the inevitability that he was staying in the race, that the time for him to make a different decision had passed.

Now here he was, on the phone, telling me otherwise.

131 Days to the Election

* * *

As soon as he walked onto the debate stage in Atlanta, I could see he wasn't right. He'd had neuropathy in his feet for years. Then he'd fractured his foot playing with one of his dogs. His doctor had prescribed a boot, but he was too stubborn to wear it, and I'm positive that screwed up his gait. Now he walked unsteadily, trying to balance himself with robotically moving hands.

He'd called me a couple of days earlier from Camp David, where he was in the middle of debate prep. It was late afternoon, and I'd been working from home in Los Angeles. I pulled up a chair overlooking our backyard.

"How's it going?" I asked.

"It's going. It's okay." He sounded downbeat and extremely tired. He didn't mention that he was coming down with a cold.

"Are you getting some rest? You need to take a break, you know."

Debate camp is awful. They break you to make you. They prod at all your missteps, all your weaknesses; find holes in your arguments; savage your delivery. It leaves you feeling barely competent. From there, they build you back up, running through every possible line of attack until you feel invulnerable. With the debate fast approaching, Joe should have been in that second phase. By the time he made that call to me, he should have been more upbeat. But he didn't sound that way, and it worried me.

I reminded him about the tactics we'd previously discussed in dealing with Trump: alternate brushing him off like lint on your shoulder or striking back aggressively. His voice lightened as he recalled how his mother had once promised him a quarter if he went back and punched the bully who'd been picking on him. He did, and she gave him fifty cents. Telling the story seemed to put him in better spirits, so I wished him luck and, trying to buck him up, told him he was going to kill it. I hung up feeling sorry for him. I knew he didn't want to do this debate, and it seemed like he just needed to talk to someone who would understand what it feels like, what it would take.

Within the campaign, there'd been a whole debate about whether he *should* debate. Joe had seemed reluctant from the start. Jill didn't seem to think he should, either. Trump's refusal to debate during his party's primary had cleared a plausible path for avoiding it. Nancy Pelosi, for one, argued that Biden didn't need to lower the dignity of the presidency by appearing onstage with a convicted felon who'd tried to subvert the last election. But some of his most trusted advisers were insistent that this would be the split-screen moment he needed. The campaign was stuck, fighting with Trump for the same limited pool of disengaged or undecided voters.

Doubts about Biden's age and capacity had been fueled by the report of Special Counsel Robert Hur on his retention of classified documents. Hur had concluded that he couldn't get a conviction because a jury would perceive Biden as a "well-meaning, elderly man with a poor memory." The report had detailed concerning lapses. I knew very well that when he was tired, his age showed, and I also knew that depositions can be grueling. And this one began October 8, the morning after Hamas had viciously attacked Israel, when Biden had spent long hours in classified meetings, monitoring the crisis. He would have had the weight of those events, still very much in flux and threatening regional war, on his mind. Trump's ravings had been getting progressively crazier as the campaign went on. If Biden had lost a step, Trump had, too.

Mike Donilon and Anita Dunn, another of Joe's senior advisers, had become convinced a debate at this relatively early stage could change the trajectory of the campaign. (And so it did, just not in the way they had anticipated.) These decisions were being made by his inner team, and in the end, I had to accept that they had convinced themselves that Biden could do this.

In 2012, after Barack Obama had flubbed his first debate against Mitt Romney, Biden, as vice president, had trounced Paul Ryan so badly that Sarah Palin said it reminded her of a musk ox running across the tundra with someone underfoot. The nation had just watched Biden deliver a stirring State of the Union address. Donilon and Dunn insisted that the president could do at least as well as he had against Trump in 2020.

I'd been campaigning on the West Coast in the days just before the debate—doing Spanish language press and outreach in Arizona, meeting major fundraisers in California, and attending gatherings with Black influencers in Los Angeles. That morning I'd met with the R&B superstar Usher to solidify his support on our common interest: unlocking credit for minority businesses. Then I'd taped a segment for the BET Awards, discussing issues from voting rights to abortion rights with the actress Taraji P. Henson, who gave an impassioned plea at the awards ceremony for awareness about the damaging contents of Project 2025.

In the evening, I gathered with just three of my staff to watch the debate in an overchilled conference room at the Fairmont hotel in Century City, Los Angeles. Other staffers watched in a room next door. They'd set up a tiny plate of crudités. I ordered pizza for everyone: it was going to be a long night. After the debate, I'd do a quick rallying call for campaign staff and volunteers across the country, followed by four television interviews back-to-back, immediately after Biden walked off the debate stage in Atlanta. The networks had a studio set up, ready for those live hits.

I knew there'd be something to clean up. There is always some small misstatement of fact or gaffe of some kind. Every debate has them. But because of that call from Camp David, I had a gnawing feeling about the night.

That's why the people in the room with me were the ones I trusted most. I knew I could be completely frank with them as the debate progressed. Brian Fallon, one of my senior advisers, was a seasoned media hand known for not pulling punches. While running a nonprofit dedicated to reforming the way judges are appointed, he'd given his former boss, Chuck Schumer, a C rating. Brian had concluded, earlier than most political operatives, that Trump was different in kind, not just degree. This was not business as usual—Trump was not an ordinary politician; MAGA was not a typical party. He brought a fighter's mentality to the job.

Sheila Nix, my campaign chief of staff, had come to DC from law school to work at a law firm, been recruited to help with Senator Bob Kerrey's presidential campaign, and loved every minute. Since then, she'd toggled between campaign work and issue-driven jobs, like working for Bono on poverty in sub-Saharan Africa. She'd also worked as Jill Biden's chief of staff, so she had good relations with the Biden team.

The third person in the room was my director of comms, Kirsten Allen, a veteran of tight races and high-pressure situations. I'd spotted her in 2018, working for Andrew Gillum, when he lost the Florida governor's race to Ron DeSantis by a hair, in one of the closest gubernatorial races in history. She'd been my press secretary and special assistant to Joe Biden, and had been our national press secretary for the Covid response.

Jake Tapper's first question, predictably, was on the economy. Biden answered in a thready voice, rushing through his answer. There was no light in his eyes, no expression in his voice. *They've loaded him up with too many stats,* I thought, as he blurted out numbers. *The first question is always difficult. He needs to warm up. He'll settle down; he'll get on top of it.*

The next question was on the military. *He's got so much material on this—Trump calling our fallen soldiers "suckers and losers."* He managed to get off that line but had stepped on it earlier by saying no one had died in wars overseas on his watch, seeming to forget the thirteen marines who died in the bomb blast at the airport during the evacuation of Afghanistan. I'd been on Air Force Two when it happened, and we had to change our flight plan to get back to DC in the face of that tragedy. *How could he overlook that day? I know his deep feelings for those men and women. It's personal to him.*

Trump, meanwhile, was using his words like a weapon, but shooting before he aimed, spouting lies, unburdened by the truth. Biden, striving for accuracy, often stopped midsentence to correct himself, which left him sounding hesitant and garbled. I knew the important policy points he was struggling to convey, and I knew he knew them. He is a master of this material, but that was not coming across at all.

And then, at the end of a string of convoluted sentences in which he twice confused millions and billions, Joe lost his train of thought entirely, looked disoriented, and blurted out, "We finally beat Medicare."

Trump's reply: "Well, he's right. He did beat Medicare. He beat it to death."

As the ninety minutes ground on, my staffers watched with one eye on the big screen, the other on the small screens in their hands. They were tracking reactions on social media: "Disaster." "Train wreck." "Embarrassment." Kirsten and Sheila were texting each other: Are other people seeing what we're seeing? Is it as bad as we think?

Doug, at a watch party with Hollywood donors, was getting an earful. Rob Reiner had screamed at him: "We're going to lose our fucking democracy and it's your fault!"

During the final commercial break, I went to another room to quickly get makeup and hair touched up. Brian handed me the talking points the campaign had prepped. I glanced down at them.

"JOE BIDEN WON"—all caps, highlighted. "He fought through his cold as he is fighting for the American people."

Are you kidding me?

I threw the paper back on the table. Then Michael Tyler, Biden's campaign communications director, called from Atlanta with a similar account of what they expected me to say.

No. Don't feed me bullshit. Everyone saw what they saw.

I couldn't help but think of the Richard Pryor joke where his wife catches him in bed with another woman. "You gonna believe me or your lyin' eyes?" he says.

I was not about to tell the American people that their eyes had lied. I would not jeopardize my own credibility. This night had turned into a disaster, and I was fully aware of the importance of what I was to say. How we handled this, right now, would have a long-term political effect, not just for him but for me. I had to acknowledge what people saw and then try to give them a way to make sense of it.

I got on the phone for the previously scheduled call to the campaign staff and volunteers. I wanted to calm them down, but I needed to speak the truth. I told them that as the debate progressed you could see that Biden wanted to debate on facts, but Trump didn't. I read to them from the notes I'd scrawled on Trump's numerous lies.

It was just a few paces to the makeshift studio, but it felt like a death march. My staff crowded around me, stressed, knowing the weight I had to carry. Even in that dark room, I could see Brian sweating. He was nervous that we hadn't had time to game out a better line of response than the worthless campaign talking points.

I looked at him and said, "I'm ready."

As I squared my shoulders to face Anderson Cooper on CNN, I shooed the team out of my line of sight. I needed to focus on the real audience, and I couldn't be distracted by their anxious faces.

Anderson lit straight in. "Some within your own party are wondering if President Biden should even step aside. What do you say to that?"

"Listen, people can debate on style points, but ultimately this election and who is the president of the United States has to be about substance . . . Donald Trump lied over and over and over again, as he is wont to do. He would not disavow what happened on January 6.

He would not give a clear answer on whether he would stand by the election results this November. He went back and forth about where he stands on one of the most critical issues of freedom in America, which is the right of women to make decisions about their own body." As I went on to point out that women suffering miscarriages had been denied emergency care, he tried to interrupt me, saying that the president hadn't been able to clearly make that case.

I shot back that what mattered more is a president's actions in office, pivoting to what Trump had done in inciting the attack on the Capitol. I talked about the bipartisan infrastructure bill, about Joe's daily work as I'd witnessed it: in the Situation Room, keeping Americans safe; in daily meetings, carefully weighing briefings with the intelligence community and military leaders; on the world stage, where I'd often witnessed leaders leaning on his long experience, seeking his advice. And then I just lost my patience with his line of questioning. "So I'm not going to spend all night with you talking about the last ninety minutes when I've been watching the last three and a half years of performance."

Anderson pressed. "This was a debate that your campaign wanted . . . Can you say," he asked, "that you are not concerned at all having watched the president's performance tonight?"

I had to tell the truth. "I get that this is the after-play for the debate, this conversation that I'm in, and I understand why everyone wants to talk about it. But I think it's also important to recognize that the choice in November between these two people that were on the debate stage involves extraordinary stakes. And there's one person on that stage who has the endorsement of their vice president, and that's Joe Biden."

Anderson tried to jump in, but I pushed right on.

"Mike Pence is nowhere to be found in supporting Donald Trump, and that's why he has to look for someone else to run with him, who, as we know, will embolden and rubber-stamp whatever he wants because they're going to have to make a choice to not be Mike Pence and to put Donald Trump over their country."

And then Anderson said: "Neither person on that stage tonight made the argument as coherently as you just did."

As Anderson returned to his panel of pundits, I scrawled one word on a note card and slid it beneath the gaze of the camera to my staff: *Feedback?*

They slid back an answer: *Keep saying 3 ½ years vrs 90 mins. Mike Pence.*

Then I was on with the other networks.

Meanwhile, on Cooper's follow-up panel, CNN's national correspondent John King kicked off his remarks: "I just want to make an observation about your interview with the vice president . . . I think one of the greatest acts of political malpractice I have seen in my lifetime doing this is that they kept her under wraps for three years. Now she's on the road, she has great appeals . . . She also has potential star power. And on issues like reproductive rights and in the Black community, she is a great asset to this team, and they have kept her under wraps."

107 Days to the Election

* * *

On the coffee table at the vice president's residence, the thousand pieces of the harvest festival jigsaw puzzle lay scattered. My grandnieces pounded up the stairs to find their parents, Nik and Meena. Meena was in the closet, packing for the trip home to Palo Alto.

My sister, Maya, had been only seventeen, still in high school, when Meena was born. I was in the midst of my undergrad degree at Howard and had been admitted to law school at Georgetown. Instead, I came home and did my law degree at Hastings so I could help with the baby as Maya went to Berkeley and then got her law degree at Stanford. Meena did her undergrad at Stanford and law at Harvard. She is now a writer, producer, all-round firecracker. And she is a daughter to me.

She was folding clothes when her two girls burst into the room.

"Mommy, Mommy!" Amara exclaimed. "Auntie says everyone has to come downstairs!"

Meena went on packing. "In a minute, honey. We need to get going to the airport soon—"

"*No!*" Amara waved her hands. "Auntie said"—she scrunched her small face into the best imitation she could muster of the urgent look I'd just given her—"come downstairs *right now*!"

Meena dumped the clothes and ran down the stairs to the second floor, just as my brother-in-law, Tony West, came sprinting up from the first.

I first heard about Tony when Meena was four years old and kept talking about "my friend Tony." I finally asked Maya about this little friend of Meena's. Maya confided that Tony wasn't a preschool pal; he was her law school classmate and the president of the *Stanford Law Review*. Maya and Tony married soon after graduation.

Tony is a brilliant lawyer and has been a brother to me for thirty-six years. Even though he had been number three at the Department of Justice, and is now chief legal officer at Uber, Doug and I have taken to affectionately calling him our fifty-year-old teenaged son, given how much we love taking care of him when he stays with us.

He is also an astute political thinker, working on campaigns since he was a teenager, first for Representative Norm Mineta, then for Michael Dukakis, John Kerry, and Barack Obama. A year earlier, he had started what he called the "Red File." With a president in his eighties, he suggested, it would be malpractice on my part to be unprepared if, God forbid, something should happen. In such a traumatic moment, it would be prudent to have a plan for the first twenty-four to forty-eight hours, so people don't have to make a lot of decisions in the pressure of a crisis. He had thought through the first twenty-five calls I would need to make to world leaders, the first twenty-five to political colleagues, when to make my first statement, and what the rules of transition are. I didn't want to dwell on such an eventuality: I left it in his hands.

As the pressure for Joe to drop out had mounted, he'd pulled out the Red File and started adding to it. I did not want to be a part of any such discussions, so while Tony was in town for the family weekend, he'd gathered four members of my core team, without me, for a meeting in the pool house.

Tony had opened the meeting saying, "Let's assume he's dropping out tomorrow."

"That's not going to happen," replied Brian Fallon, my chief of communications. "He's got Netanyahu this week."

When I sent Nik out to get Tony, the group was on a Zoom call with the DNC convention chair, Minyon Moore, in Chicago. She was midsentence, explaining the delegate process, when she suddenly looked down at her phone, distracted. "Guys, hold on for a second," she said. Quentin Fulks, Joe's deputy campaign manager, had called. Biden had just told him he was dropping out. At that same moment, Nik appeared at the pool house door.

"Tony, she needs you in the house."

I was still on the phone with Joe as Tony burst into my office. When I put the phone down, Tony and I stared at each other, shocked at what had suddenly happened, concerned for what was at stake.

"If this isn't handled right, he will crap all over his legacy," Tony said.

We waited for the promised call back from Joe, anxious as the minutes passed. News was starting to leak. Then, the call.

There was no postponing the announcement of his dropping out, Joe said. "But the statement endorsing you will go out a few minutes later."

"Joe, thank you for this," I said, relieved. "I will do you proud. I am so looking forward to carrying on the work we've done together."

"You're gonna do great, kid."

His announcement that he would not be seeking reelection hit social media just twenty-two minutes after we hung up. Twenty-seven minutes after that, he endorsed me as the Democratic candidate for president of the United States.

From all over the city that hot Sunday afternoon, my staff dropped whatever they were doing and rushed to my side. Some hurried over in their workout clothes. But Steven Kelly, one of my speechwriters, always immaculately dressed out of respect for his White House role, had taken time to put on a suit and tie. "Steven, today you can ditch the tie," I told him.

The group from the pool house, who had expected to be here for a short what-if meeting, canceled their plans for the rest of the day. The table that had just been the site of a relaxed family meal was suddenly covered in binders and notepads. It became a boiler room, a site for the rolling calls we needed to make right away to secure support from Democratic delegates gathering for our convention in Chicago in less than a month, as well as from the former presidents, elected officials, and labor leaders who would be attending.

I knew I had everything I needed to do this. With Joe's endorsement and more name recognition than anyone else who might challenge, I had the strongest case. I'd also proven in the midterms that I could help flip seats. I had appeal for moderates and independents.

I also had a powerful personal contact list. On the road for the past four years, touring college campuses to build youth support and, more recently, on my tour for reproductive rights, I'd made a point of inviting local elected leaders to my events. Later, I'd have a moment with them, take a picture, have a brief chat. I would meet fifty to a hundred people a day in this way, and I had made it a point to follow up and keep those connections alive. During the delegate selection process, I'd pressed to include people who were my enthusiastic supporters, not just Joe's—people I'd known for years. I don't think too many people grasped the strength of the relationships I'd forged. This was not going to be a coronation. It would be the result of years of work.

But the one person I hadn't talked to was Doug. He wasn't answering his phone. I asked Meena and Tony to try calling our son, Cole, also in Los Angeles, to see if he had any idea where his dad was.

On a bike at SoulCycle in West Hollywood, as it turned out. He was catching up with a partner at his former law firm who'd come out as gay during the Covid pandemic. After their workout, Doug was grabbing coffee with Mitch and his boyfriend, Bob, when Bob glanced down at his phone.

"Doug," he said, "I think you need to see this." It was Biden's announcement about withdrawing from the race.

"Guys, I gotta go."

Doug lurched from the table and sprinted the hundred yards to his car, where he'd left his phone. There was steam coming out of it. As well as missed calls from me, every member of his family had texted: *Call Kamala.*

"Where the hell have you been?" I demanded. "I need you!"

"I don't see an endorsement. What's going on?"

"Don't worry, it's coming," I said. We strategized for a few seconds on how to get him back east, and then I had to take another call.

Maya, meanwhile, had jumped on the Acela in New York, but got stuck when the train broke down not far outside of the city. Nia, my personal assistant, took the little girls to play basketball on the half court that Mike Pence had installed in the backyard. Meena, social media savvy from her work as a producer, huddled with my comms team to create new Kamala HQ messaging for my Twitter account. Someone suggested we put a coconut tree as a logo in my bio. "Absolutely fucking not!" cried Meena, dropping her voice as she realized I was on the phone to former presidents in the next room.

She couldn't help edging toward the door to eavesdrop. She overheard Bill Clinton yelling for Hillary, who was in another part of their house in New York, and then the two of them struggling to create a conference call. Their reaction was effusive. Others were more guarded. To all of them, I said: *I'm in it to win. I intend to earn this. I hope I have your support. I welcome your ideas.*

In my notes of the calls:

Barack Obama: *Saddle up! Joe did what I hoped he would do. But you have to earn it. Michelle and I are supportive but not going to put a finger on the scale right now. Let Joe have his moment. Think through timing.*

The Clintons:

> **Bill:** *Oh my God, I'm so relieved! Send me anywhere. Make this your own campaign.*

Hillary: *We're thrilled the president endorsed you. We'll do whatever we can—we'll jump on a plane, we'll get on Amtrak. I want to be part of your war council.*

Jim Clyburn, the dean of the Congressional Black Caucus, whose support had lifted Biden to win the South Carolina primary: *Let's go. I'm all in.*

Josh Shapiro, governor of Pennsylvania: *How you holding up? You will have my support. I have a lot of Trump voters in my state. You have ability to draw them away.*

Wes Moore, governor of Maryland: *You've been loyal. I respect that.*

Pete Buttigieg, my primary opponent in 2019, now a close friend: *You're going to be a fantastic president.*

Roy Cooper, governor of North Carolina and a fellow former state attorney general: *Before you say anything, I'm all in.*

Chuck Schumer: *I believe we will win with you at the head of the ticket.*

Bernie Sanders: *I supported Joe because he was the strongest voice for the working class. Please focus on the working class, not just on abortion.*

Gretchen Whitmer: *I believe you'll win, but I need to let the dust settle, talk to my colleagues before I make a public statement.*

Nancy Pelosi: *I'm so sad about Joe. It's so tragic. My heart is broken. But now it's you! It's important there's a process, we have a great bench. We should have some kind of primary, not an anointment.*

J. B. Pritzker: *As governor of Illinois, I'm the convention host. I can't commit.*

Gavin Newsom: *Hiking. Will call back.* (He never did.)

Mark Kelly, senator from Arizona, tweeted his endorsement even before I reached him.

I went from call to call with the clarity that comes when stakes are high, stress is through the roof, and there's zero ambiguity. Some people I called would offer me support and then ask, "What do you think the process should be?"

If they thought I was down with a mini primary or some other half-baked procedure, I was quick to disabuse them. How much more time would it have taken to pull that off? I could imagine the chaos of even trying to decide *how* to do it, much less actually doing it, as precious days slipped away.

"*This* is the process. If anyone wants to challenge me, they're welcome to jump in. But I intend to earn the support of the majority of the delegates and I'm doing it right now." Each call took no more than two or three minutes. Outside, in the fierce afternoon heat, a media scrum swarmed.

A few hours into this day of frenzied, nonstop calls, I realized I needed centering. I stopped everything to call my pastor. Reverend Dr. Amos C. Brown is a Baptist preacher who marched with Dr. King. Of course he had already heard the news. I put him on speaker so the whole table could listen to his wise and sonorous voice, and we prayed. He talked about Queen Esther, who saved her people when they were threatened. "You were born for a time such as this," he said, and I teared up. He asked God to protect me, my family, my team, and to give us an understanding of our purpose in this moment. It grounded us all.

Then we were back on it. Outside, the sky darkened. Storm Horncastle, my indispensable social secretary, got us sandwiches, ordered pizza. Maya abandoned her stalled train and got an Uber for the long drive to DC. Doug hadn't been able to get a flight that night, so he arranged a plane to get him to campaign headquarters in Delaware the next day. He made calls on my behalf from our home in Los Angeles into the evening, until a neighbor came to the door: "It's about to get serious: you need to come have a drink." They tossed down some Johnnie Walker Blue Label as he let his new reality sink in.

At 5:29 p.m., staff alerted me that the British singer-songwriter Charli XCX had posted: *Kamala is brat*. *Brat* was the title of her latest album and identified me with her brand: edgy, imperfect, confident, embracing. From then on, our rebranded Kamala HQ social media site was awash in her signature color, lime green, and posts supporting us used that color.

At ten p.m., I finally decided it was too late to call anyone else. We had been going for eight hours. I'd spoken to more than a hundred people. Every single call had mattered. I'd had to be entirely present for each one, giving out and taking in important information. Now the dining room table was strewn with scrawled notes, sandwich crusts, and the greasy remains of a pizza with anchovies—my favorite, no one else's. I was still in my workout clothes, my unbrushed hair tangled in its scrunchie. Despite that, I decided we needed to record the moment. Before I went upstairs to take a long-overdue shower, I gathered my team.

"Things are going to get wild," I said. "There will be hard days ahead. We have a lot of ground to cover. But you are the best team in the world, and I know we can do this. Let's take a photo."

And there we all are: seventeen rumpled, messy, smiling people. Joyful warriors, about to go into the battle of our lives.

106 Days to the Election

Rollout

* * *

My campaign rollout would happen that afternoon in Delaware. But first I had other duties.

I was vice president of the United States. The VP always has a daily schedule crammed with myriad responsibilities. My staff secretary, Oliver Mittelstaedt, would deliver the schedule and the fat briefing binders for the events of the next day to my residence late the evening before. The schedule outlined in exquisite detail every move of every person around me, described to the inch and the minute, down to which people will ride the elevator with me at each location. If there will be a photo line at some point in the day, even the number of camera clicks will be noted, indicating whether the shots are going to be with groups or individuals. Dozens of people are involved, from Secret Service to White House staff to traveling press, and all of them must be choreographed. Within this elaborate dance, my moves are indicated by the word "**YOU**" in bold letters.

Whatever is start time on that sheet, I will be up two hours earlier. A man can work out, shower, shave, pat down his hair, and grab one of half a dozen identical blue suits. As any woman in a public-facing job knows, it takes us longer. Women need to add time for hairstyling, makeup, and more complicated apparel choices, including not repeating the same outfit too often. For me, pantsuits have been a practical choice: if you're going to be photographed getting in and out of numerous SUVs and climbing stairs on windy tarmacs, they offer less chance of a wardrobe malfunction. As trivial as it may seem, women are still judged on all this. Get it wrong in one direction, you're a frump. Go too far in the other, you're vain and frivolous. Like our tone of voice or our uninhibited laugh, it has the potential to be noted ahead of the consequential matters we're engaged in, be it national security or a billion-dollar infrastructure deal.

I'd barely slept.

The mythology of America says anyone can grow up to be president. But most people don't think that's really possible for them.

Did I grow up as a kid with a dream to be president? No.

My mother told me I could be anything, and I believed her, but president wasn't on my list. I was in my first year as a senator before it crossed my mind—oddly, as a result of a throwaway remark. Doug and I were home in Los Angeles for the weekend, having breakfast at a popular hangout in our neighborhood, when Lawrence O'Donnell, the political commentator, walked in. He wandered up to our table to talk about the dire consequences of a second Trump term. "*You* should run for president," he said. I honestly had not thought about it until that moment. The idea took root in my imagination, and, as a result of running against Joe for the nomination in 2019, I wound up as his VP.

I now know that there is only one apprenticeship for president of the United States, and that is being vice president. I'd been a heartbeat away for three and a half years. I knew the job; I knew I could do it. I wanted to do it. I wanted to do *the work*.

I want to keep people safe and help them thrive.

For me, it's always been about that work. From the time my mother told me to look after my little sister, I have been a protector. As a prosecutor, my work was protecting vulnerable people, especially women and children, from sexual predators. As California's attorney general I protected our state from cartels, homeowners from predatory banks, and I made the criminal justice data from the second-biggest justice department in the country open, accessible to reporters and researchers, so we could transparently test our system and see what was most effective. In the Senate, it was getting money to community banks, the most effective funders of small business. In the White House, I was able to work on so many issues that mattered to me: small business, maternal health, child poverty, climate action, infrastructure, repairing our global alliances.

As president, there was so much more I could do. I wanted to see Gen Z given the tools they needed to become a new Greatest Generation, and I had so many ideas on how to help them. I wanted to create a secretary of culture to uplift the immense creative talent of this country. I wanted to change the way we think about our workforce, to assign value based on an individual's skill, to open up government jobs to talented people who didn't necessarily have a college degree. I wanted to increase home ownership. All these things, and so much more, all grounded in the fundamental values of dignity, fairness, and opportunity.

My thoughts darted from these promising horizons to gnarly thickets of logistics. I was up at six, reviving with a brief workout on the elliptical as I watched the news.

The previous day's labors had paid off: the Associated Press had surveyed delegates and reported that I had enough support locked in to win the nomination, although that wouldn't be official till a roll call in fourteen days.

Trump's public reaction was to claim I'd be easier to defeat than Biden because I was even further to the left—a "dangerous San Francisco radical." But reports from inside his campaign revealed dismay. Later that day, Trump whined on Truth Social: "They also mislead [*sic*] the Republican Party, causing it to waste a great deal of time and money" on political advertising targeting a candidate who was no longer his opponent. After the debate, after the assassination attempt, the Republicans had believed they were on a glide path. Now a boulder had rolled onto the runway, and they had to recalculate their approach.

At breakfast I found Maya, who'd arrived after midnight. She was excited for me. She had been by my side, doing the heavy lifting for every campaign, taking time from her own work as a leader at the ACLU, the League of Women Voters, and the Ford Foundation. She was realistic about what this would mean for me, for our family. She also knew how well I could do this job, and she knew why I wanted to do it. Only a sister, raised with the same values and sense of purpose, could see so clearly how I felt.

I had briefings with my team about my events at the White House and what we had to accomplish in Delaware that afternoon. Some had suggested I do my first big event as a candidate in Pennsylvania, but I pushed back hard. "There are people in Wilmington who have been working round the clock for months. They're going to be feeling a lot of emotions. I need to see them first."

I called David Plouffe, who'd run Obama's 2008 campaign. He dove right into the details. I took notes: *I don't have fidelity with what's happening on the ground. But I know Trump is doing better than he did in '16, in '20. The assassination attempt pushed his turnout 20 percent. Whatever you think his turnout will be, add 10 percent. Don't listen to anyone who says rely on paid media. Take risks. TikTok, podcasts—risky but important. Four things you can't mess up: Rollout, First Interview, Convention, Debate. Nail the big moments and don't sweat the small speed bumps.*

At 10:30 a.m., my motorcade left for the White House. It was College Athlete Day, and a crowd of over a thousand students were gathering on the South Lawn to be recognized as champions in the 2023–2024 National Collegiate Athletic Association season. Since the president had Covid, I'd been asked to stand in his place. Now those routine remarks had new significance and needed rapid revisions. I was determined to recognize the weight of the moment and to honor the president for his achievements.

Stepping up to the podium, I looked across the lawn at the spectacular array of young athletes in front of me. I could feel their excitement.

I told them the president was sorry his Covid recovery was keeping him from being there and went on to say that in one term, he had already surpassed the legacy of most presidents who served two. I shared a bit of our personal story, telling them I had gotten to know Joe Biden through his son Beau.

Beau and I had been state attorneys general, me in California and he in Delaware. In the aftermath of the Great Recession of 2008, he had stood with me against the big banks who had defrauded so many borrowers, people who'd lost homes. I'd pulled California out of the national negotiations when the banks proposed a settlement that I thought was crumbs on the table given the harm caused by their malpractice and fraud.

Delaware didn't have nearly as many folks underwater as we did in California, but it did have a lot of influential banks who wanted to get out of their mess by paying the least possible penalty. In an act of political courage and principle, Beau was by my side as we stared down the big banks, and I eventually got $20 billion for Californians who'd been harmed. I will always admire Beau for taking that risk.

Beau and I talked often, comparing notes on our work and becoming close friends. When he died from brain cancer, everyone who knew him, knew his character and gifts, was devastated at the loss for his family, his friends, and for the United States. I flew across the country to be at his funeral. Beau always spoke so admiringly of his father, of his integrity and commitment. I shared that with the crowd, adding my gratitude for Joe's service to America. Then I went on with my prepared remarks, focused on the young athletes' achievements.

As I stepped down from the podium, the band struck up Queen's anthem: *We are the champions, my friends. And we'll keep on fighting till the end . . . No time for losers.* With Trump on the ballot and the threats to freedom outlined in Project 2025, this was the time for fighting. No time to lose. Only 106 days till the election.

A hundred and six days to remake a campaign deployed over a year earlier for the reelection of a familiar eighty-one-year-old guy who had been part of the political scene for the last half century, to repurpose it as the historic campaign of a woman, whom many voters still didn't know very well, born almost a quarter century later with a completely different set of experiences and accomplishments.

Less than a month to redesign a convention made for Joe into a celebration of an entirely different kind of candidate.

Two weeks to vet and choose a vice president—a choice that would not just reverberate through the campaign but would be integral to the success of my administration.

It would be the shortest campaign in modern presidential history. This, in a country used to having a year or two to learn the plans, policies, values, and character of their presidential candidates. Against a man who had been campaigning for almost ten years, ever since he came down the escalator at Trump Tower in 2015.

As we headed through a sudden downpour to Joint Base Andrews and made the quick hop to Delaware, I worked on the speech I would soon be giving, one of the most important of my life. My usual process for major speeches was to work with Adam Frankel, who had been my senior speech writer since 2021. A deep thinker who had authored a book on the intergenerational trauma of Holocaust survivors, his Democratic Party DNA could be traced in several directions, including to the JFK administration. I would share broad concepts for what I wanted a speech to get across, and after we talked it out, he'd put it down on paper, trying to capture my voice. I'd go over it many more times before it went on the teleprompter, making sure it was words for the ear, not the eye.

But this speech was different. I knew what I needed to say about Trump's character, his record, and his horrible agenda. For the first two weeks of this campaign, I would have nothing but the benefit of my own instincts. Polling hadn't been done, messages hadn't been tested, but I didn't need polling that day to know what I wanted to say and exactly how I wanted to say it.

Doug's flight had landed ten minutes earlier. He was waiting in the forward operating base when Jill Biden returned the call he'd made to her the day before, when he first heard the news.

"Be careful what you wish for." Her tone was desolate. "You're about to see how horrible the world is."

When my plane landed, Doug bounded up the steps of Air Force Two and wrapped me in a hug. There wasn't time to talk. We were once again about to walk through the fire together. He and I both knew it. It did my heart good to receive that big, bearish hug. Sometimes, in a marriage, that's how everything is said.

The Biden–Harris Campaign HQ had been built in Wilmington, Delaware, because it was Joe's town. The key staffers were his people, his loyal longtime operatives. We were both on the ticket and the campaign had been tasked to work hard for both of us. There had been an early understanding that Joe would mostly campaign from the White House while I did the heavy lifting on the trail, so I was already aware of how extensive the travel demands would be. But it was a Joe-shaped organism that would need to adapt very fast. There was no way to know if it could.

As I stepped into the room, the place erupted. Young faces everywhere, cheering and crying. In the twenty-four hours since I'd declared my candidacy, the campaign had taken in $81 million. Everyone in the room knew that funds had all but dried up after the debate, and this sudden gush of money was proof of life. I was surprised to see how quickly they'd switched out the Biden–Harris signs and covered the walls with newly printed HARRIS FOR PRESIDENT posters.

My first order of business was to put out a small brush fire. Jen O'Malley Dillon—JOD, as everyone called her—was chair of the campaign, a seasoned pro who had led us to a win in 2020, the first woman campaign manager for a successful Democratic ticket. I had called her on Sunday to ask her to stay on in the role. But there were questions about how the campaign would need to be reshaped, and when David Plouffe called her to discuss strategy, there was confusion. In a quick meeting, I reassured her that I wanted her and the campaign manager, Julie Chávez Rodríguez, to remain in their roles. I didn't have time to build a new plane; I had to fly the aircraft available. It would have been a self-inflicted disaster to blow it up, 106 days from the election. Everyone in that HQ was dedicated. They often worked around the clock. Many had given up jobs, hauled themselves across the country, to live in Delaware and do this work.

But I had my concerns. Some, like Mike Donilon, one of Joe's closest advisers, had moved from the West Wing to the campaign because he was expert in channeling Joe; he knew Joe's every whim and inflection. It was unclear how that expertise could work for me. In fact, he left the campaign and returned to the West Wing less than two weeks later.

For several months, the Biden–Harris campaign team had been holding meetings in what's called the "tennis hut," a pavilion on the grounds of the White House. These political briefings often made no sense to me. Mike Donilon would filter the data from the polls and present the numbers in soothing terms: that the razor-thin, within-the-margin-of-error results were no cause for hair on fire; that really there was nothing to see here. Doug had wanted to stop sitting next to me because he got tired of me kicking him under the table when I asked a question and got a nonanswer. My chief of staff, Lorraine Voles, turned to me as we left one of these meetings and said, "If I ever organized that sort of dog-and-pony bullshit for you, you'd have my head on a platter."

I'd had to learn from the news, a month earlier, that there was a planned $50 million ad buy, even as big donors were sitting on their hands. I didn't see how we were going to fix the problem by throwing money at it, even if we had the money to throw. There were no specifics about which swing states to prioritize, which demographics to target, just happy talk about how we were "going to right the ship."

On July 5, I was on Air Force Two, headed to New Orleans for *Essence* magazine's Festival of Culture, one of the most significant gatherings of Black talent in the country, when Joe's chief of staff, Jeff Zients, reached me. "I'm willing to fight to the death for this president," I told him. "But the campaign can't have us out there like the emperor with no clothes. My name is on this ticket, so I don't want to hear XYZ is happening or not happening when the facts just don't support it." I'd become concerned that the data was being filtered to manage Joe's mood and lift his spirits. "I need straight talk. We have many pollsters—are they all in agreement on what's being presented at these meetings?"

My team members, like Kirsten Allen, Sheila Nix, Brian Fallon, Ike Irby, Josh Hsu—the people clear about what I wanted—would now have to elbow their way into the campaign structure. I told JOD that my own pollster, David Binder, who had been with me since I ran for district attorney, would be taking a more significant role. One of the first calls I'd made was to Kristin Bertolina Faust, a key political strategist who had been with me since my race for attorney general. When we hung up, she packed and left her husband and two teenagers in Sacramento, arrived in Wilmington, and did not leave till November 6.

David Plouffe, I said, would join us as a senior adviser as soon as he extricated himself from existing commitments. Room also needed to be made for the raft of young people newly drawn to my candidacy. We'd keep the Delaware HQ but would open two new offices right away in Northern and Southern California, where we could tap the talents of people who had supported me for years, and deploy them to Nevada and Arizona.

An entirely new digital campaign would be spun up—digital for me looked entirely different from digital for Joe. Kirsten Allen immediately started briefing comms and digital staff in more detail on my background and values so that anything they created would give an accurate reflection.

Although Joe had felt differently, I made the immediate decision to go on TikTok. The @KamalaHQ TikTok would be a five-person Gen Z team in their twenties. We would give them a few rules of the road and then let them trick it out.

Insta would have a Millennial flavor, X would be directed at political junkies, and Facebook would target the Boomers.

Outside of the campaign, we already had the KHive, an online presence that had sprung up organically in 2017 and swarmed back, in force, to support me throughout the campaign. These digitally savvy fans, most of whom I did not know, had an encyclopedic knowledge of my record and would vigorously rebut anything inaccurate that was posted about me.

We put polls in the field that day. There was an urgent need to find out what voters knew about me and what their impressions were so that we could shape our messaging.

I knew I needed to leave these details in the hands of others. We would fail if I tried to micromanage them. I'd just have to go with God and trust the team. There's no such thing as a low-key event in a presidential campaign. I had to be 100 percent present for the thousands of voters I'd be meeting every day. I couldn't be constantly evaluating and questioning everyone else. It wouldn't be good for their confidence or my peace of mind. Nonetheless, the buck stopped with me, and I was aware of that from the get-go.

At five p.m., it was time to move to the stage. Over a floor speaker came Joe Biden's raspy voice. I could sense enormous effort. He was trying to sound upbeat, but you could hear the hurt as he hesitated over his words.

"If I didn't have Covid, I'd be sitting there with you—standing there with you. I—I'm so proud of what you've all done. And—but this Covid has been keeping me out of—out of people's hair for the next three or four days. But I'm going to be on the road, and I'm not going anywhere. I'm going—it's—it's kept me away a little bit, but, you know, I want people to remember that what we have done has been incredible, and we get—so much more we're going to get done. And so, I want to say hello to Kamala if she can hear me. I know she's going to be speaking shortly. And I want to say to the team: Embrace her. She's the best. I wanted to call today to thank everybody—everybody in this effort. I know yesterday's news is surprising and it's hard for you to hear, but it was the right thing to do."

He gained speed as he went on, praising the sacrifices of the campaign workers and promising to continue to bring the fight to Trump in his final months in the White House. The applause, when he finished, was warm and heartfelt. I hoped it lifted his spirits.

All the questioning about his capacity had wounded him badly. He didn't want to get out of this race; he didn't want to stop being president. I was determined that he at least have his dignity. My feelings for him were grounded in warmth and loyalty, but they had become complicated, over time, with hurt and disappointment. At that moment, the warmth predominated. So when I took the stage, I spent the first third of my remarks effusively praising him before I launched into my own campaign speech. I would do that for several weeks until my campaign strategists urged me to stop: "It's time this campaign was about you." It was David Plouffe who would eventually put it to me more bluntly: "People hate Joe Biden."

It was hard for me to hear that.

The rapport between Joe and me was genuine. For two people who seemingly couldn't have been more different, our values were incredibly aligned. We cared about working people, we'd given our lives to public service. We would outdo each other quoting sayings from our parents, and we both liked to secretly and affectionately make fun of the British, drawing on our respective colonial ancestry—his Irish, mine Jamaican and Indian. Before the campaign got into gear, we met regularly for lunch in the private dining room just off the Oval Office. He'd have a club sandwich; I'd have grilled fish. And then, with a conspiratorial grin, he'd order us up a chocolate shake or a sundae. We discussed everything from my bilateral meetings with leaders like France's Emmanuel Macron, the Philippines' Bongbong Marcos, and Ghana's Nana Akufo-Addo, to the latest political gossip from the Hill.

But Plouffe was a realist. He knew that the president's approval rating of 41 percent was a ball and chain dragging on my campaign. It would take time, too much time, before I acknowledged this truth.

But what I knew for certain: I faced an opponent who majored in malice, and I was damned if I was going to join the chorus of cruelty. Our administration had achieved great things: getting Covid under control; creating fifteen million new jobs; standing up for democracy at home and abroad, passing bipartisan legislation that nobody thought would be possible in such a bitterly divided Congress, including a bipartisan infrastructure bill and the most significant climate-saving measures ever. In this first speech, in many that followed, and when elected president, I was determined to recognize Joe Biden for that.

Then I turned to the job at hand: defining my own campaign and reminding people what I brought to the table.

"Before I was elected as vice president, before I was elected as United States senator, I was the elected attorney general of California. And before that, I was a courtroom prosecutor. In those roles, I took on perpetrators of all kinds . . ."

This politically savvy crowd was several jumps ahead; they knew where I was going and loved it. They signaled their approval with laughter and applause.

"Predators who abused women, fraudsters who ripped off consumers, cheaters who broke the rules for their own gain. So, hear me when I say . . . I know Donald Trump's type."

The crowd exploded.

There are phrases in English that can do a lot of work for you. "I know his type" is one of them. We've all said it about someone of low character whom we've personally known. It chimes with memories of bad boyfriends, obnoxious bosses, shady businessmen. The kind of person you warn your kid not to befriend.

I went on: "As a young prosecutor, when I was in the Alameda County District Attorney's Office in California, I specialized in cases involving sexual abuse. Donald Trump was found liable by a jury for committing sexual abuse.

"As attorney general of California, I took on one of our country's largest for-profit colleges and put it out of business. Donald Trump ran a for-profit college, Trump University, that was forced to pay $25 million to the students it scammed.

"As district attorney, to go after polluters, I created one of the first environmental justice units in our nation. Donald Trump stood in Mar-a-Lago and told Big Oil lobbyists he would do their bidding for a $1 billion campaign contribution."

At this example of Trump's massive corruption, booing erupted.

"During the foreclosure crisis, I took on the big Wall Street banks and won $20 billion for California families, holding those banks accountable for fraud. Donald Trump was just found guilty of thirty-four counts of fraud."

Pivoting, I said that our campaign was about more than the stark contrast between my record and Trump's. The campaign, I stressed, was about two very different versions of our country going forward, one focused on the future, one mired in the past. Trump wanted to take us back to failed trickle-down economics that had never done a thing to lift the middle class and instead brought only more inequity. He romanticized a time when freedom and rights were limited and denied to so many Americans.

I was born into a fight for freedom and stood in that tradition. Freedom to vote, to control one's own body, to breathe clean air and drink clean water, to be free from the fear of weapons of war on our city streets and in our children's classrooms. Freedom from anxiety about health care costs, childcare costs, a retirement spent in poverty. Freedom to afford a home, build wealth, provide our kids a good education. The freedom not just to get by but to get ahead. And the freedom to simply be.

Finally, I wrapped up with the kind of call-and-response familiar to me from the church of my childhood:

"Do we believe in the promise of America?"

The crowd affirmed it.

"And are we willing to fight for it?"

"Yes!" they cried.

"And when we fight . . ."

"We win!"

105 Days to the Election

* * *

The bleachers in the very warm gym of West Allis Central High School just outside Milwaukee were packed. Hundreds more supporters crammed the floor in front of the stage, fanning themselves for some relief from the heat. When the cheering finally died down enough to allow me to start speaking, I told the crowd, "The path to the White House goes through Wisconsin." I would campaign in the state seventeen times before Election Day, the venues getting ever larger to accommodate swelling crowds. But this was the first rally of my campaign: my first chance to define the intersection of what Joe stood for and what I stood for, and how, as much as we were alike, we were also very different.

With my staff, in the prep room, I'd come up with a new line for the speech. Trump's slogan, "Make America Great Again," was very telling. "*Again.*" His agenda was to drag America backward. Not a goal of progress, but regression. I also wanted to remind the audience how cruel and chaotic his first term had been.

"We're not going back."

As soon as I delivered the line, the audience, unprompted, began chanting it back at me emphatically. Backstage, Ike, Brian, and Sheila nodded. "That works."

I'd been trying to draft the speech at home the night before, after Doug, Tony, and I returned from Delaware. It had been an emotional seesaw of a day: the poignancy of Joe's remarks and then the enthusiastic reception that had followed.

Meena had stayed on at the VP residence, wanting to be helpful. She also, I think, wanted the girls to experience this moment in history. But my baby nieces weren't all that interested in history. They were interested in making meatballs. I wasn't the candidate embarking on the fight for the future of their country. I was still just Auntie. While I huddled with Tony and Doug, trying to work on the next day's priorities, the girls zoomed around the house, oblivious.

"What's for dinner? What movie can you watch with us?"

It was Doug who gently pointed out that, at this moment, it was a level of multitasking above even my capacity. The girls, he said, would need to head back home. When I left for Milwaukee, they traveled with me in my motorcade, two munchkins flanked by burly Secret Service agents, to the landing zone for Marine Two. I blew a kiss and waved goodbye to them as the chopper rose over the rooftops of Washington, DC.

As I was delivering my speech in Milwaukee, Doug was in McLean, Virginia, for an event that had long been on his schedule: a roundtable with people affected by the *Dobbs* decision, held at a reproductive health clinic that had opened in response to the overturning of *Roe v. Wade*. It was serving not only Virginians, but also rising numbers forced to travel from states with abortion bans. Since *Dobbs*, Doug had made it a big part of his role to talk to men about why the crisis of reproductive freedom was an issue for all of us, not only women. He was determined to keep the clinic on his schedule to highlight what he termed "the post-*Dobbs* hellscape."

Doug was staffed by a tiny team—all that had been necessary for campaign events of a Second Spouse. At most of his previous events, there might have been one or two local reporters. Now there were scores of national media. As he left the meeting, reporters shouted questions. One asked for his reaction to a remark about me that Trump had posted on Truth Social. "Lyin' Kamala Harris destroys everything she touches!"

"That's all he's got?" my Jersey boy shot back.

My Dougie.

I had kissed a lot of frogs before fate—and my best friend, Chrisette—delivered me the amazing Douglas Craig Emhoff, first Second Gentleman of the United States.

Doug was born into a loving Jewish family in Brooklyn. His dad was a shoe designer, and they moved to New Jersey when Doug was about five. He had most of his schooling there, and the guys from his kindergarten remain some of his best friends. They're still on a group chat that's active every day. When he was sixteen, the family relocated to California, and that's where he went to college and law school. Money was tight, so he worked full-time parking cars, waiting tables, and slinging burgers at McDonald's so that he could afford to go to college part-time. (Later in the campaign, when Trump put on a McDonald's apron, serving fries as a stunt, it was particularly galling. Doug, my sister, Maya, and I had all sweated over those McDonald's deep fryers in our teens—I vividly remember my annoyance when I learned that my cousin, who was bagging groceries that summer, made more than me. Meanwhile, Trump got handed $413 million from his daddy—and then his companies went bankrupt four times.)

Chrisette met Doug when he quickly resolved a lawsuit for her family that had dragged on for years. She was impressed by his smarts and his sense of humor. When she set us up on a blind date in 2013, she implored me: "Don't google him." She was afraid I'd see some corporate headshot of a bland white guy and back out of the date. I was attorney general at the time; he was a successful law firm partner, specializing in entertainment law and intellectual property. (One of his cases centered on who had created the character of the Taco Bell Chihuahua.) He was divorced, parenting two young teens with his ex-wife, Kerstin.

As a child of divorced parents, I was determined to take it slowly.

I didn't want to come into Cole's and Ella's lives unless this was going to be serious. Doug, however, already knew it was. "I'm too old to play hide the ball," he emailed me after our first date. "I want to see if we can make this work." We were married less than a year later, with Maya officiating. So much for slowly.

Doug hadn't been particularly into politics before we met. He was always a Democrat; he always voted. But like many people busy building a career and raising kids, he mainly tuned in around election time and wasn't deep in the weeds. I'd run virtually unopposed for my second term as AG, so the first year of our marriage was politically uneventful. We were able to take weekends away and do relatively normal date nights. Poor Doug didn't realize that politics is *hard*.

When Barbara Boxer announced she wouldn't be running for senator in 2016, we sat out by the firepit in the backyard with a big yellow legal pad and wrote out the pros and cons of running for her seat. If I ran, I thought I would be elected to serve just as Hillary Clinton would make history as the first woman president. It didn't go that way, and we arrived in Washington, DC, to endure Trump's first era of chaos and cruelty.

There was good work to be done pushing back against that agenda. I'm proud of holding feet to the fire in Senate hearings, asking tough questions that revealed the nature of Bill Barr, Jeff Sessions, and Brett Kavanaugh. I'm proud that we secured billions for community banks and that we raised federal relief for wildfires to the same level as other natural disasters. And I'm proud that as a member of the Senate Intelligence Committee we investigated and then declassified our findings of Russia's interference in the 2016 presidential race.

But the job was frustrating. As a former AG, I was used to being in charge: I'd make a decision and I'd get something done. Because Democrats were in the minority, the Trump-era Senate sometimes felt frustratingly performative. I yearned for a bipartisan era when senators could reach across the aisle to accomplish real improvements in people's lives.

———

I was lucky to have Doug at my side. It's helpful to have a husband who wakes up with a smile on his face. He's also very protective. Once, when I was giving a speech, a man leapt onto the stage, trying to grab the mic. Doug barreled down the aisle from the very back of the hall and shoved the guy offstage. The fierce expression on his face went viral. Sometimes, at home, I would see him staring into his laptop with a pained expression, and I'd know he'd found something malicious about me. I'd adopt a resonant voice, like a horror-movie protagonist warning her partner not to go down in the basement: *"Don't . . . read . . . the . . . comments!"*

Doug soon learned that American politics isn't built for male spouses. In DC, there are long-standing social structures and well-understood roles for wives. Not for the very few husbands. While I was a senator, it didn't matter too much, since Doug still had the law firm work that he loved. But the day I got the call to be vice president, he made a huge sacrifice, gladly and without bitterness. He knew it was essential that there be no appearance of conflicts of interest in our new roles. So that was his last day at his law firm.

But what was his new role? No one even knew what to call him. I came up with the title Second Gentleman, off the cuff, during a live interview on CNN. (When I got back to the house he said, "Okay, I guess we figured that one out.") Now, in White House–speak, SGOTUS is an established awkward acronym, just like POTUS and VPOTUS. Since, as VP, I was also president of the Senate, Doug became the president of the Senate spouses, upholding the traditions of luncheons and events originally designed for an all-female association.

At the vice president's residence, we'd been given an organizational chart showing how the household was meant to function. Under the heading "Second Lady," an arrow pointed to "Family Life," which turned out to be a euphemism for "housekeeper." While there were naval enlisted aides who helped with household tasks if I was in the residence, they vanished when I was traveling. Because it was a secure facility, we were precluded from hiring our own outside help. If Doug needed laundry done, he had to do it himself or else hide his clothes in my laundry basket and hope that they'd take pity. Since I'm the cook in the family, I needed to make big batches of food and freeze them for him, so he'd have something decent to eat when I was gone.

After warmly welcoming us into the Biden family at the beginning of the campaign, there seemed to be a change of temperature after the election. Understandably, after all the tragedy they had endured—Joe's first wife and daughter killed in a car crash, Beau's brain cancer, Hunter's addiction—the Biden family was extraordinarily tight-knit. I had always admired Jill for her fierce loyalty to her family and also her dedication to teaching. But I suspect Jill hadn't quite forgiven me for the 2019 primary debate, when I'd gone hard at Joe over his early opposition to busing. Although I had regular working lunches with Joe, there wasn't a lot of family socializing.

So, three years in, when we suddenly received an eleventh-hour invitation for the two of us to join the Biden family celebration at the White House on Fourth of July 2024, it came as a surprise. We'd planned on being home in Los Angeles, where, for the past three years, we'd used Fourth of July as a chance to thank the Secret Service detail and the local police and first responders who looked after us whenever we were able to be home. Doug fired up the barbecue, and we personally cooked and served hot dogs for all two hundred of them in our backyard. July 3 is also Doug's father's birthday, a big family occasion. He was turning eighty-seven, and at that age, every birthday is precious to us. Because of the sudden request from the Bidens, we had to abruptly change the date for his celebration.

The holiday came after a terrible couple of weeks for Joe. In his first sit-down television interview after the debate, he told George Stephanopoulos that he couldn't recall if he'd rewatched it or not. This was supposed to be the corrective interview that would fix perceptions; instead, it reinforced them. Then there would be revelations that two radio interviewers had asked him pre-scripted questions provided by his campaign staff. It wasn't uncommon for staff to ask interviewers what subjects they would be touching upon, but in his postdebate context it was damning. The chorus for him to step down would reach a crescendo, with Democratic members of Congress speaking out and celebrities such as George Clooney writing biting op-eds.

The campaign had asked me to call members of Congress to assess support for him. That made me uneasy. I said I'd call only those I knew well: people who wouldn't misconstrue the call as some kind of self-serving fishing expedition. Amid all the chatter, gossip, and malevolence, I never let even those closest to me engage me in the conversation about whether Joe should drop out. I know how this town works. Information is its most prized capital. What you know and what you're prepared to trade are the keys to power. Everyone is in this swap meet: politicians, lobbyists, the press. Intentionally or not, word would spread that I was passively gauging their support for me. And I didn't want to hear anyone saying to me, You *should run*. There was no good way for me to respond to that.

The last thing our ailing campaign needed was rumors of a rift between the president and me. What I didn't know then was that some of his senior staff didn't share that concern. In their own calls trying to quell the rebellion, they'd been talking me down, saying, *If Joe goes, you'll get* her, strongly implying that I wasn't up to it.

It was just one of the many ways his staff was responding badly to the crisis. They'd started cramming his schedule with more events, knowing full well that when he was tired, he did poorly. Hunter Biden's trial was underway, and I suppose the campaign wanted to distract from that and wanted Joe to be seen as functioning vigorously as president despite the personal burden he was carrying. Instead, they were exhausting him. Whose idea was it to have him stand in the broiling sun at a Juneteenth celebration for *three hours* until, worn out, he was described as "comatose"?

Many people want to spin up a narrative of some big conspiracy at the White House to hide Joe Biden's infirmity. Here is the truth as I lived it. Joe Biden was a smart guy with long experience and deep conviction, able to discharge the duties of president. On his worst day, he was more deeply knowledgeable, more capable of exercising judgment, and far more compassionate than Donald Trump on his best.

But at eighty-one, Joe got tired. That's when his age showed in physical and verbal stumbles. I don't think it's any surprise that the debate debacle happened right after two back-to-back trips to Europe *and* a flight to the West Coast for a Hollywood fundraiser.

I don't believe it was incapacity. If I believed that, I would have said so. As loyal as I am to President Biden, I am more loyal to my country.

What I do know is that he needed rest, and you're not going to get it during a presidential campaign. They don't call it "running for office" for nothing. Any campaign is a full sprint. A presidential race is sprinting through a marathon. Like a marathon, it is a test of endurance. Unlike a marathon, tomatoes are being thrown at you every step of the way.

There was a distinction between his ability to campaign and his ability to govern. I was right beside him as he navigated successfully through intensely dangerous world events: Putin's threat to use tactical nuclear weapons on the Ukraine battlefront; the missile exchanges between Iran and Israel that might have escalated into regional war if we hadn't rallied the diverse coalition that protected Israel during those attacks. His judgment, his experience, and the relationships he had developed were expertly deployed.

As for campaigning, I *did* have concerns. His voice was no longer strong, his verbal stumbles more frequent. Apart from the superhuman stamina required, communicating is the main game. Before he stepped aside from the top of the ticket, I had planned to do many of the big public rallies and a lot of the crazy travel while his team fashioned a White House–based campaign for him.

Even so, his inner circle, the people who knew him best, should have realized that *any* campaign was a bridge too far, and that in its rigors, he'd be perpetually, increasingly, unavoidably exhausted. They should have counseled him accordingly. Instead, it seemed that the worse things got, the more they pushed him. And the more they pushed, the faster and more visibly his energy seemed to drain. I had never, in three and a half years at the White House, in the Oval Office or the Situation Room, witnessed anything remotely like the level of confusion, incoherence, and debility we saw on the debate stage.

When Doug and I arrived at the White House on July 4, I greeted Joe with our usual hug. He felt so frail. One of the staff drew Doug aside. The First Lady wanted to speak with him. He was led to the Blue Room, where Jill Biden was standing alone. She seemed tense, even angry.

"What's going on?" she demanded. "Are you supporting us?"

Of course, Doug said. Of course we are supporting you.

"Okay. That's really important. We need to know that."

When I joined him, Doug was wearing a grim expression. Doug runs cool. He's slow to anger. But I could tell something had gotten to him.

Later, he unloaded. "They hide you away for four years, give you impossible, shit jobs, don't correct the record when those tasks are mischaracterized, never fight back when you're attacked, never praise your accomplishments, and now, finally, they want you out there on that balcony, standing right beside them. Now, finally, they know you are an asset, and they need you to reassure the American people.

"And still, they have to ask if we're loyal?"

104 Days to the Election

* * *

T he first stop on the day's calendar had been planned months earlier. At a meeting in the Oval Office discussing her work uplifting Black executives and entrepreneurs, Dr. Stacie NC Grant had invited me to address the annual gathering—the Grand Boulé—of her sorority, Zeta Phi Beta.

Now I was in Indianapolis, looking out over a convention center packed with six thousand powerful women in dark blue dresses and white jackets. I'm a member of a different sorority, Alpha Kappa Alpha, the first Black women's Greek letter organization, founded at Howard University in 1908. But these women are my sisters, too. We're all part of the Divine Nine, the Greek organizations founded when segregation was law in the South and standard practice in the North. W. E. B. Du Bois and Thurgood Marshall were early members of the first Black fraternity, Alpha Phi Alpha, founded at Cornell University in 1906. The Divine Nine has been an engine of uplift for generations of Black college men and women, instilling a love and celebration of excellence, philanthropy, and service to all mankind. My Divine Nine family would show up for me throughout the campaign. That day I was so pleased to see the young president of Phi Beta Sigma, Chris V. Rey, and the esteemed president of Delta Sigma Theta, Elsie Cooke-Holmes.

Throughout my career I've maintained that people in positions of power must be required to ask of themselves: *Who am I not hearing from?* Then make it their business to seek those folks out. I came to the White House knowing that the people in that building needed to hear from a wider range of voices.

As vice president I'd been given several roles by Joe Biden. But one role I created for myself was building up the diverse coalition that our party encompassed. I made it my business to get out there and make sure that no community was overlooked, especially those that had been taken for granted in the past. Black women, the Democrats' staunchest, most reliable voting bloc, was one such community. The boulé in Indianapolis was one of a dozen Divine Nine gatherings I'd addressed since taking office.

On this day there was a new energy in the room as I walked onto the stage. A Black woman was slated to be the Democratic nominee for president. It was us. And everyone there understood what it meant: that this would be a journey of both joy and pain. I was in a room full of people with whom, because of our shared experience, certain words did not need to be said. There is an emotion that comes from being in a place where people see you, support you, know you. The kindness and the love in that room penetrated the armor I usually wore, armor I'd need to put back on as soon as I left that room.

The biggest applause came when I started to say what I would do to restore the rights of *Roe v. Wade.*

"When I am president—"

A roar erupted that drowned out the rest of that sentence.

That roar told me they could see it. Clearly, for the first time. This could be, and it should be. It was not because of gender or because of race, but despite it.

I thought, as I often did, of Shirley Chisholm, and I know they did, too. The first Black woman elected to the US Congress and the first woman to run for our party's nomination. She had blazed the path, and now I was standing on it.

From Indianapolis we flew on to Houston to meet with emergency management staff and get a briefing on recovery efforts after the devastation of Hurricane Beryl. The Category 1 hurricane's eyewall had slammed Houston, bringing down power lines and leaving vulnerable people without air-conditioning or water during triple-digit heat indexes. At least twenty souls had died. The economic damage—in the billions—was still being reckoned.

These kinds of briefings are sadly familiar to me. As DA, I'd witnessed the aftermath of Hurricane Katrina. As senator, I'd been to Puerto Rico after Hurricane Maria and I'd toured the communities in my home state that had been ravaged by wildfires. It was heartbreaking to see the scale of these losses and the exhausted faces of individuals standing in the ruins of a lifetime's work, a lifetime's dreams. It was infuriating to see how predators swarmed like cockroaches, price gouging, spreading misinformation. But it was also inspiring to talk to the first responders who ran toward danger, sometimes helping strangers even as their own homes were at risk. And then there were the regular people who stepped up to help in whatever way they could: collecting toiletries, making sandwiches, organizing clothing drives.

In my life I've seen over and over that it is often the people with the least who give the most.

As I shook hands and thanked the police and emergency workers one by one, in each I saw a hero. The kind of person who answered a calling with a sense of duty to the well-being of people they've never met. A reporter in the press pool shouted a question about Biden's upcoming speech. It was just after five p.m. in Houston, and the president would be addressing the nation from the Oval Office later that evening.

I watched it at the hotel that night. It was a good speech, drawing on the history of the presidency to locate his own place within it. But as my staff later pointed out, it was almost nine minutes into the eleven-minute address before he mentioned me.

"I want to thank our great vice president, Kamala Harris. She is experienced, she's tough, she's capable. She's been an incredible partner to me and leader for our country."

And that was it.

I am a loyal person.

During all those months of growing panic, should I have told Joe to consider not running? Perhaps. But the American people had chosen him before in the same matchup. Maybe he was right to believe that they would do so again.

He was, by some measures, the most consistently underestimated man in Washington. He'd been right about his tactics for pushing his agenda through a resistant Congress.

It was just possible he was right about this, too.

And of all the people in the White House, I was in the worst position to make the case that he should drop out. I knew it would come off to him as incredibly self-serving if I advised him not to run. He would see it as naked ambition, perhaps as poisonous disloyalty, even if my only message was: *Don't let the other guy win.*

"It's Joe and Jill's decision." We all said that, like a mantra, as if we'd all been hypnotized. Was it grace, or was it recklessness? In retrospect, I think it was recklessness. The stakes were simply too high. This wasn't a choice that should have been left to an individual's ego, an individual's ambition. It should have been more than a personal decision.

I was well aware of my delicate status. Lore has it that every outgoing chief of staff always tells the incoming president's chief of staff Rule Number One: *Watch the VP.* Because I'd gone after him over busing in the 2019 primary debate, I came into the White House with what we lawyers call a "rebuttable presumption." I had to prove my loyalty, time and time again.

When Fox News attacked me on everything from my laugh, to my tone of voice, to whom I'd dated in my twenties, or claimed I was a "DEI hire," the White House rarely pushed back with my actual résumé: two terms elected DA, top cop in the second-largest department of justice in the United States, senator representing one in eight Americans.

Lorraine, my chief of staff, constantly had to advocate for my role at events: "She's not going to stand there like a potted plant. Give her two minutes of remarks. Have her introduce the president."

They had a huge comms team; they had Karine Jean-Pierre briefing in the pressroom every day. But getting anything positive said about my work or any defense against untrue attacks was almost impossible.

An example: In 2021, I was dispatched to the Élysée Palace to help reset our tattered relationship with France after we signed the Australia-UK-US security pact. Australia had agreed to buy submarines from France but scrapped that contract when we and the UK agreed to supply Australia with nuclear subs under the new AUKUS agreement instead. This had caused tremendous friction.

In our meeting, Emmanuel Macron and I warmed the chill by focusing on our many areas of cooperation, such as space exploration, climate change, transatlantic security, cybersecurity, the Sahel, and the Indo-Pacific.

On that trip, I was invited to visit the renowned Pasteur Institute, where my mother had worked on mRNA research related to breast cancer. I was speaking informally with the scientists there about how I wished politicians would more closely follow the scientific method: testing a hypothesis and adjusting according to results, rather than coming in with the Plan, as if they had all the answers up front.

I said "the Plan" with exaggerated emphasis and air quotes. Fox News, the *New York Post*, and Newsmax went wild, claiming I'd faked a French accent. This was total nonsense, but the White House seemed glad to let reporting about my "gaffe" overwhelm the significant thaw in foreign relations I'd achieved.

Worse, I often learned that the president's staff was adding fuel to negative narratives that sprung up around me. One narrative that took a stubborn hold was that I had a "chaotic" office and unusually high staff turnover during my first year.

The plain fact is many people who come to work with a new administration in the White House haven't done it before. It's a job unlike any other, and not every person, no matter how talented in their former position, can step up into such a high-stress, round-the-clock role. Others find they just don't want a job that doesn't pay particularly well, takes a massive toll on family, and rules out anything resembling a normal life. I'm not going to keep people on who can't thrive in their jobs—it's not fair to them and it's not good for the country.

So the first year in any White House sees staff churn. Working for the first woman vice president, my staff had the additional challenge of confronting gendered stereotypes, a constant battle that could prove exhausting.

I was the first vice president to have a dedicated press pool tracking my every public move. Before me, vice presidents had what's called a "supplemental pool," as the First Lady does, covering important events. Because of this constant attention, things that had never been especially newsworthy about the vice president were suddenly reported and scrutinized.

And when the stories were unfair or inaccurate, the president's inner circle seemed fine with it. Indeed, it seemed as if they decided I should be knocked down a little bit more.

"The VP should take on irregular migration."

From March 2021, my assignment was to attack the root causes of the misery that was driving people from their homes and villages in Guatemala, Honduras, and El Salvador. Because I'd prosecuted cartels and human traffickers from the Northern Triangle, I was up to speed on the region and its problems, and had ideas about the kinds of investments and other interventions that over time would reduce irregular migration, help to bring stability, and offer people a safer future in their own community.

Most people don't want to leave home. They don't want to leave their grandmother, their church, their friends, their language. And when they do, it is usually for one of two reasons: they fear for their lives, or they can't make a living. Much of that region is rural, and farmers are increasingly hit by climate events such as floods and droughts. If you can no longer grow food where you are, and if there's no other livelihood, you will leave, because there's simply no choice. Corruption and gangs thrive when there are limited resources.

When Republicans mischaracterized my role as "border czar," no one in the White House comms team helped me to effectively push back and explain what I had really been tasked to do, nor to highlight any of the progress I had achieved. I won commitments of $5.2 billion in new investments by private companies for the region. I had already seen almost a billion of that money deployed, thanks to enthusiastic partners such as Mastercard, Microsoft, and Nespresso.

I held numerous bilateral meetings with leaders throughout the region, especially with President Alejandro Giammattei in Guatemala, and later his successor, President Bernardo Arévalo. I had multiple calls with Giammattei, warning him that I expected free and fair elections, sending my national security adviser Phil Gordon to reinforce the message in person, and publicly supporting Arévalo once the election was called.

I met with activist groups fighting corruption and for human rights in El Salvador, Guatemala, and Honduras. Cabinet members pitched in: Tom Vilsack at the Department of Agriculture accessed resources to train farmers in the latest methods to increase yields.

I worked closely with Mexico's president, Andrés Manuel López Obrador, and later his successor, President Claudia Sheinbaum, on our mutual border concerns. The investment I was bringing was a bargaining chip with regional governments to crack down on corrosive levels of corruption. These American companies, I told them, would not invest unless real steps were taken. The investments I encouraged have connected communities to the internet and brought people into the formal financial system, creating jobs and opportunity.

In the locations where I was able to bring new enterprises and greater stability, data showed it was working. Our investments had created seventy thousand new jobs, reached over a million people with training programs, and connected 2.5 million previously unbanked people with banking services and access to credit. These people were staying put. I wanted to get that good news out. But White House staff stalled. "Not yet. We need more data." The story remained untold.

Instead, I shouldered the blame for the porous border, an issue that had proved intractable for Democratic and Republican administrations alike. Even the breathtaking cruelty of Trump's family separation policy hadn't deterred the desperate. It was an issue that absolutely demanded bipartisan cooperation at an impossibly partisan, most uncooperative time.

No one around the president advocated, *Give her something she can win with*.

Then the *Dobbs* decision came down.

Here was a huge issue on which the president was not seeking to lead. Joe struggled to talk about reproductive rights in a way that met the gravity of the moment. He ceded that leadership to me. I initiated a national tour and rallied the outrage in red states and blue states alike. As well as big public events, I convened roundtables, starting out with ten or twelve state legislators whom I would connect with resources in the Justice Department or Health and Human Services. Soon, advocates started attending, then health care providers, then families affected by restrictive laws. There would be hundreds of people at these meetings, building a national coalition. All this work upended the narrative that we were doomed to a shellacking in the midterms. We defied historical precedent because of our efforts on this issue. (Since 1934, the president's party has lost an average of twenty-eight House seats and four Senate seats in midterm elections. We lost just nine seats in the House and retained control of the Senate.)

Joe was already polling badly on the age issue, with roughly 75 percent of voters saying he was too old to be an effective president. Then he started taking on water for his perceived blank check to Benjamin Netanyahu in Gaza.

When polls indicated that I was getting more popular, the people around him didn't like the contrast that was emerging.

In Selma, Alabama, at the commemoration of Bloody Sunday, when civil rights marchers were attacked and beaten once they'd crossed the Edmund Pettus Bridge, I gave a strong speech on the humanitarian crisis in Gaza. Desperate people had been shot when they swarmed a food truck, and I spoke of families reduced to eating leaves or animal feed, women prematurely giving birth with little or no medical care, and children dying from malnutrition and dehydration. I reiterated my strong support for Israel's security and called on Hamas to release the hostages and accept the ceasefire agreement then on the table. I also called on Israel for greater access to aid. It was a speech that had been vetted and approved by the White House and the National Security Council. It went viral, and the West Wing was displeased. I was castigated for, apparently, delivering it too well.

Their thinking was zero-sum: *If she's shining, he's dimmed.* None of them grasped that if I did well, he did well. That given the concerns about his age, my visible success as his vice president was vital. It would serve as a testament to his judgment in choosing me and reassurance that if something happened, the country was in good hands. My success was important *for him.*

His team didn't get it.

103 Days to the Election

* * *

"Y our entry has electrified this race," said Randi Weingarten, president of the American Federation of Teachers. Her union had been the first to endorse me in an announcement on July 22. We were waiting backstage at the Houston convention center where I was to speak to more than three thousand teachers gathered for their annual convention. We could hear the crowd chanting, call-and-response: "Kamala!" "Harris!"

I took the stage to a standing ovation. Again, I led with Joe.

"So last night, our president addressed the nation. And he showed once again what true leadership looks like," I said. "And over his entire career, Joe has led with grace and strength, and bold vision and deep compassion."

In the meat of my speech, I hit our key policy differences with Republicans: "We want to ban assault weapons, and they want to ban books." I gave teachers the love they so deserve: these dedicated, underpaid professionals who change lives. I spoke of the teacher who'd changed mine: my first grade teacher, Mrs. Wilson, the remarkable woman who had stayed in my life and shown up for my law school graduation.

Afterward, the motorcade drove to the airport through a downpour, water running across the highway in cataracts. It made me concerned for Houston, for the impact of the next Beryl, and the next hurricane after that; concerned for all the great American cities and communities under threat from the weather disasters made more frequent and more intense by climate change. Everyone who said we couldn't afford to make the necessary changes to achieve net-zero carbon emissions didn't seem to grasp that we couldn't afford *not* to. What sort of American economy would we have in a future where even Wall Street itself could be drowned by rising water?

I had been the deciding vote for the Inflation Reduction Act, which was the most consequential climate bill ever enacted into law. My senior policy adviser, Ike Irby, is a climate scientist. It's an issue about which I am passionate and one on which the US president needs to lead. Part of the challenge with this very short campaign was that we had to focus on needs that felt more immediate, like how to deal with the grocery bill or the cost of childcare. Talking about the benefits that would flow from our green energy investments was too distant.

We had offered generous rebates to low- and middle-income families to help them install heat pumps and other energy-efficient appliances that would lower emissions *and* utility bills, but people hadn't yet had a chance to feel those savings. It was hard to get people excited about the prospect of much lower utility bills in the future—that the battery technologies we'd invested in would be cheap enough for every home to make and store its own power from sunlight.

People were focused on the cost of things *today*. I needed to emphasize that I had plans that would swiftly lower the cost of housing, that would stop price gouging. Climate policy was a much longer, more complicated conversation. It had to include explaining our plans for a just transition, one that wouldn't leave workers employed in the fossil fuel economy behind. I knew that one in five voters, and an even higher percentage of younger voters, identified as being very concerned about climate change. On my college tour young people had spoken frankly to me of "climate anxiety"—their fear that my generation's failure to act was robbing them of a healthy planet, a healthy future. I knew I risked leaving those votes on the table by not talking more about this issue.

In this short campaign, I just didn't have time. I had to triage issues so that key information could sink in. Sometimes I felt like the triage nurse who makes the call in *The Pitt*: each one of those souls is important, but with the limited resources you have, you must choose among them. It was frustrating that I had to leave so much out. But as the advertising industry has long known, people must hear the same message three times before it even starts to penetrate.

After the exhilaration of being with the teachers, people I greatly admired, I was heading to a meeting with Netanyahu, about whom I was more ambivalent. What I'm not ambivalent about is Israel's security. As a young girl I carried around a little blue box for the Jewish National Fund, soliciting support to plant trees in Israel. I believe Israel was right to respond to the atrocities of October 7. But the ferocity of Netanyahu's response, the number of innocent Palestinian women and children killed, and his failure to prioritize the lives of the hostages had weakened Israel's moral position internationally and created angry dissent within Israel itself.

People like me, who understand the importance of a Jewish homeland, who value Israel as a democracy and as an ally, sincerely believed that the scale of the response and the denial of food and medical supplies to civilians were doing Israel grave harm. I'd been on almost every phone call between the president and Netanyahu since October 7. Soon after the pogrom, I met with the distraught parents of American hostages. Many in Israel feared that Netanyahu's priority was his own political survival, not the desperate predicament of their captive children.

I had low expectations for our bilateral meeting. It was important to demonstrate our continuing support for our longtime ally especially after such an atrocious attack. It was also critical to show that we were continuing to press our plan for a ceasefire that would bring the hostages home to their families and spare innocent Palestinian civilians.

But as I stepped off Air Force Two at Joint Base Andrews, I was forced back into campaign mode. Trump, being Trump, had backed off on his willingness to stick to the September 10 debate he'd agreed to. He'd been rubbing his hands at the prospect of another round with Joe. Now that it was me, he suddenly wasn't so keen. I stood under the wing on the tarmac and told the assembled reporters:

"You have been asking me about the debate and I'll tell you I'm ready to debate Donald Trump. I have agreed to the previously agreed upon September 10 debate. He agreed to that previously. Now, here he is backpedaling. I'm ready, and I think the voters deserve to see the split screen that exists in this race on a debate stage."

With the Israeli prime minister due at my ceremonial office in the Eisenhower Executive Office Building, I walked to the waiting SUV without taking questions. I met Netanyahu in the vast, beautiful space containing Teddy Roosevelt's mahogany desk. The inside of the top drawer has been signed by every vice president since the 1940s. It is an eloquent testimony to national pride in the peaceful transfer of power through the years.

Netanyahu's hooded gaze and disengaged demeanor made it clear to me that he was running out the clock. He denied Gazans were starving and blamed Hamas for looting food. I interrupted to reiterate the need for an immediate ceasefire and a day-after plan that gave Palestinians some kind of political horizon. Netanyahu wanted only a temporary ceasefire to get hostages back but did not want to end the war. It was clear that nothing would be accomplished. We'd outlined the terms of negotiation for the ceasefire back in May and made frustratingly little progress with either Israel or Hamas.

Netanyahu was bent on undermining Joe Biden, one of Israel's staunchest allies. I had pleaded with Joe, when he spoke publicly on this issue, to extend the same empathy he showed to the suffering of

Ukrainians to the suffering of innocent Gazan civilians. But he couldn't do it: while he could passionately state, "I am a Zionist," his remarks about innocent Palestinians came off as inadequate and forced.

That loyalty meant nothing to Netanyahu. He wanted Trump in the seat opposite him. Not Joe, not me. Netanyahu wanted the guy who would acquiesce to his every extreme proposal for the future of Gaza's inhabitants and add his own plan for a land grab by his developer cronies.

It was distressing to see how this issue was dividing Americans. Ten thousand incidents of anti-Semitic harassment, vandalism, and more than 150 physical assaults. A six-year-old Palestinian child stabbed to death, his mother wounded, by their own landlord in Illinois. Synagogues, temples, and Jewish community centers scrambling to protect themselves with new security measures. Three Palestinian college students shot in Vermont, leaving one a paraplegic. Posters of Israeli hostages defaced and torn down from walls in New York City. Campus protests, some of which harassed and threatened Jewish students and created an atmosphere of tension and fear. These rising expressions of hate were chilling.

Long before October 7, Doug had become a leading voice in our administration combatting anti-Semitism, speaking at the United Nations and representing the United States at Holocaust commemorations in Poland and Germany. Doug was proud of his Jewish heritage and its history of social justice. He was proud that Rabbi Abraham Joshua Heschel had marched beside Dr. King. Doug worked to inspire and reinforce that pride in young Jews, taking the press with him to visit his old summer camp and talking to the kids there about celebrating their identity. He believed in the idea of *tikkun olam*, the obligation to repair the shattered world, small shard by small shard. We were the first family at the vice president's residence to have a mezuzah on the doorpost. The one we affixed came from a synagogue in Atlanta where Dr. King preached when it opened its doors to Black worshippers after their church was burned by segregationists.

For any enduring peace, we have to let go of extreme rhetoric on both sides. The war in Gaza is not a binary issue, but too often the conversation about it is. I wanted to acknowledge the complexity, nuance, and history of the region, but it seemed very few people had the appetite for that or the willingness to hold two tragic narratives in their mind at the same time, to grieve for human suffering both Israeli and Palestinian. Loud voices on either side claimed there were no innocents on the other, a position I found inhuman. And I know Secretary of State Tony Blinken, who was tirelessly hauling himself from Jerusalem to Doha to DC, sincerely wanted to end the suffering on all sides.

Right from the beginning of the campaign, protesters who thought we hadn't done enough for Gazans tried to disrupt my rallies.

I was born amid dissent. Civil rights were won through protest. My parents took me to demonstrations when I was still in my stroller. The people at my rallies had every right to do what they were doing. I understood them, I understood why they were angry. Usually, the crowd drowned them out, and I went on with the business of my speech. But at a rally in Detroit, as I was detailing Trump's threats to climate policy and the Affordable Care Act, a noisy group chanted: "Kamala, Kamala, you can't hide. We won't vote for genocide." The threat to withhold their vote got to me. It felt reckless. Either Trump or I would be elected. The issue was not binary, but the outcome of this election certainly was.

"You know what? If you want Donald Trump to win, then say that. Otherwise, I'm speaking."

Why weren't they protesting at Trump rallies? I wondered. I wished they would understand that sitting out the election or voting for a third candidate would elect Trump and kill any effort for a just peace, any hope for a two-state solution.

I wrapped up that unproductive meeting with Netanyahu in under an hour and walked out to address the press. I sincerely reaffirmed my commitment to Israel's right to defend itself. I added that *how* Israel did that mattered.

I said that Hamas triggered the war when it massacred 1,200 innocent people and committed horrific acts of sexual violence. I listed by name the five American hostages still living and the three whose remains were still held by Hamas.

Then I told the press that I had discussed with the prime minister the dire situation of innocent civilians in Gaza. I described the agonizing "images of dead children and desperate, hungry people fleeing for safety, sometimes displaced for the second, third, or fourth time." I said, "We cannot look away in the face of these tragedies. We cannot allow ourselves to become numb to the suffering, and I will not be silent." I described our discussions on the proposed ceasefire.

"To everyone who has been calling for a ceasefire and to everyone who yearns for peace, I see you and I hear you. Let's get the deal done."

102 Days to the Election

* * *

M y days now started with a fifteen-minute briefing on how the campaign was landing in the news.

But the big news of the day for my campaign wasn't news to me. Barack and Michelle Obama had decided the time was right to endorse me. They'd wanted to make a film of them calling me, and it was now up on social media.

Netanyahu had flown down to Mar-a-Lago to see Trump. I learned that he was enraged by my remarks after our meeting. The briefing digressed to note that Trump had stopped wearing the bandage on his ear, almost two weeks after the bullet had nicked it.

Then there was a second briefing with my staffers Dean Lieberman and Ernie Apreza. Dean, a deputy national security adviser and skilled strategist, would update on international events, and Ernie, my press secretary, on domestic news.

There was a note before the next item on my schedule: "Hold for hearty breakfast." It's a reality of campaign life that a grown woman needs to be reminded to make time to eat. But what followed would be a day of almost back-to-back calls with little pause for refueling. There would be a DNC Finance Committee call with good news about the scale of donations large and small that were continuing to pour in. There was a call in to the faith coalition hosted by my pastor, Reverend Brown. And we had to keep moving on the search for the person who would join my ticket.

I had to find a vice presidential candidate, and I had to find one fast.

From the day I got Joe's call I had sixteen days to do it, and now I had exactly eleven left. When Joe picked me, he'd taken over nine weeks to thoroughly consider all his options. My deadline was August 6, a day after the roll call that would formally nominate me. Ohio's ballot had an August 7 closing date, and they needed two names to print on the ballot. It was an excruciatingly tight time frame. My choice would impact not just the race but also the shape of my administration.

Being a vice presidential pick is an enormous gift, vaulting someone who might have local or state recognition onto the bigger, brighter national stage. But it can also mean taking a job that, as FDR's VP John Nance Garner so memorably said, may not be "worth a bucket of warm piss."

Jimmy Carter, having lived through the assassination of JFK and the resignation of Nixon, knew that the vice president had to be ready to take over. He remade the role. His vice president, Walter Mondale, was the first to have an office in the West Wing. Ronald Reagan also understood that the vice president needed to be prepared, as did Bill Clinton. George W. Bush went further, ceding unprecedented power to Dick Cheney. But it remains true that the vice president's role will be as little or as much as the sitting president desires. That can be a hard pill to swallow.

A couple of likely candidates, such as Michigan's Gretchen Whitmer and North Carolina's Roy Cooper, would preemptively withdraw from contention. We'd put a poll in the field to determine who among the other possibilities had name recognition and, of those, who had the kinds of positives and negatives that might help or hurt us. The results turned out to be useless. None of the names moved the needle either way. So that put the onus on what would turn up during vetting and what my personal chemistry with each candidate was like. I wanted someone who shared my vision and had the practical chops to implement our plans.

We narrowed it down to eight possible candidates and asked them to submit material such as financial disclosures, ads from previous political campaigns, and information about their personal lives that might not yet have found its way into the public record.

My vetting team was led by Jen O'Malley Dillon, my campaign chief of staff Sheila Nix, former Attorney General Eric Holder, and former White House counsel Dana Remus.

There's a reason we had top cops and lawyers on the team. It's a prosecutorial process, as I had learned four years earlier when I sat across a table from the lawyer vetting me. The final stage, after the investigation, was an interrogation that lasted nine hours. The attorney took every aspect of my past, especially the sensitive or difficult moments, and pressed me on them. Not because she didn't know the answers, but to see how I would handle the pressure. Did I get my back up? Could I pivot? Would my answers pass the smell test? She would periodically ask me if I wanted to take a break. I declined. We didn't get up from that table until she had fine-tooth-combed my entire life.

Biden had won the nomination because Congressman Jim Clyburn, leader of the Congressional Black Caucus, had thrown his support behind him. The Black vote in the South Carolina primary—especially Black women's vote—had thrust him to victory. The pressure was on him to pick a Black woman running mate.

The press knew I was on the short list, so they had our DC apartment building staked out. When Doug and I stepped out to go somewhere, they'd follow. Occasionally I'd save them the trouble. I'd wander over to their van and say, "Doug and I are just going for coffee, can I bring you something?"

Getting to my interview with Joe was choreographed like a spy movie. Andy Vargas, my body person, drove me in our Audi to a strip mall, where I switched to an SUV and was instructed to duck as we approached a big house in northern Virginia. I was led downstairs to the bottom level, to a room with closed drapes, where Jill and Joe would meet me. It was the height of Covid, so we were all wearing masks.

Once you are chosen as VP candidate, you barely have time to blink before your life becomes unrecognizable. Prior to getting the call from Joe to tell me he had picked me, I'd been visited by a friend, Carol, who has a remarkable garden. She wanted to give me a box of her late-season tomatoes. I was feeling stressed, knowing that Joe was about to decide and that the world was watching. When I'm stressed, I like to cook. I greeted Carol in the lobby of my apartment building—both masked—and carried the box back upstairs, rolling up my sleeves to make a big batch of marinara for the freezer.

I never made that sauce. Right after Joe's call at 2:00 p.m., cars started pulling up on the street outside, spilling out national campaign staffers with briefing books on every aspect of the campaign. I took the binders and gave each staffer a handful of ripe tomatoes in return. I hate wasting food.

And now I was about to cause the same sudden swerve in someone else's life.

Of the eight names on the list for vetting, I might as well say that Pete Buttigieg was my first choice. Harvard grad, multilingual Rhodes Scholar, business consultant, naval intelligence officer, twice-elected Midwestern mayor, cabinet secretary, loving husband and father: he was well qualified in so many respects. I love Pete. I love working with Pete. He and his husband, Chasten, are friends. He is a sincere public servant with the rare talent of being able to frame liberal arguments in a way that makes it possible for conservatives to hear them. He knows the importance of taking our case to people who aren't usually exposed to it and is magnificent at sparring with opponents on Fox News.

He would have been an ideal partner—if I were a straight white man. But we were already asking a lot of America: to accept a woman, a Black woman, a Black woman married to a Jewish man. Part of me wanted to say, *Screw it, let's just do it.* But knowing what was at stake, it was too big of a risk.

And I think Pete also knew that—to our mutual sadness.

101 Days to the Election

* * *

We were on Air Force Two en route to Pittsfield, Massachusetts, in the heart of the Berkshires. This was an event that had been planned when enthusiasm for the campaign was flagging; now it was through the roof. We'd had a target to raise $400,000 at this event, but that had shot up to over $1.5 million.

"Thank God you guys are top of the ticket. We weren't going to make payroll," a senior campaign finance official on the plane confided to Sheila. Until that moment, my team had no idea how bad things had been.

The streets were lined with people waving handmade signs saying MADAM PRESIDENT and singing the Woody Guthrie anthem "This Land Is Your Land."

One sign, LOTUS FOR POTUS, might've confounded anyone who didn't know Sanskrit. It came from a meme posted by a fifty-three-year-old South Asian pediatrician right after Biden endorsed me. "In Sanskrit, Kamala means LOTUS. In America, Kamala means POTUS."

Pittsfield is a city of about forty thousand, and despite its picturesque location in rolling, wooded hills, it struggles with many of the issues of small-town rural America, such as a stubbornly high poverty rate and opioid addiction. But in summer, an influx of affluent arts lovers, drawn to the rich cultural offerings at nearby Tanglewood, masks those realities.

The event at the historic Colonial Theatre had been planned as a fundraiser for the Biden Victory Fund but had been quickly rebranded as the Harris Victory Fund. Solidly blue Massachusetts wasn't used to seeing the presidential candidate this close to the election, when swing states generally get the lion's share of a candidate's time, and organizers had half expected, now that I was top of the ticket, I'd send a surrogate. But I'd wanted to keep my commitment.

The concert would feature A-list talents such as James Taylor and Yo-Yo Ma, both longtime Democratic supporters. The two Massachusetts senators were there: Elizabeth Warren, whom I'd come to know when fighting the big banks as California AG, and Ed Markey, whose wife, Rear Admiral Susan Blumenthal, had helped Doug find his way in the foreign land of the Senate spouse.

It was a warm, familiar crowd, slightly on the older side, dotted with longtime supporters and friends who'd driven west from Boston and Martha's Vineyard. As the campaign went on, the venues would get bigger and the crowds more diverse: posses of young girls taking selfies, dads with their kids on their shoulders, tattooed teenagers ushering a grandma to a better vantage point. People of all ages, colors, wallet sizes. All standing shoulder to shoulder, being immensely kind to one another. I could feel the intensity of emotion, and my only thought, when glancing down at a tear-streaked face or grasping a hand on the rope line:

There is so much at stake. I cannot fail these people.

100 Days to the Election

* * *

That Sunday I hunkered down at the vice president's residence to work on plans for the convention and to go over campaign strategy. Maya and Tony were staying with us. We worked on logistical plans for the large group of friends and family who would be attending the convention to support me. It's more than a notion how much planning needs to go into that: where they will stay, where they'll eat, who will look after the elderly ones, how to get them to and from the convention site. Who will field the 101 questions they will have of me when I can't possibly take that call. National politics is one thing; family politics can sometimes be just as gnarly. Maya, as always, took up the slack.

The convention chair, Minyon Moore, started her political career with Jesse Jackson's presidential run in 1984 and worked for both Clintons and as an adviser on the Biden–Harris transition in 2020. She'd been tasked with planning a showcase for Joe. But because she is a subtle and strategic thinker who sees six moves ahead, she had formed a group called the What-If Committee to prepare for all kinds of contingencies, such as what would happen if the Republicans deposited hundreds of migrants from the border, as they had been doing in Chicago, right at the convention door. The possibility that

Joe might drop out was also on the what-if list, but rated significantly below ensuring that the media narrative that this convention could be a rerun of 1968 did not come to pass.

Minyon's task benefited, in the end, by the Biden team's failure to engage with her to nail down Joe's convention theme. She was free to order up graphics for my theme: FOR THE PEOPLE, FOR OUR FUTURE.

For the program, we had to figure out what to keep and what to throw out from what had been planned for Joe. Some of it was a given: there are large procedural segments, there will always be elected officials and union leaders and some celebrities. Anyone running for office lobbies hard for a speaking slot in prime time.

In this case, they would need to be slotted in before Joe Biden's speech on night one, the vice presidential nominee's on night two, and my acceptance speech on the final night. Each of us would have friends and family speaking as our lead-ins.

We needed to tell my story in the production, and one aspect I wanted to highlight was my work as AG. I think that the elected attorneys general are some of the most talented and dedicated officials in the country, and I wanted to throw a spotlight on them as well.

The convention exists on two planes at the same time. It must work for the delegates in the hall—those committed community leaders from every state and every walk of life who live and breathe Democratic politics—and also for the television audience, who may have only just started to focus on the election as they deal with their daily responsibilities. I believe it is also in the party's interest to highlight our stars, while we make it as entertaining as possible.

When I became VP, I had a secret project—I called it the Stars Project—that only my senior team knew about. We'd brainstorm about the younger talents in the party and then, on Friday afternoons, I'd invite one or another to visit my office in the West Wing or the residence. As I'd offer a seat on the couch across from me, more than one nervously confessed: "I feel like I've been called into the principal's office." I would laugh and say, "No, I think you're very talented. What are you working on, and how can I help you?"

Many of those on my list spoke at the convention: Lauren Underwood, Robert Garcia, Angela Alsobrooks, Lateefah Simon, Maxwell Frost, Joe Neguse, Lina Hidalgo, Jasmine Crockett.

Stephanie Cutter, a trusted adviser and veteran strategist, aided by Reggie Hudlin, my best friend Chrisette's award-winning film-maker husband, had started pulling together the short biographical video usual for the vice president, but now that I was top of the ticket we had to scramble to find much more material. This video and my speech would be my introduction to the large numbers of people who had just tuned into the campaign and really didn't know who I was.

I would finally have control of the podium to reclaim my narrative and my identity.

Early that evening I got a call from Joe. For months, I'd been working on delicate negotiations to bring home former US marine Paul Whelan and *Wall Street Journal* reporter Evan Gershkovich from their unjust imprisonment in Russia. While attending the Munich Security Conference in February, I'd used the opportunity to arrange private meetings with German Chancellor Olaf Scholz and Slovenian Prime Minister Robert Golob. Germany had in custody the inmate of most value to Vladimir Putin, the assassin Vadim Krasikov, who had killed a Chechen separatist in Berlin. Slovenia had two other Russians of interest to Putin; Poland and Norway each had one.

It was a chess game, with many states' interests in play. Chancellor Scholz is a serious, thoughtful man who weighed his options carefully. As with all the European heads of state, there was a heightened sense of the threat Putin represented. Eastern Europeans, especially, had experienced oppression under the kind of Greater Russia that Putin romanticized and yearned to re-create.

There was also a melancholy sense that the United States was not the ally it had once been. Trump's first term had proven that our leadership of NATO, the world's greatest military alliance, was not constant and might be fleeting. Their knowledge of what happened in the 1930s is far greater than what they perceive ours to be. They can feel it in their blood and in their bones. And they legitimately fear we might abandon them. When I would say, "America is back," they would say, "For how long?" I always reassured them, while silently praying that what I said would remain true.

It was no small ask of Chancellor Scholz to release a murderer serving a life sentence. But he was motivated by the possibility of securing the release of Alexei Navalny, the leading opposition figure in Russia, who had been saved from Russian poisoning by German doctors, before bravely returning to Russia knowing he'd be imprisoned. A small team at the NSC and the Office of the Special Presidential Envoy for Hostage Affairs at the State Department had worked around the clock on the details of this complex negotiation, never forgetting for a minute that lives were at stake—as we tragically learned.

Just before I was due to speak at the Munich Security Conference, we received dreadful news: Navalny was dead in his icy gulag, almost certainly murdered. I began my speech expressing deep sorrow for his death, saying it was another instance of Putin's brutality. "Whatever story they tell, let us be clear: Russia is responsible."

Navalny's widow, Yulia, had not been scheduled to speak at the conference, but she arrived, red-eyed and heartbroken, and took the podium after I spoke, giving a courageous call for resistance. The killing of Navalny made me even more motivated to achieve this prisoner swap, even though the chessboard had just been so violently overturned.

Now, Joe was calling to say the pieces were finally moving into place. It looked like we'd soon be able to tell the families of Paul Whelan and Evan Gershkovich that their ordeal was finally over.

99 Days to the Election

* * *

I had expected to debate J. D. Vance and had started to prep for that. Now we began to prepare to debate Donald Trump instead.

The first session happened around the table in the vice president's residence. Later, we'd move to the basement at Howard University, fitted out to mimic the set on which the real debate would take place. I'd started my political career freshman year at Howard, running for a seat on the liberal arts student council, against a smart, tough Jersey girl. I still consider it one of my hardest races.

That day, we started with the broad strokes of debate strategy. For better or worse, a presidential debate is a television event, not a contest on who knows the most about policy. The aim, my team stressed, was not to be the biggest wonk on the stage. The aim was to walk off leaving the voters comfortable that you have what it takes to be president. A lot of that is demeanor. You need to be confident, clear, and unrattled. The person who is winning, the team reminded me, is the person who is having the most fun. I got into the habit of drawing a little smiley face at the top of the blank pad that was placed on the podium so that I would keep that in mind. Then I drew a line bisecting the page. On one side would go a note about a Trump assertion; on the other, my response.

Karen Dunn was the leader of my debate prep team. She is an experienced trial lawyer, a veteran of big, complex cases. If you need a wartime consigliere, she is the one. She is a taskmaster, very smart, and she really cared about me.

Among the advice I got that first session:

- Be on offense continually, especially on issues perceived to be vulnerabilities.
- He will try to rattle and distract you. Don't fall for it.
- Be prepared to say "That's a lie."
- Remember, the economy is what keeps people up at night.

With Rohini Kosoglu, my former Senate chief of staff and domestic policy adviser, we started to create the debate book, a binder of issues that we gradually reduced to a stack of cards on which we developed and refined talking points, lines of attack, rebuttals to the kinds of lies Trump might spout. We had a card for every nuance of every subject, and once I memorized what was on that card, I'd draw a big, loopy *X* across it.

I am not a trained seal; I'm not going to memorize lines and spout them. I have to understand the logic and building blocks of every argument so I can present it clearly and defend it persuasively.

We also addressed the painful matter of imagining what kinds of personal attacks Trump might mount against me. A man who had no floor, who could go infinitely low, get infinitely cruel. He'd disparaged the war hero Senator John McCain, mocked a reporter's disability. The gutter was deep for this guy.

I'd had quite a big team in the room to get the most diverse range of input I could on how answers would land. But for the part of the prep focusing on personal assaults, I narrowed the group to less than a handful.

"He might ask you if you've ever had an abortion," one adviser said.

If he did, the response would be: *That's none of your business and that's not what we're here for.* Someone made a dark joke that if he got that personal, I should ask if he took Viagra. Another: Had he ever paid for an abortion?

In the end, he didn't go down that track. He probably knew a question like that would be exceedingly thin ice for him—and would infuriate just about every woman in America.

98 Days to the Election

* * *

There were ten thousand people at the rally in Atlanta.

It was the first rally designed specifically for my candidacy, not as a supporting act to Joe, and I wanted to liven it up, broaden the cultural appeal, and bring more creativity and fun. Having Megan Thee Stallion opening for me and Quavo as a speaker was one way to do that.

Both artists are committed activists. In 2022, Quavo, a talented hip-hop artist, witnessed his nephew and band member shot and killed. He became an ardent activist dedicated to ending gun violence. Megan is a generous philanthropist in her hometown of Houston and has done innovative work supporting education and financial literacy for women and girls nationally and abroad. She is also a red-hot rapper, famous for provocative lyrics stressing body positivity. She embraced the nickname "Stallion," given to her in her teens for her tall, strong physique. "I know my ladies in the crowd love their bodies," she told them. "If you want to keep loving your bodies, you know who to vote for!" She and her backup dancers performed in blue pantsuits—a witty nod to my style, even though theirs were of a cut and fit very different from the kind I wear.

There had been a question about whether I should have *any*

celebrities at my rallies. Would it seem too California, too Hollywood? I thought that the right surrogates could help expand the crowd and add excitement. There were questions about whether Megan was the right choice. As well as the usual online trolling, there were anxious remarks from supporters: "You need to be more middle of the road— you're not projecting the right image as you come out of the box." I knew they were people who cared about me, but I also knew they were wrong. We needed to welcome everyone into this campaign, and that meant people who listened to music that ranged from Bruce Springsteen to Lil Wayne.

By the time I got to the podium, the audience was on fire. In my speech, I talked about the threats to women's reproductive freedom. I berated Trump for sinking the bipartisan bill that would have helped with border security—"as my friend Quavo would say, he does not walk it like he talks it."

And then I went after him for backing out of the debate. "But he and his running mate sure seem to have a lot to say about me." As the audience howled, I added, "If you've got something to say, say it to my face."

By the next day, national polls revealed we'd made up all the ground lost since Joe's debate. I was in a statistical dead heat with Trump. Later, I read the reporting on that rally with amusement and some chagrin. Many of the reporters now traveling with us hadn't covered rallies I'd been having as vice president. My college tour events had often been standing room only, same with my rallies for reproductive rights. If they had covered those events, the enthusiasm in Atlanta might not have come as such a surprise.

97 Days to the Election

* * *

In the summer of 2021, during her final trip to Washington as German chancellor, I hosted Angela Merkel for breakfast at the vice president's residence.

I am a stickler for being on time—I feel it's a mark of respect. Everyone's time is valuable. But sometimes schedules go sideways, and I fall short. That wouldn't happen with the chancellor. Germans value punctuality, and I was determined we wouldn't come off as overly casual Americans. I asked to be passed a note when we had five minutes left, so that I could wrap the discussion gracefully and end precisely on time.

Contrary to how the press had covered the personality of this extraordinary leader, she was warm, with a great sense of humor. I thought about the injustice of that portrayal as we spoke about many issues: the catastrophic flooding that had just ravaged western Germany, my own experience with extreme weather events in California, and the imperative for multilateral action on climate policy. We discussed speeding up the global flow of Covid vaccines. Drawing on her fifteen years as the putative leader of Europe and her experiences dealing with four presidents, she spoke bluntly about her concerns over the vulnerabilities in US global leadership post-9/11. She had opposed Bush's Mideast wars and been concerned by Trump's fundamental misunderstanding of the NATO alliance.

When my staffer handed me the requested note and I started to wind up the discussion, she waved me off.

"Let me tell you a personal story," she said. As a woman and an outsider who had risen to the highest level of her nation's government, she had particular advice she wished to share. She detailed how difficult her rise in politics had been, as a woman from East Germany at a time when her party was dominated by West German men. As it became clear how formidable she was, the attacks became personal, mean.

"They used to call me . . ." She turned to her translator, whom she'd barely consulted during our meeting, and said a German word.

"It is a very ugly bird," the translator explained.

"They used to call me this—this ugly bird," she said. "And at first, it hurt me deeply."

She leaned forward.

"Don't you ever let them make you cry."

On July 31 I was aboard Air Force Two, en route to Houston, where I would address Sigma Gamma Rho, another of the Divine Nine sororities. Four days earlier, a supporter had offered to add a fundraiser ahead of that event. They thought, at such short notice, they might raise a million dollars. They'd raised $2.5 million. I would spend that night in Houston, and the next day I would deliver a eulogy for the trailblazer congresswoman Sheila Jackson Lee, my sorority sister, a distinguished lawyer and judge, and a smart and strategic legislator whose district encompassed most of central Houston. She was a breast cancer survivor, but pancreatic cancer had taken her life.

I was in my cabin polishing the eulogy, when Kirsten, my media adviser, and Lorraine, my chief of staff, rapped on the door.

"Trump just said you're not Black."

He was onstage at the annual meeting of the National Association of Black Journalists in Chicago, being interviewed by a three-woman panel. It wasn't a comfortable crowd for Trump. He got off to a rocky start, branding ABC reporter Rachel Scott "nasty" and "rude," after her first question, about why Black voters should trust him, in which she'd quoted his own racist language. Then she asked her second question: Republicans had said I was a DEI hire. Did he think I was only on the ticket because I was a Black woman?

He replied that he had always thought I was Indian. "I didn't know she was Black until a number of years ago when she happened to turn Black and now she wants to be known as Black."

It was the same old divisive playbook, using race as a wedge. He'd used it on Obama with all the birther libels. He'd even used it against Nikki Haley, deliberately mispronouncing her given name, Nimrata, and pretending he didn't know if she was eligible to be president since her parents were Indian-born. He's an expert at suggesting that someone is a fraud—that you cannot believe this person. Which I believe some psychologists would call "projection."

Hurtful and degrading comments are, sadly, part and parcel of running for office these days. You can't endure it at this level unless, above all else, you care about the people you want to represent and the things you will be able to do to make their lives better. If you do care about that, then there's no time to wallow in self-pity or lament the unfairness of it. Not that you don't feel it. Not that it's okay. It is what it is. And it was familiar to me.

Where it crosses the line is when opponents go after family members. That same day, anti-Muslim activist, 9/11 conspiracy peddler, and far-right Trump booster Laura Loomer posted on X about an affair Doug had, fifteen years earlier in his previous marriage, with a teacher at his children's school. It was quickly picked up by the *Daily Mail* and the *New York Post*. Of course, I knew about this. Doug had told me about it when we were dating. We disclosed it during my vetting for VP.

By marrying me and taking a very public stand at my side, Doug had knowingly put himself in the line of fire. His former wife, Kerstin, had not, and neither had the kids—nor, for that matter, the teacher, who was soon being ambushed by paparazzi in the driveway of her home. I hated what was happening: that the kids had to be reminded of this awful period, that their friends would talk about it all over again, that Kerstin would have her privacy invaded, and that all of them would be dragged back into a miserable time.

But I was running for president. I told Doug that he would need to deal with it: I couldn't look away from the job in front of me. He handled it like the mensch that he is, issuing a statement taking responsibility and expressing regret. Kerstin bravely and forthrightly issued a statement of her own, saying: "Doug and I decided to end our marriage for a variety of reasons, many years ago. He is a great father to our kids, continues to be a great friend to me and I am really proud of the warm and supportive blended family Doug, Kamala, and I have built together."

People like Loomer do their dirty work hoping their target will lash out and say something inappropriate or be personally wounded to distraction. I don't want my family to be hurt, and I think that's true for every honorable human who runs for office. If we were holding on to norms of decency, families should be off-limits. Sadly, they are not.

The "happened to turn Black" remarks blew up all over the media. Trump's team pulled out an online cooking show where I'd made masala dosa with Mindy Kaling and chatted with her about my maternal grandparents, using it as "proof" that I claimed to be Indian. I am proud of my Indian heritage.

I was running to be president, not to be an American history professor. It wasn't my duty to school the former president on America's racial history—the one-drop rule; the one-eighth law—and how this history had been, and still is, weaponized.

When my mother came alone to this country from India as a nineteen-year-old student in 1958, there were still very few South Asians in the United States. She knew that with a Black Jamaican-born father, Americans would see us as Black children. She raised Maya and me to be proud Black women.

I could hear my mother's stern voice: "Kamala, don't ever let anyone tell you who you are. *You* tell *them* who you are."

On the plane that day when I first heard about Trump's remark, we patched in Brian Fallon from DC on a call to strategize a response. Brian wanted me to punch back with a big speech about my racial identity, like the one Obama had given. I was so pissed that I didn't hold back.

"Are you fucking kidding me?" I was not about to take Trump's bait. He lies all the time, I told Brian. He throws out outrageous statements to distract from the real issues. "Today he wants me to prove my race. What next? He'll say I'm not a woman and I'll need to show my vagina?"

Brian, on the other end of the phone, fell silent. I imagined the deep crimson of his blush.

96 Days to the Election

* * *

E van Gershkovich and Paul Whelan were on the move.

The complex diplomatic effort that spanned six countries and involved the biggest prisoner exchange since the Cold War was forged of international friendships, the tattered relationships that Joe Biden and I had painstakingly mended after Trump had shredded them in his first term. This result was a product of exactly the kind of skilled diplomacy that Trump and Vance, in their deep and willful ignorance, scorned.

Evan and Paul were out of prison, along with fourteen other political prisoners. With the Russians there was always the risk of a last-minute hitch, so we waited anxiously until we had news they were in safe airspace, in flight to Turkey. From there, they'd be flown home to America. Joe Biden had the happy task of alerting their next of kin.

I called Yulia Navalnaya. I'd met and spent time with her in Munich. Her husband, Alexei, should have been on that plane. She is an immensely strong and courageous person, but I knew this day would be hard. On the call, I said that while we couldn't bring her husband home to her, I promised we would do our utmost to keep his dream of a free Russia alive.

Then I left for Fallbrook Church, to celebrate the life of my friend

Sheila Jackson Lee. From 1995, she represented the people of Houston in Congress with exceptional tenacity. President Clinton joked that her name was on the shortest list in his White House—the "Just Say Yes" list, because you knew she was one of the people who would never stop until she got the thing she wanted from you. So, you might as well say yes right from the get-go.

After the service, at the Houston airport, I was able to speak to the traveling press about the good news that Russia's unlawful detentions and mockery of justice were finally over. We landed at Joint Base Andrews. The plane carrying Evan and Paul was not due to arrive there till almost midnight, so I went home, changed out of my funeral attire, did a couple of hours' work, and then headed back to greet them. The president and I spent those few joyful minutes on the tarmac with the families who had waited in anguish for so long.

Paul Whelan, who had been incarcerated the longest, was first down the aircraft steps. As I stood by, the president got so involved in the delighted reunion between Paul and his family that he didn't notice Evan stepping off the plane. There was an awkward moment for Evan as he stood uncertainly at the base of the steps, alone, a bemused expression on his face: *What about me?* The minute I noticed, I walked forward, arms outstretched. He broke into a big grin. He was finally home.

95 Days to the Election

* * *

That Friday morning, the VP selection committee received final vetting memos on the three candidates we'd narrowed down as finalists. The committee would be going through the memos to make sure there were no last-minute surprises before we called them in for face-to-face meetings over the weekend. The residence was staked out by the press, and the media chatter was all about when I'd be interviewing. It felt like we were holding a papal conclave in the residence and the press outside were waiting for the white smoke. Getting those candidates in and out discreetly, without exposing them to a barrage, was going to take some cloak-and-dagger shenanigans.

I'd need to make the decision by Monday at the latest, since we'd announced that I'd appear with my chosen running mate Tuesday night in Philadelphia. The announcement location had been picked well in advance, simply because Pennsylvania was the most critical swing state, with nineteen electoral votes. Secrecy around the interviews was important. It built excitement and momentum for the campaign. I planned to announce my decision by video, text, and email to supporters just before the Philly rally.

The short list had been closely held. It was so secret that even my personal schedule identified the finalists only as Candidate 1, 2, and 3. But media were reporting that some on the longer list who'd been considered earlier had cleared their schedules, canceling events in case they got the call to meet with me that weekend. Some big egos were about to take a bruising. And these were important people with vital work to do. It was wrong to keep them in the dark. We decided to let CNN know that the three finalists were Mark Kelly, Josh Shapiro and Tim Walz.

Trump, of course, immediately took the most divisive tack he could think of, musing publicly that Josh Shapiro's Jewish identity would cost me the votes of Arab Americans. It was a typical dog whistle, except that now the frequency was audible to more than his Charlottesville tiki-torch acolytes.

The timing of my running mate announcement had been driven by the virtual roll call of Democratic convention delegates that had started the night before. I couldn't announce a running mate until I officially held the nomination. There was zero suspense about that, since mine was the only name on the ballot. Because of our superhuman effort on the day Joe dropped out, we'd made it clear that I had the support needed, and no other candidate competed to get the three hundred signatures required by party rules to challenge me.

The balloting was open till Monday evening, but word came through about 1:00 p.m. Friday from the party chair reporting that I'd crossed the threshold in the vote tally, making me the nominee.

I was pressing on with the business at hand when Sheila grabbed me by the arms and said, "Please just take thirty seconds! You need to appreciate the historic thing you've just accomplished!"

Trump had been saying he'd decide about debating me once I'd clinched the nomination. Sure enough, he released a statement on his Truth Social platform. It was classic Trump. Yes, he would debate me. But he'd reneged on the agreement negotiated for that debate. According to him, it would now be on September 4, not 10; it would be on Fox News, not ABC; and "the Rules will be similar to the Rules of my Debate with Sleepy Joe, who has been treated horribly by his Party – BUT WITH A FULL ARENA AUDIENCE!"

I'm sure his team leaned on him to keep the rule that mics would be silenced during the other debater's time. That was the one rule I wanted changed. I knew I could handle his disruptive asides, and I wanted viewers to see and hear how undisciplined and bullying he could be. His team knew that his crazy ranting didn't play well, so they'd kept that requirement in place. The wording of his statement made it sound as if I'd agreed to all the other changes.

Nope.

We could sense an air of panic in the Trump campaign. That day we'd announced that we'd taken in $310 million in the last month alone, more than double his donations over the same period. So we decided to punch back hard. I responded that I would be in the ABC studio on September 10 whether he was there or not and would be glad to use the ninety minutes of airtime exclusively.

94 Days to the Election

* * *

When we moved into the vice president's residence, I'd worked with a craftsman to design a table for the dining room. It comprised three squares that could fit together as one long table for big dinners or staff meetings, but could also be separated for smaller, more intimate occasions, with drop leaves that could be raised to make them round.

On Saturday morning we arranged the room for the next day's interviews. There was just a single square table in the center of the room. I would sit on one side; my potential VP would sit on the other. Either Sheila Nix or JOD would be on the sofa across the room, out of the candidate's line of sight. They would alternate as my second pair of eyes and ears. I didn't want to overstaff what was already a stressful situation.

Very few people have ever made this decision. I called Hillary and Bill Clinton, because they knew what it was like and would give me candid and confidential advice. *One of your strengths,* they said, *is that you bring a joyful energy to the campaign. You have to choose someone who won't work against that.* They told me to be aware that over the course of the campaign, people will be able to tell if it is a genuinely good relationship or a political marriage of convenience. Bill: "You have to level with them and watch how they answer."

Bill said that Al Gore was good for him "because he knew things I didn't know. We were as different as daylight and dark and it worked." They both emphasized that I'd be offering this person the chance of a lifetime, so they'd better know it. If they were someone dying for immediate public recognition, it might not be the job for them. They might have to swallow a lot of crap.

My staff and I spent much of the day going over the briefing books on each finalist, working out what we needed to glean from this final interview. We had the data. The main question remaining was: Are they going to be compatible?

I'd recruited my invaluable social secretary and residence manager, Storm Horncastle, to collect each finalist in her '99 Jeep Wrangler. The press was used to seeing her coming and going from the residence, so if her passenger ducked, no one would know he was here. We dubbed it Operation Veep in a Jeep.

I had an ulterior motive for recruiting Storm for this job. Storm is from Norway, not especially political, and had mostly worked in embassies prior to taking the job with me at the vice president's residence. She has an exquisitely tuned sense of protocol, is an excellent judge of character, and does not hold back her opinions. I thought it would be telling to see how each finalist treated her. Over the years I'd learned it's one thing how people treat me, it's another to see how they behave toward someone they perceive as less powerful. I'm especially sensitive to this because, as a child, I saw how my mother, a small brown woman with a foreign accent, would be treated in a fancy department store and other public places: as if she didn't belong or couldn't afford to be there. She was a distinguished scientist doing groundbreaking research, but often I saw her encounter derision and disrespect.

I needed to know that my running mate was a person who valued the dignity of everyone and would take a moment to show it.

93 Days to the Election

* * *

The pack of reporters staking out the gate to the Naval Observatory that Sunday had no idea that Storm had secretly arranged to come and go through an alternate entrance that hadn't been used for about twenty years. Inside, I would be making one of the most difficult decisions of my life, against a background of international tension.

On July 31 Israel had pulled off the audacious assassination of Hamas's political leader right in the heart of Tehran—at the guesthouse of the Revolutionary Guard, no less. We expected Iran to respond. The question was how, when, and with what consequences. There's campaigning, and there is governing. That weekend I would have to divide my focus between my role as a candidate for president and my most solemn duty, as sitting vice president, to help protect our nation's security.

We had decided to hold a pre-brief before each interview and a debrief after. I knew all three men; we'd worked together. But this encounter was going to be very different. Josh Shapiro, governor of Pennsylvania, arrived first.

Storm had picked him up from the parking lot of an elementary school in Glover Park. At the last minute, Storm had traded her Jeep for a vehicle with tinted windows, since discretion in this process was so important to us. Josh went to get in the front seat, but Storm instructed that he needed to be in the back, so he could duck and not been seen. She thought he seemed a little disappointed by that.

When he learned she was the residence manager, he peppered her with questions about the house, from the number of bedrooms to how he might arrange to get Pennsylvania artists' work on loan from the Smithsonian.

In our meeting he was, as always, poised, polished, and personable.

I told him how much I admired his work. He was great on the stump, a wonderful campaigner, very compelling and very bright. Our careers synced in many places. While employed as a political adviser on Capitol Hill, he took night classes to get his law degree at Georgetown and then ran for the Pennsylvania statehouse. He had been twice elected state attorney general.

I'd had a chance to see how his mind worked when we were both Rodel Fellows at the Aspen Institute in 2006, when he was a member of the Pennsylvania statehouse and I was San Francisco DA. That two-year bipartisan program for young, elected leaders included seminars on the founding documents of democracy and ethics, as well as international trips exploring global issues.

Josh had been elected governor in 2022 and was popular in a state with nineteen electoral votes that we badly needed to win.

We talked about how to handle the attacks he'd confronted on Gaza and what effect it might have on the enthusiasm we were trying to build. Big protests at the convention were a major concern. As a student, he'd written an op-ed stating that peace with Palestinians was impossible, and this decades-old article had been dragged out to smear him as "Genocide Josh." He said he felt he'd been able to deal with critics by stating clearly that his youthful opinion had been misguided and that he was fully committed to a two-state solution. He had also publicly called Netanyahu "one of the worst leaders of all time."

I asked him if he understood the job of vice president. "Because if you do, you'll be good at it and our administration will be strong."

He peppered me with questions, trying to nail down, in detail, what role I saw for my VP. At one point, he mused that he would want to be in the room for every decision. I told him bluntly that was an unrealistic expectation. A vice president is not a copresident. I had a nagging concern that he would be unable to settle for a role as number two and that it would wear on our partnership. I had to be able to completely trust the person in that role.

"Every day as president," I said, "I'll have ninety-nine problems, and my VP can't be one."

Apart from apprehensions for myself, I was also concerned for him. I thought his frustrations with the job might impact his performance in the role. And why take an effective Democratic governor out of a job he liked and was good at? But could I afford to turn my back on such a talented political athlete in such a critical state? Josh assured me he'd do everything to help me win Pennsylvania whether I chose him or not, "because this is the most important election we've faced."

I had time to hash out these thoughts in a debrief with my team. Meanwhile, Storm returned Josh to the pickup location. Storm instructed the state trooper who was arranging transport on an alternate route that would avoid driving by the vice president's residence on Massachusetts Avenue. She assumed that the press would notice official vehicles with Pennsylvania plates. She was disappointed, ten minutes later, to see those very cars on CNN, cruising right by the residence. That lack of discretion did not play well with her.

She picked up Minnesota Governor Tim Walz from a nearby dog park. He was amused by the cloak-and-dagger shenanigans. On the drive, they talked about her Norwegian background—his state has a large Norwegian community—and when he arrived, he seemed touched that Storm had his preferred beverage, Diet Mountain Dew, on the table ready for him.

It was quickly clear to me that Tim had walked into that room feeling he wouldn't get the job. The first thing he said as he sat down—I don't even know if the door had closed behind him—was:

"Whether or not you pick me, I'm going to do everything I can to get you elected."

He was immediately self-critical. "I'm not a good debater." "I've never used a teleprompter." He was less polished than Josh. But he had an appealing authenticity and was genuinely self-deprecating. A lot of people in politics act self-deprecating, but it's just that, an act. If anything, Tim over-indexed his own liabilities.

On the face of it, we had nothing in common. I'm West Coast; he's Midwest. I was born in Oakland and grew up in a working-class urban neighborhood. He's from a rural town of four hundred on the Nebraska plains. I worked at McDonald's in the summer; he worked on his family's farm. Despite those differences, Tim reminded me of everyone I grew up with. He was plainspoken, hardworking, strong, kind, and a fighter for what he believes is right. And he had a sense of humor.

Never mind the teleprompter, here was a guy who knew how to put an engine together. A guy who could talk knowledgeably to a farmer about hogs and soybeans. A guy who knew what it meant to hunt in fall to put food in the freezer to last through winter. None of it was shtick. It is just who he is.

He would make the case for the people who were not in the room. Even more valuable, Tim would *notice* who was not in the room and would know how to reach them. Of the three candidates, this quality was authentic and unique to him.

As a farmer, factory worker, Army National Guardsman, social studies teacher, football coach, and Democrat who had beaten a six-term Republican to win a congressional seat in 2006 and hold it through five elections, Tim had the most diverse life experience. He and his wife, Gwen, had struggled with infertility and had their daughter, Hope, through intrauterine insemination. Their son, Gus, still in high school, had special needs. Tim had the empathy that came from living those experiences. He knew what it meant to suffer as much as he knew what it meant to succeed.

His record as a two-term governor was impressive. He'd pushed for and signed legislation codifying reproductive rights, providing free school meals, making college tuition free for low-income families, and requiring universal background checks for gun buyers. Under his leadership, his state was designated one of the most business friendly in the nation. These were issues that mattered to me. They were the kinds of achievements I wanted for my administration. I felt like Tim knew how to help me get them done.

He said he had no ambition to be president, that his aim as vice president would be doing meaningful work to improve people's lives. It's no bad thing for a vice president to want to be president, unless that ambition plays a corrosive role in the relationship and causes disloyalty. That wouldn't be an issue with Tim. He had no fixed ideas about what the role of vice president should be, saying he would do whatever I found was most useful for him to do.

Finally, Storm set off to collect Mark Kelly, senator from Arizona. As she drove up to the agreed meeting point, he texted her: *I'm in the Tesla by the dumpsters.* For an astronaut who had walked in space, it was a very down-to-earth location for a rendezvous.

By the time I sat down with Kelly, Shapiro and Walz had both impressed me in completely different ways. There was very little weight on the scale favoring one over the other. The choice between them was tough enough. Now, an American hero had entered the room, a Navy baseball cap paired handsomely with his business suit.

Kelly served twenty-four years in the US Navy, retiring as a highly decorated captain with over five thousand flying hours and thirty-nine combat missions. He and his twin brother, both astronauts, have dedicated their lives to our country in the most noble way. Scott Kelly spent almost a year in space to study the effects of long-duration space travel on the human body. Because they are identical twins, retired astronaut Mark, down here on Earth while Scott was in space, was the perfect control subject.

Mark Kelly had also been put to the test by personal tragedy when his wife, Congresswoman Gabby Giffords, was shot in the head in an assassination attempt. I had watched as he stood beside her every step of her long, difficult recovery and fought tirelessly for sensible gun reform. We'd worked together on that issue in the Senate. They had both been supportive friends ever since I was AG.

Since I was also in charge of overseeing the National Space Council, I'd sought Mark's opinion on how to maintain a thriving aerospace industry for civilian and military ends. He'd advised me on one of my proudest achievements, the Artemis Accords, which provide a forward-looking set of international principles for how humanity uses the resources of space, the moon, and Mars. One of its most immediate concerns is creating a legal framework for how we deal with ever-proliferating "space junk," as the number of satellites increase and older ones decay and fall to Earth. When I took up my role at the Space Council, only nine nations had signed on to the accords. After my meetings with Narendra Modi, Emmanuel Macron, Andrés Manuel López Obrador, and many other world leaders, it's now fifty-five. Mark and I shared this passionate interest.

I was impressed that Mark had won his Senate seat in a traditionally red state, helping to turn it purple. He was pro-business in a way that mattered to me and could be helpful in countering the Republican narrative that I wasn't. As a senator for a border state, he'd broken with our party's preferred language on migration, calling the situation "a crisis." I agreed with that characterization and had argued that the White House should also use that word. Irregular migration *was* a crisis—a global one—to which we, America, always a beacon for the poor and the threatened, could not be, and were not, immune. Politically, I rarely emphasized that point, because it could be mischaracterized as a lame excuse.

But Mark's slowness to sign on to the PRO Act, protecting unions' right to organize, had raised a red flag. He had come out in full-throated support as recently as July 24, aware, maybe, that I would only choose a running mate who was unquestionably pro-labor.

I admired Mark Kelly. He would be magnetic.

As I sat across from him, what I saw was our American ideal of selfless service. Untarnished. He also hadn't yet had an "oh shit" moment in his relatively short political career. I wasn't sure how he would cope with the kind of garbage Trump would throw at him. Could a captain, used to deference and respect, adapt to an opponent's national campaign specifically designed to disrespect him, to cut a hero down to something small? John Kerry, a war hero, had been swiftboated—defamed in an untrue campaign about his military record that had unfairly damaged his reputation. The guy who led that effort, Chris LaCivita, was now one of Trump's top campaign aides. I realized that I couldn't afford to test Mark Kelly in that ugly grinder.

When Kelly left, I got on a Zoom call with the selection committee and my chosen committee of advisers: Senator Catherine Cortez Masto, Labor Secretary Marty Walsh, former Congressman Cedric Richmond, and Tony West. We reviewed what we'd heard from each of these exceptional men and weighed the pros and cons. Their concerns were how adeptly and passionately each of them would defend me. In short, who would be most loyal and effective at the job. The ambition must be for the job, not for the political future beyond.

To get a young person's opinion, I called my godson, Alexander Hudlin, seventeen years old and very much a creature of the zeitgeist. He was for Walz. "Auntie, I like him."

My senior staff, to a person, strongly favored Tim.

A confidential group within the campaign had already mocked up announcements pumping whichever of the three I chose, ready to press "send" once my decision could be announced. This helped me envision the narrative of our ticket.

It was late when I finally sat down in the family room. Maya and Tony were staying with us. They both liked Walz. Maya especially liked the fact that he was not trying to be anything but the best VP for her sister: "He's loyal, he'll have your back on the trail, and it's clear that you like him," she said.

Doug and I went back and forth. He had known Josh longer and leaned that way.

It was always going to have to be my decision. I told my staff and family that I didn't want any more input, and I went to do something practical: I made a tasty rub and seasoned a pork roast.

By the time I went to bed, I'd decided on Walz.

92 Days to the Election

* * *

In the morning, as usual, Doug was up before me. He likes to make his coffee from scratch. I've pointed out to him that there are machines that grind the beans and make the brew so that it's all ready for you when you wake up, but he's not interested. He likes his system.

I was standing there in my bathrobe, waiting for the noise of the grinder to stop.

"Honey," I said. "Have I made the right choice?"

I hate being indecisive, but there I was. Doug turned and gave me a look. "Your gut is always right. Trust it."

I knew very well that wheels were already in motion. Sheila had assembled a small, trusted team who were en route to Minnesota to brief Tim and get the whole family ready for the rally that night. Ink was already flowing onto hundreds of Harris–Walz posters.

I recalled an earlier conversation with Barack Obama. He'd also narrowed it down to three finalists: Joe Biden, Evan Bayh, and Tim Kaine. I asked him how he'd finally decided on Joe.

"I chose Joe because we were very different," he said. "Different types, different sets of experience. You cover more ground."

That accorded with my thinking and made me feel good about my decision. While I worked out, I turned on the television to see

what the American people were watching. So much political pun-
ditry feels to me like high-class gossip, usually based on speculation
with minimal facts. That morning's chatter was no exception.

It was time to call Tim. I got my campaign videographer ready to
film the call for social media. Then I sat down at the table and tapped
in his number. It went to voicemail. I called again. Same.

Tim, at home in Minnesota, saw "blocked number" on his cell
phone and figured it was a spam call. He didn't pick up. He didn't
want his line to be busy, just in case I called.

I had to get Sheila to text him and tell him to pick up the damn
phone.

The cat out of the bag, Gwen, his wife, videoed the call on their
end. She caught him sitting down by the window in his camo baseball
cap as he finally answered.

"Hi, this is Tim."

"It's Kamala Harris, good morning, Governor . . . Listen, I want
you to do this with me. Let's do this together. Would you be my running mate? And let's get this thing on the road?"

"I would be honored."

My next job was to quickly contact Josh and Mark. The news
had already started to leak, and they should hear this from me, not
the media. Dana Remus later let me know that Josh had been trying
to reach me earlier that morning. The only reason I could imagine
for him calling was that he'd intuited he wouldn't be the choice and
wanted to withdraw first, so it would be seen as his decision. But
nothing was said about that, and he graciously offered to introduce
us in Philly. I'd been concerned that holding the rally there, as long
planned, would seem disrespectful to him, since so many had expected and wanted him to be my choice. But he dismissed those concerns and said that he knew such a major event couldn't be relocated
at the last minute, even if he had wanted me to, which he did not. It
would, he said, be a great opportunity to show party unity around the
newly decided ticket. I appreciated his leadership.

Mark Kelly was equally gracious, promising that I had his support and that he and Gabby would do everything they possibly could. He lived up to that promise throughout the rest of the campaign.

Of course, the world had not conveniently paused as I managed the VP process. The White House sits at the center of a hailstorm of events, national and global, and that barrage doesn't stop for an election. As I'd been interviewing and making my decision, I was acutely aware of the rising tensions between Iran and Israel.

That afternoon I headed to the Situation Room, where the president had convened a meeting of the national security team. My first duty as vice president was to be there to help assess the intelligence and advice, and to offer the room, and the president, my perspective. I'm only the eleventh sitting vice president to run for president. When speaking on the campaign trail or facing Trump on the debate stage, the gravity of moments in the Situation Room weighed heavily on my heart and mind.

I will never discuss, here or anywhere else, the conversations in that room, the middle-of-the-night calls to gather there, the dramas that unfolded. Unlike the current national security team, we did not hash out our plans on Signal. America's national security relies heavily on classified information that our adversaries try very hard to acquire. Why make it easy for them? And where is the professionalism, where is the self-discipline?

As soon as I became vice president, I disabled the text capability and even the camera on my phone. For four years, I didn't receive or send a text message of any kind, official or unofficial. As for matters of national security, whatever the hour or the day of the week, the president and I and our entire team hauled our asses out of bed and into a SCIF—a sensitive compartmented information facility—or the Situation Room. Sometimes, in the middle of dinner or watching a show, I would receive a certain call and immediately get up and leave the room. Doug would say, "There she goes again," aware that he'd never know from me what crisis had interrupted us.

Our task that afternoon was to assess current intelligence and make sure we were doing everything we could to calm tensions. Back in April, Iran had launched more than one hundred ballistic missiles at Israel. It could have led to an uncontrollable escalation. It hadn't, thanks to intense diplomatic efforts by our administration. We and our regional allies had rallied to Israel's defense and limited the damage.

We have not had diplomats or a CIA station in Iran for almost a half century, since students occupied our embassy and took our people hostage in 1979. We know the threat posed by the regime of the ayatollahs, but the United States has not always aligned with our Israeli allies on how best to contain it. The Joint Comprehensive Plan of Action, the nuclear deal painstakingly brokered by the Obama administration, had paused Tehran's march to the bomb and given us the ability to see into Iran's nuclear program through regular International Atomic Energy Agency inspections. Netanyahu had encouraged Trump to tear up the plan, which he did in 2018, shutting down that ability and unshackling Tehran.

Differences of opinion existed even within our national security team. As with every national security issue, the president would hear from the generals. He would challenge the heads of the intelligence community. He would seek a global view, teasing out how any given action we might take in one region would be perceived by our allies or our adversaries elsewhere. His years of experience in foreign policy clearly showed in those discussions. He was always focused, always commander in chief in that room.

My job was to sit at his right hand, hear all views, test assumptions, ask hard questions, and help him make the best decisions he could.

91 Days to the Election

* * *

I hadn't met Tim's family. From the vetting file, I knew that his wife, Gwen, had been a teacher for two decades, and that she and Tim had met when their underfunded public school in Nebraska had to install a flimsy partition dividing one classroom into two. She taught on one side, Tim on the other. I also knew that she'd championed criminal justice reform and stressed the role of educational opportunity in diverting youth from crime. I knew we'd be closely aligned on these issues.

While she was known as an important adviser to her husband, she hadn't taken a high-profile public role as Minnesota's First Lady. I wondered how she'd manage the glare of the next ninety-one days.

It didn't take long to find out. Gwen got right in there and proved to be a force. As wife of a two-term governor and a guy who'd held congressional leadership positions, she was no neophyte on the trail, exuding warmth, heart, and soul. A campaign like ours is something you do as two couples, two families, two partnerships, combining to form a third. It forges intimacy and brings you close.

I adore Gwen.

Our first encounter was in the locker room of the Temple University gym, appropriate enough for Coach Walz. It was my idea for the campaign to lean into Tim's brand as coach, a role that conveys both strength and caring. Tim was a relative unknown nationally, but there was so much about him that would be familiar to people's everyday relationships and experiences. Not many people have met an astronaut, and they might not love politicians, but most people can relate to a high school coach. And with early voting starting in forty-five days, that immediate connection was important. Knowing that, I'd asked the team to print up COACH signs that people could hold up at rallies.

Their kids, Hope and Gus, understandably seemed a little shell-shocked by the sudden change in their young lives. Doug and I understood what they were going through. Our kids had been there four years before. I sent the staff away. We wanted to have a moment where we were just two families getting acquainted. I was concerned for the kids and wanted them to know this was going to be okay and that we cared about them as people, not just props to walk onstage with. We pulled chairs into a circle and chatted, getting to know one another a little, before it was time to go.

As we stood, Tim gathered us in a huddle, like we were his team in the locker room about to run onto the field. We put our hands in the circle and raised them with a cheer.

Ten thousand people had gathered to hear from us. The roar that met us when we walked out onstage was so deafening we could barely hear ourselves. Tim, unused to crowds of that size, looked astonished.

My first job that night was to introduce Tim Walz to the country. This was not hard: the man has a biography that could provide scripts for several Hallmark movies. I led with how he'd coached a perennially losing high school football team—they hadn't scored a single touchdown in the first six weeks of the season before he became coach—to winning the state championship.

I went on to tell the story of how a student who wanted to start the first gay-straight alliance at the school had gone to this storied football coach to ask for his support. Walz immediately agreed to become the group's faculty adviser. Tim said he thought it would send a message of inclusion if the adviser was a football coach, a soldier, straight, and married.

Waiting in the wings with Doug, Gwen was visibly nervous. When it came time for them to join us, Doug said, "Follow me!" and swept her out onto the stage.

As the four of us stood for applause, Tim grabbed Doug, rather than Gwen, for the big hug. (Cole and Tony later joked that Doug had never hugged them as passionately as he hugged Tim that night.)

When Tim clasped my hand to thrust it high in an enthusiastic victory gesture, he was so tall that the entire front of my jacket rose up. It felt like I was dangling from a jungle gym while wearing a suit. Not the best look. I made a mental note to tell him: *From now on, when we do that, you gotta bend your elbow.*

We rode the high of the crowd that night. It was a room full of joy. The campaign was fresh, alive, vibrating with energy. It seemed like anything was possible.

90 Days to the Election

* * *

I t was a perfect summer day in Wisconsin: red barns against a rinsed blue sky, emerald fields ripe with the promise of a good harvest. I lived in Wisconsin for a while when I was a preschooler and my parents had teaching jobs there. The beauty of the state on days like this brings back strong childhood memories.

I'd left a muggy, overcast Washington, DC, for my first full day on the trail with Tim. When I boarded Air Force Two, I checked in with my team in the front cabin. Sheila and my dedicated deputy chief of staff, Erin Wilson, were among those staffing me that day. Then I headed back, through the cabin containing my Secret Service detail, for a few minutes of off-the-record chat, or OTR, with the traveling press. These informal sessions before wheels up were useful for both of us. They got to ask me anything and, as the different reporters who joined us covered diverse beats, the topics could be wide-ranging. My responses were candid and would often inform the on-record questions they would ask me later. For my part, I got a preview of the issues that might shape the day's news cycle.

Pool reporters work hard, fast, and selflessly. Since not every reporter can fit on the plane or in the West Wing, representatives of each media organization rotate the responsibility for being with me or the president, and send out the first quick drafts of what is going on for the use of all their colleagues. They are on duty whenever we are engaged in public events, and in a campaign that can be a long day's work.

Pool reports generally start with the words "Pool swept"—meaning they and their belongings have been checked by security—"and loading, rolling at" some ungodly hour. They generally end late at night, with the word "Lid." This indicates that there will be no more news that day, although not because I've finally gone to bed.

My day continues with briefings, prep, sometimes radio interviews, live or recorded. My personal "lid" often doesn't go on until the very early hours.

On the way back from the OTR with the press pool to my cabin up front, I had a cherished ritual. I always high-fived the head of my Secret Service detail, who would stand as I walked by.

"Max!" I'd exclaim as our hands met in the air.

"Ma'am!" he'd crisply reply.

The Secret Service assigns code names to its protectees. Mine, aptly, was Pioneer. Doug's, Playmaker. The kids, who also had Secret Service protection, were allowed to choose their own names, so long as they started with *P*. Ella, with her quirky sense of humor, chose Pickle. Cole became Pirate.

We landed at Chippewa Valley Regional Airport to be greeted by local officials and Girl Scout Troop #3307. I asked the girls about their summer plans, and one asked about mine. I said I was planning on going somewhere in ninety days, and we shared a laugh.

I got into my motorcade, but we weren't pulling out. I asked Max why we weren't leaving. That was when I learned we were being held up by J. D. Vance. He was out of his car and walking toward Air Force Two, in violation of every rule of security and protocol.

I later learned that he told reporters he was there because "I just wanted to check out my future plane."

Had I known he was pulling that juvenile stunt, I would've been inclined to step from my car and use a word I believe best pronounced correctly. It begins with an *m* and ends with *ah*.

By now, I suppose, he will be well acquainted with that old plane. It came into service for Al Gore in 1998 and it's hard to replace, since Boeing no longer makes a jet as compact yet high-powered, able to take off and land at smaller airports like Chippewa Valley Regional. Vance will have learned that the vice president's seat resists adjustment when you want to move it, but flies unexpectedly forward at inopportune moments. He'll know that the door to the restroom doesn't always stay closed, or may not even open. Wrestling with that door as we were trying to fix America's infrastructure problems, I knew this was one infrastructure problem I would not be able to fix.

When press would cover me hustling up the stairs to board, it wasn't because I relished the luxury of that plane. It was the thought of the comfy Uggs I kept on board, when I could finally kick off my high heels.

It is probably just as well that I didn't know about Vance's sophomoric comment that day, since I was already annoyed. As Maya Angelou famously said, "When someone shows you who they are, believe them the first time." He had dared to accuse Tim Walz of "stolen valor"—a grievous smear pieced together from the most threadbare scraps. Walz entered the National Guard at seventeen and served for twenty-four years, including an overseas deployment to Italy. He could have retired after twenty years but re-upped after 9/11 and continued to serve until deciding to run for Congress in May 2005, flipping a solidly red seat. His unit was notified of a deployment two months after his retirement and actually deployed a full eight months after that.

Vance picked on Tim's statement, when arguing for an assault weapons ban in 2018, that "these weapons of war that I carried in war" had no place on civilian streets. Walz hadn't seen combat during his deployments. Neither had Vance, who served four years as reporter in the Marines' public affairs department. But that didn't stop him from spinning Tim's minor misstatement into a swiftboat-style slander. He also implied that Tim's retirement had been timed to avoid the Iraq deployment, even though it had been entirely driven by the timing of his run for Congress.

These attacks went against everything I knew and admired about the military code of honor. I was appalled that Vance would stoop so low to wound and rattle a fellow veteran, a better man.

Our motorcade turned down a dusty road toward a vast field colorful with twelve thousand people and resonant with the strains of the band Bon Iver finishing a live set. Some people had abandoned their cars a mile from the field and walked the rest of the way. Many held their blue Harris–Walz signs over their heads for protection from the brilliant sunshine.

A local farmer introduced Tim as "a lifelong Midwesterner" who "understands rural America." Tim proved it as he spoke, connecting to the enthusiastic crowd and finding a Midwestern cadence in which to talk about reproductive rights, LGBTQ+ issues, and how Trump's Republicans infringed on basic freedoms.

"Even if we wouldn't make the same choices for ourselves . . . there's a golden rule: Mind your own damn business," he said. "I don't need you telling me about our health care, I don't need you telling us who we love, and I sure the hell don't need you telling us what books we're going to read."

Then he took a sly swipe at J. D. Vance, who was over at an aviation equipment manufacturer in nearby Eau Claire, busy lying about Tim's record.

"Just like all of us in regular America we go to Yale, and then we have our careers funded by Silicon Valley billionaires, and then you write a book about the place you grew up and you trash that place . . . We're better than that."

When I took the podium after Tim, the crowd was in high spirits. As I talked about Trump, a chant started: "Lock him up!"

I disliked that chant when Trump aimed it at Hillary, and I wasn't about to encourage it at my rallies. In the democracy I cherish, we don't lock up people because they are our political opponents. They are locked up if a jury determines they have committed serious crimes. As a former prosecutor I know what it means to ask that someone be locked up; I know the seriousness of depriving someone of their liberty. It's not something I have ever taken lightly. I carried the moral weight of it. I would never reduce it to a chant to please and entertain a crowd.

I held up my hand and interrupted the chants. "Well, hold on. You know what? The courts are going to handle that part of it.

"What we're going to do is beat him in November."

That evening, we held an even bigger rally in a large airport hangar at Wayne County airport near Detroit. The crowd spilled out of the hangar and across the tarmac where Air Force Two had landed. There were several giant screens for the outdoor crowd that couldn't see the rally stage.

The size of the crowd unnerved Donald Trump. He would later post on Truth Social that "nobody" had been there and the crowd pictures were fake.

He was getting rattled.

Supporters gleefully posted their own photos from the rally. Lavora Barnes, chair of the Michigan Democratic Party, playfully posted a photo of herself addressing the crowd from the podium and thanked "whoever made the AI image" for being "kind enough to include me at the lectern. That AI crowd was really loud," she wrote, "my ears just stopped ringing from their imaginary cheering."

David Plouffe's post on X was less tongue in cheek. "These are not conspiratorial rantings from the deepest recesses of the internet. The author could have the nuclear codes and be responsible for decisions that will affect us all for decades."

89 Days to the Election

* * *

Shawn Fain, president of the United Auto Workers, has union in his DNA. His grandparents came up from the South to work in Indiana car plants—two at GM, one at Chrysler. He was hired at Chrysler in 1994, just in time to watch UAW courage evaporate and corruption take hold as auto jobs moved to nonunion plants that they'd failed to organize or out of the country entirely. As president, he led an audacious series of strikes that won workers more than 25 percent pay increases. He sometimes wears a pin commemorating his take-no-prisoners approach to those acrimonious contract talks. It's a disc with a tiny spinning arrow reading FUCK. The arrow points variously to words on the pin's rim: THIS, OFF, and YOU.

I stood on the picket line with UAW workers during the strikes and I admired the way Fain's leadership had revived the union. Tim and I met with him and 170 union members at Local 900 Hall in Wayne, Michigan. Fain said the union had endorsed me because "Kamala Harris is one of us. Tim Walz is one of us." As he talked about the "Trump–Vance disaster," members in the hall interjected "Felon!" "Racist!" "Scab!" He asked the members to show up for us in the campaign, putting into action the organizing capacity that has always made unions integral to Democrats' electoral success. When Tim spoke, he underlined that message: "Eighty-nine days. We can do anything for eighty-nine days. Tell people, 'Sleep when you're dead, you've got work to do.'"

88 Days to the Election

* * *

Trump had been sitting on his gilded furniture at home in Mar-a-Lago for a week, letting me dominate the news cycle. Perhaps realizing this, and worried for his candidacy, he'd finally agreed to debate me on September 10 and suggested that two more debates should follow. I said I'd be glad to discuss terms for those.

As Tim and I barnstormed Arizona, meeting with small business owners at a Latino-owned restaurant and talking about border security, Trump headed to solidly red Montana for the purpose of undermining the principled Democratic Senator Jon Tester, whom he had campaigned against and failed to unseat in the previous election cycle.

It was at his rally in Bozeman that he once again pretended he didn't know how to pronounce my name. "Ka-*mar*-la, sometimes referred to as *Kar*-ma-la, you know, she's got about nine different ways of pronouncing the name. And because the press is so dishonest, no matter how you say it, they'll say you were wrong. You were wrong! I don't care if I get it right. Actually, I couldn't care less." He was playing up the disrespect, but the secondary intent was to reinforce the notion that I was alien, other, too different to lead America. He lied and said I'd refused to debate him, when he'd been the one throwing up obstacles, and then said I'd refused to do a press interview. "You know why? 'Cause she's dumb."

I read the volley of insults as a signal that he was unnerved by the crowds I was drawing and the continuing flood of funds to our campaign. Comments to reporters that day by Montana Senator Steve Daines, the chairman of the National Republican Senatorial Committee, seemed to confirm that. "There's definitely a honeymoon period going on," he said of the enthusiasm for my candidacy. He predicted it would continue through the Democratic National Convention and the mood would change by mid-September.

It turned out to be more complicated than that. And he was off on the timing.

But he wasn't entirely wrong.

87 Days to the Election

* * *

There had been hecklers at the rally in Phoenix the night before, and once again I'd addressed them directly. I'd been talking about health care as a human right when a small group of Gaza protesters interrupted.

"Okay, guys," I said. "Let's talk Gaza for a moment. We all want this war to end and to get the hostages out, and I will work on it full-time when I am president, as I have been."

That morning, we woke to news of an Israeli strike that had killed at least eighty people in Gaza. As I left the hotel I took questions from the press in the parking lot, underlining yet again that even though Israel had every right to go after Hamas, far too many civilians were being killed and that Israel had a responsibility to avoid these deaths.

It was a blisteringly hot afternoon in Phoenix, and when we arrived in Las Vegas a little before 4:00 p.m., it was even hotter: 109 degrees. Since I'd joined the race, volunteer numbers in Nevada had surged 400 percent, thanks in large part to the organizing work of Megan Jones. She came to me five years earlier, schooled in the Harry Reid style of politics, and like him, she knew how to throw a punch on behalf of people who needed defending.

There was a long line of supporters still waiting to get through the magnetometers into the university arena where we'd hold the rally. I was concerned for so many people standing outside in that extreme weather, especially when I heard ambulance sirens. People were collapsing from heatstroke. Local officials wisely made the call to close the doors to avoid more casualties. Four thousand were turned away.

On that occasion, the officials made the right, humane call. But there were other times, other venues, where my deputy chief of staff, Erin, had to argue with fire marshals who wanted to shut the doors and turn crowds away long before the posted safe capacity had been reached. Sometimes this happened when the lines were still long and whole sections of seating had yet to be filled. It was political gamesmanship, pure and simple. I was lucky to have a tough-minded team to push back against it. But they did not always prevail.

So many people stand behind a candidate, doing unglamorous, indispensable work. Juan Ortega oversaw my advance team, the people who wrangle venues, hotels, drop-in visits, liaising with local communities, smoothing over all kinds of problems. One person I saw almost every day was Alexia Lewis. She was there, in the wings, at every rally. I would walk from the venue's green room to a designated spot backstage where, if there was a monitor, I could watch the remarks of the person introducing me. Then I would move to the wings at the side of the stage. It would be just me, Alexia, and the Secret Service. Alexia would stand, her right hand held out in a stop sign, and I would wait obediently behind her. "Freedom" would play and at the exactly right moment, Alexia would turn her hand over in a go-ahead gesture, and I would head for the stage. She was my human traffic light.

To the twelve thousand who had made it inside at that Las Vegas rally, I expressed gratitude to the Culinary Workers Union, which had endorsed us, and I promised to work to increase the minimum wage. The CWU's members are mostly women, mostly immigrants. They prepare the food, make the beds, clean the rooms, do the invisible work that allows visitors to have a great time. They are the people you don't see: hardworking, unsung, underpaid.

The CWU had asked, in earlier discussions, that we eliminate tax on tips, and my policy team had been working on our proposal before Trump's half-baked announcement. I'd much rather give a tax cut to low-wage service workers than to billionaires. But unlike Trump, I worked to pair the exemption idea with an increase in the minimum wage, because the sad fact is that most tipped workers are so underpaid that they don't earn enough to owe any federal taxes. For those people, eliminating the tax on their tips would be meaningless. I stressed that the exemption would be crafted to ensure affluent professionals didn't start restructuring their compensation to take advantage of the loophole.

Las Vegas was the last stop on this swing state tour.

Air Force Two was heading next to San Francisco, where my political career began.

86 Days to the Election

* * *

One reason I'd come home to the Bay Area was to address nearly seven hundred key supporters who together just that evening had raised over $12 million for my campaign.

There were many long-standing friends there, but two of the faces I was happiest to see were Amara's and Leela's. They dashed into my arms, and I hugged and loved them up. It had been only a couple of weeks since I'd waved goodbye to them from my helicopter, but so much had happened.

When Nancy Pelosi, vivid in a fuchsia pantsuit, walked onstage to introduce me, the audience stood in applause. She had been the most skilled House Speaker since Tip O'Neill. Branded a "San Francisco liberal," her opponents soon learned that she was genetically a Baltimore girl: steely, pragmatic, and resilient. Everyone in that room believed she'd been a factor in changing the fate of this campaign. In her pointed public statements and in private, she'd brought some realism to Joe and his inner circle, forcing them to confront the dwindling money and tanking polls.

When I ran for San Francisco DA in 2003, Nancy had supported the incumbent I was running against. When I won, she praised my strategy. She had been blunt about preferring a mini primary after

Joe stepped down. But she'd quickly offered her full support to me once she realized I had the numbers and the vocal support of so many other party leaders.

Before my speech, I had a meet and greet with some high-level donors. I pulled aside one of the most long-standing and generous, a leader in Silicon Valley. My head close to his ear, I said, "I'm concerned about Musk. Are you guys on top of it?" I wanted reassurance that the tech people who supported democracy were putting resources into combating mis- and disinformation. We needed a counterforce to whatever might be brewing, and I knew that the campaign I'd inherited didn't have the skill set or the resources for it. The people I knew in Silicon Valley had a much better grasp of how deep the roots went, how far they spread.

Elon Musk had set off my spidey senses long before his MAGA-fication and his endorsement of Trump. Both SpaceX and Tesla sprang to life in California, and millions of California taxpayers had helped the companies prosper. But when Democrats tried to tie electric car subsidies to workplace standards—Tesla had been sued for labor violations, including racial discrimination and suppressing union organizing efforts—Musk began a rightward pivot. It accelerated during Covid, when he refused to close the Tesla plant to protect the health of his workers. When he moved his operations to Texas, he claimed it was because the state offered more "freedom," which was the height of hypocrisy, since Texas, with its draconian abortion ban and the privacy-shredding policies around it, violated the most basic of human liberties.

Musk is a talented entrepreneur. But there are genius engineers behind the cars and rockets, such as Tesla's former longtime chief technical officer, J. B. Straubel, who deserve just as much credit.

Despite what I think of Musk, I believe Joe Biden made a mistake in not inviting him to the White House in 2021 for an event promoting our electric vehicle policy. I shared this view with his team. Behind the president on the lawn that day were electric Fords, Chevys, Jeeps. American-made Teslas, then the world's most innovative and successful electric cars, were nowhere to be seen. Biden, loyal to the UAW, was sending a message about Musk's anti-union stance. But as president of the United States, if you are convening the nation's manufacturers of electric vehicles and the biggest player in the field is not there, it simply doesn't make sense. Musk never forgave it.

Since he had acquired Twitter and sacked its content moderators and fact-checkers, the platform had become a den of conspiracy theories and alt-right bile. It was also, increasingly, Musk's personal megaphone for boosting Trump and denigrating me. Musk had announced that he would interview Trump live on X the next evening. He would deliver Trump the opportunity to spew his lies, free of fact-checking.

And in the days that followed, he would deliver a whole lot more.

85 Days to the Election

* * *

"This space is not available." That was the message in the dead air of what was supposed to be the live stream between Trump and Musk. The conversation, due to start at 8:00 p.m., finally kicked off at 8:42 p.m. Musk couldn't even run a live stream in the year 2024.

What followed, eventually, was the usual litany of insults and lies—at least twenty false claims, according to CNN fact-checkers—as the two edgelords stroked each other's egos.

I thought back to meetings I'd convened with other business leaders and CEOs when we were advocating our Build Back Better agenda; people who had shown that you can build great companies while taking care of your workforce and the planet. Among them were Hamdi Ulukaya of Chobani, Alison Whritenour of Seventh Generation, Jenna Johnson of Patagonia, and Josh Silverman of Etsy. All the leaders I'd invited ran highly successful businesses that also supported childcare and/or paid leave policies for their employees.

We would discuss how our agenda would support childcare and therefore help the corporate bottom line. When families don't have reliable, quality care for their kids, it increases absenteeism, lowers productivity, and leads to higher turnover. The estimated losses to earnings and revenues are $57 billion a year.

These younger leaders in the corporate world understood that paid leave gave a good return on investment. It was not only the right thing to do, but it made economic sense. It's a win-win for workers and the companies. People work more productively and without distraction if they know their kids are well cared for.

Our goal in the Build Back Better legislation was to ensure that no parent who wants to work, or who has to work, would end up paying more than 7 percent of their income on childcare.

The Republicans, of course, mischaracterized these provisions in the legislation. They call it socialism; I call it capitalism, and a great ROI.

78 Days to the Election

The Convention, Day 1

* * *

It was supposed to have been Joe Biden's convention. Covid had robbed him of a big celebration when he won the nomination in 2020. And now, I suppose, a part of him felt robbed again.

The long signs prepared for the crowd to wave during his climactic speech that night inadvertently told the whole story. WE ❤ JOE, they read. And in small print: "Paid for by Harris for President."

I was sensitive to how he and his family must be feeling. It was not the end any of them had wanted for his fifty years of public service.

But I was also extremely proud of what we had accomplished in four years. This convention would have the big emotional beats, the important speeches, but it would also be fun. We'd put thought into engaging young delegates. There was a special area set up for social media influencers, and DJ Cassidy was going to turn the sometimes tedious roll call into a nationwide dance party, spinning music organic to each state.

I love our conventions. I love running into delegates from Alaska and American Samoa, Mississippi and Maine: Americans united by a passion for democracy. I love that at this huge event—the jumbotrons,

TV cameras, lights, speakers—there's a real intimacy in the hall. Local organizers and political icons rubbing shoulders. Elected leaders and grassroots activists and big donors thrown together for an intense four days.

At my very first convention, in Los Angeles in 2000, I'd been a committed young Dem who hadn't yet run for anything. My bestie, Chrisette, who later introduced me to Doug, attended with me, sitting high up in the rafters, cheering for Al Gore.

Twelve years later, as California AG, I had my first speaking role. It didn't go to plan. The convention that year was held in Charlotte, North Carolina, and I was cochair of the rules committee with Martin O'Malley, then the governor of Maryland. The city had rushed to get ready for the incoming hordes. It didn't quite succeed. Parts of the hotel booked for our California delegation remained under construction, with the manufacturer's stickers still on the elevators and no hot water in the showers. When I spoke at the delegates' breakfast, I led with a line from the Eagles song: "Welcome to the Hotel California."

I was supposed to give a report on the rules committee meeting and then, two nights later, a speech on my work as AG taking on the big banks. When I rehearsed, the convention director had sage advice: "Walk out there like you bought that podium. You own it. It's your podium."

I was trying for that confident strut—head up, shoulders back—when my stiletto sank right through the floor. It had found the trapdoor in the stage.

"If anything goes wrong with the prompter," I'd been instructed, "don't worry. There's a copy of your speech on the shelf of the podium."

It was the opening of the convention. The arena was filled with delegates for the very first committee report. As I looked up at the screen where I expected to see the text of my rules committee remarks scrolling, I realized that they'd loaded, instead, my speech for two nights later. As I improvised—"We had a great meeting of the rules committee, we talked about the rules . . ."—my hand was groping for the promised paper speech on the podium shelf. It wasn't there.

No matter how many speeches I've made since then, the memory of that teleprompter fail has always been at the back of my mind. I knew it would be with me even as I walked out to accept the nomination.

Of all the conventions I've attended, this was the most united in years. There'd often been undercurrents—not-quite-mended rifts: Hillary supporters sour that she'd been run over by Barack, Bernie supporters resentful of Hillary's win.

It was hard to detect anything but relief in this hall. We could have been staring down a very different four days. It could have been a contested convention, a messy floor fight. Instead, there was gratitude that Biden had passed the torch to me, relief that I'd been able to grasp it, a sense of unity and enthusiasm.

Delegates wore T-shirts—some homemade—with a range of slogans. A simple ,LA was popular: a playful instruction on how to pronounce my first name. KAMALA IS BRAT (a Charli XCX reference) abounded. SAY IT TO MY FACE, quoting my debate challenge to Trump, and CHUCKS & PEARLS, referencing my habit of pairing Converse sneakers with my favorite pearl necklace, were also abundant.

I appreciated a shirt that read: VOTING IS MY "BLACK JOB." A delegate and dear friend from San Francisco, Matthew J. Rothschild, proved to be a favorite with press photographers, sporting a boater hat bedazzled with sprays of glittery stars, red, white, and blue ribbons, and a Kamala doll head.

It's not tradition for the nominee to speak on the first night, but I planned to make a "surprise" appearance to welcome everybody and to praise "our incredible president."

Backstage, I met up with two of the most important people from my childhood. They would speak that night, following a short biographical video about me. Stacey Johnson-Batiste was my best friend in kindergarten and remains one of my closest confidantes. Her mom,

Doris Johnson, and my mother were dear friends. I remember them laughing; they would always cut up together.

When she looked at me, held my hand, and said, "Your mother would be so proud of you," I knew she was standing in for my mother and I could feel my throat constrict. But I would not let myself cry. I told myself, *I will not do that tonight.*

After I went onstage for my brief remarks, I joined the audience to sit next to Doug and Tim.

I'm not sure when I started to worry. But at some point, I realized that things were running behind. I knew the program; I knew what we had to get through. If they didn't pick up the pace, I feared that Joe's speech might get pushed right to the edge or even out of prime time in the East.

I wanted Joe to have his moment. I couldn't figure out what was up. None of the speeches seemed to be running noticeably over time. Although I did observe that Shawn Fain—sporting a TRUMP IS A SCAB T-shirt—finished his timed remarks, which had been loaded in the teleprompter, and then continued his rousing defense of unions from additional notes he'd somehow smuggled onto the podium. And while the introduction said *Senator* Raphael Warnock, the person who actually walked onto the stage was *Reverend* Warnock, the head preacher at Ebenezer Baptist Church. Needless to say, he was not brief.

I learned later that Biden's people were backstage, reaming out anyone and everyone. Parts of the program were untouchable. Jill Biden had to speak, then their daughter, Ashley, would introduce Joe. To gain back time, something would have to be cut. In the end, a performance by James Taylor and a video about Joe that Steven Spielberg worked on were regretfully sacrificed.

He was supposed to go on at 9:44 p.m. Even with those program cuts, when Joe walked onstage to an almost five-minute audience chant of "Thank you, Joe!" it was 11:30 Eastern time.

He spoke for nearly an hour, detailing the accomplishments of our administration. It was a legacy speech for him, not an argument for me, and he was entitled to it. But if we waited for some personal stories about working with me and what qualities he had seen that led him to endorse me, they weren't there.

And then, at last, a fulsome, generous endorsement: "Selecting Kamala as my vice president was the very first decision I made when I became our nominee. And it was the best decision I made in my whole career."

Given that his career spanned half a century, that was saying something.

77 Days to the Election

The Convention, Day 2

* * *

Tim and I left the convention that day to get back on the campaign trail. We couldn't afford four days out of the battleground states, but the only night they could spare me was the night of Doug's speech, which made me unhappy.

Milwaukee was the closest battleground city, and it was the same stadium where the Republicans had held their convention the previous month and where the Democrats would have convened but for Covid in 2020.

In a perfectly timed and choreographed piece of stagecraft, the convention producers pulled off a live feed between the rally and the convention. I walked out onstage in Milwaukee just as the roll call concluded in Chicago with my California delegation giving me their votes.

The roll call is alphabetical, other than the nominee's home state, which is given the honor of being last. On the big screens in the Milwaukee stadium, I recognized all the beaming faces of the California delegates bunched around the microphone. There were people who had been with me my whole career, some who had worked on my very first campaign, stuffing envelopes under my mother's guidance. It was an emotional moment for me. And it was wonderful to be able to thank those delegates and share the high excitement of the convention with the Wisconsin audience.

Flying back to the convention, we watched live on my iPad as Doug gave his speech. We were about to land as Doug wrapped up. The cabin erupted.

"DOUG! DOUG! DOUG!"

I was so proud of him. Before I became top of the ticket, Doug expected to have a minor role at the convention—a couple of minutes tucked in someplace. He was suddenly moved way up the roster.

"You're going Tuesday," he was told.

"Oh, okay, who am I on with?" he asked.

"Barack and Michelle. You three are the prime-time package."

No pressure.

He'd worked hard, writing and practicing the speech. "The words are good. I just have to do it justice, delivering it for her," he'd told Cole and Ella. He had written it with three main points: "I want people to know she's a badass, that she's spent her whole career working for the people, and I want them to know that she gives a shit."

He phrased it a little more delicately in the speech.

Other family members, including Ella, Meena, and my goddaughter, Helena Hudlin, also took to the stage to reminisce about my role in their lives. The way the kids stepped up into these highly public roles with grace and aplomb made me so proud. My baby nieces stole the show with their "tutorial" on how to pronounce my name. ("*Comma*, like a comma in a sentence, then *la*, like la la la.")

Our creative Cole had directed and narrated a funny and touching video that ran before Doug spoke. It had family pictures of Doug in his very '70s oversized bow tie at his bar mitzvah, and as an athletic hunk at summer camp. It had his official Employee of the Month photo from McDonald's, and the photo of him wearing that ferocious expression as he grabbed the guy who'd rushed the stage at my event years earlier. The video dealt frankly with the sadness of the divorce from Kerstin and told the story of how we met and the family we'd all built together.

Then Doug's speech described to the world who I was to him—in our family and as he witnessed my work in the vice president's office. It was an eloquent narrative and a bracing refutation of the ways I had been mischaracterized.

Doug's an excellent trial lawyer. He knows how to keep his cool under pressure. No one wants a lawyer who is nervous in front of an audience. But stepping out onto that huge stage, facing a forest of DOUG signs, was a whole other level.

He took a breath, centered himself, and started his speech with a shout-out to "my big, beautiful, blended family up there"—Kerstin was sitting with Cole and Ella, Doug's parents, his brother, sister, and our niece and nephew, Arden and Jasper—"and a special shout-out to my *mutha*," mimicking her Brooklyn accent, "the only person in the whole world who thinks Kamala is the lucky one, for marrying *me*."

It was a speech full of humor, love, and passionate conviction.

Dougie had nailed it.

76 Days to the Election

The Convention, Day 3

* * *

Oprah Winfrey was a surprise speaker at the convention. She hadn't been listed on the program and had snuck into the auditorium in a hat, glasses, and a face mask. In her rousing speech, she listed all the many places in America where she had lived. But it was obvious from the cheers as she took the podium that Chicago claimed her as their own.

She did her usual magic, spinning history into a unifying story of optimism and inclusion. (And she did it in under fifteen minutes.)

I was delighted to see her on the stage that night, but I must admit there was one prior occasion, in the spring of 2017, when I was even more pleased to see her.

Doug and I were heading to Cole's graduation at Colorado College. We are, as I've noted, a big, beautiful, blended family. And the group traveling to Colorado Springs that weekend kept getting bigger. Crammed in an Uber to the small hotel where we'd all be staying, my mother-in-law began to hold forth on her opinions of Donald Trump. Unsurprisingly, they were not positive. I could feel the animus emanating from the driver, and I began to worry that we might not make it to our destination.

I love my family, but there's a lot of it, and sometimes it's a lot. At one point, I crept off with Doug to have a quiet drink in the hotel's tiny bar. Sitting there, I silently prayed for patience and a bit of relief from the brood.

And then the answer. Through the door walked Oprah Winfrey. She was there, without fanfare, because one of the students from her school for impoverished girls in South Africa was also graduating, and she'd come to cheer her. That's who she is, and just one of the many things about her that I admire.

She gave me a big hug and pulled up a seat so we could catch up.

Bill Clinton, speaking for the twelfth time at a Democratic convention, delivered firm words. Like the cop who arrives at the door of a rowdy party, he wanted the music turned down a little. We were getting euphoric too soon, he warned. "We've seen more than one election slip away from us when we thought it couldn't happen," he said, clearly referring to Hillary's 2016 loss to Trump. Don't get "distracted by phony issues," he admonished. "Never underestimate your adversary."

Bill Clinton knows how to weave a tale. He's one of the best storytellers in modern politics. And why was I surprised that this night, instead of his allotted twelve minutes, he would speak for twenty-nine? He wasn't the only speaker who went long. Once again, the keynote speaker, Tim Walz, was pushed partially out of prime time in the East.

Which was too bad, because Tim gave a great speech, introducing himself to the country, making the case for me, attacking Trump on abortion and on Project 2025, presenting the values of our campaign by calling on specific examples from his own life.

He told of his and Gwen's struggle with infertility, of how it had taken years of treatments before Hope was born. When he spoke directly to his family—"you are my whole world"—Hope, in the audience, made heart hands, and a tearful Gus stood up and passionately cried, "That's my dad!"

At that moment, even the hardened reporters in the press box were reaching for a tissue.

75 Days to the Election

The Convention, Day 4

* * *

I did twenty-seven drafts of my convention speech. I knew what was riding on it.

It was my best chance to grab the attention of voters who did not know me. It would be my opportunity to introduce or reintroduce myself to the American people. I needed to tell them who I was, what had shaped me, why I was running. I needed to prosecute the case against Trump and then explain my own vision for the country. All in forty minutes.

As we worked on the final draft, Adam Frankel came down with Covid. He retreated to quarantine in his hotel room. We'd been working closely together, and he was terrified he had infected me. Fortunately, he had not. On the phone, we continued the work of refining, line by line, word by word.

While I sat in the green room waiting to go onstage, I saw that Opal, my body person, had thoughtfully placed photographs—my mother at a protest, me and my grandfather— the people I loved who were missing from the room that night.

So many people who formed me had died. I believe you can tell a lot about who a person is when you know who their people are. But many of my people aren't here. My mother, my grandfather, my "second mother" Mrs. Shelton, my aunt Mary, my uncle Sherman, my uncle Freddie. I was grateful for the ones who were: Cousin Sharada, Uncle Balu, my *chitti* Chinni. (Chinni is my mother's youngest sister.) In Tamil, there's no exact equivalent word for "aunt." The word *chitti* translates as "younger mother." I actually have two younger mothers: my *chitti* Sarala couldn't make the trip from India.)

The movie director Greta Gerwig had helped me rehearse. Her combination of gentleness and strength, modesty and smarts, made it clear how she'd managed to elicit so many great performances. "When you speak about your family," she advised, "see their faces."

A professional voice coach had also offered to come limber up my vocal presentation. She was very serious about her job, but she wanted me to stand there and emit animal noises. For cover, I enlisted my entire team to join me. We could all be embarrassed together as we made the weird hums, grunts, and trills she instructed us to produce.

We'd practiced in a room set up within the hotel to mimic the layout of the stage. In rehearsal, I walked out into the makeshift circle of stars that marked the speaker's place, waving foolishly at nobody.

When I walked out for real, the crowd was on their feet, roaring. It took many minutes to quiet them. I wanted to share the nuances of my background, including my mother's extraordinary journey, her act of love and self-determination in marrying my father—a fellow student, studying economics, from Jamaica—instead of returning to India, as expected, to an arranged marriage. Although they separated when I was five, I am grateful to my father for many things, including instilling a sense of fearlessness in me. When we'd go to the park, my mother would say, "Stay close," but he would say, "Run, Kamala, run, don't be afraid, don't let anything stop you."

I wanted people to see that in ways that matter, my story was also their story. To see themselves in our neighborhood of nurses and firefighters, in my sister and me on our banana-seat bikes, in my mother's struggle to save the down payment to finally own our own home. I wanted people to know that I, like them, cherish both my family by blood and my family by love.

I recounted how I'd chosen to be a prosecutor after my best friend in high school confided that she was being molested by her stepfather. I said that when I had a case, I charged it not in the name of the victim, but in the name of the people. Because a harm against any one of us is a harm against all of us, and no one who is a victim should stand alone. I told how every day, in the courtroom, I stood proudly before a judge and I said five words: "Kamala Harris, for the people." In my career, I said, I've only had one client: the people.

"And so, on behalf of the people, on behalf of every American, regardless of party, race, gender, or the language your grandmother speaks; on behalf of my mother, and everyone who has ever set out on their own unlikely journey; on behalf of Americans like the people I grew up with—people who work hard, chase their dreams, and look out for one another; on behalf of everyone whose story could only be written in the greatest nation on Earth, I accept your nomination to be president of the United States of America."

There had been speculation that Chicago might erupt in violence as it did in 1968 during the Vietnam War. That hadn't happened. Minyon's team had worked closely with Chicago police, everyone on the same page regarding the importance of respecting free speech and practicing de-escalation if things got heated. The Gaza protests outside the convention remained mostly peaceful. Inside, also, Minyon had made sure that every delegation had a veteran whip, someone with long experience of conventions, taking the temperature of their delegates and working for solidarity. But there was tension and some bitterness that we had not given a speaking slot to a Palestinian spokesperson.

I knew that the section of my speech dealing with the Gaza war had a lot riding on it. As David Von Drehle wrote in *The Washington Post*, it was "the rockiest, most perilous passage: her 5.0-degree-of-difficulty straddle on the war in Gaza. She charged right in and defended Israel, and just as it felt as though the room might split, she affirmed the humanity and suffering of the Palestinians. She then moved into a peroration on the subject that everyone was able to cheer for. And, behold, she had her boat through the impossible strait."

Jon Favreau, who had been director of speech writing in the Obama White House, remarked on his show, *Pod Save America*, "She looked and sounded more presidential in this convention speech than almost any other candidate I've ever seen accept the nomination . . . Her presentation, her delivery, her confidence—it was a sight to behold."

69 Days to the Election

* * *

In Savannah, Georgia, Tim Walz and I hopped on our campaign bus for a two-day barnstorming tour of southeast Georgia.

It's an area that doesn't get a lot of love from Democratic candidates, but we were after every vote in a state that was polling as evenly split and in which every vote mattered.

The big bus had been custom painted blue with a red stripe and stars and the message A NEW WAY FORWARD. Before we boarded, we spoke with a group of students from Savannah State University, Georgia's oldest HBCU. Joining us on the bus was the mayor of the city, Van R. Johnson, a former police officer who shares my passion for small business and creating opportunity for people to build wealth.

We headed out of the city, through woods draped with Spanish moss and lush wetlands, to Liberty County High School in Hinesville, where the school's marching band played for us. I told the band members that I, too, had been in my school band. I played everything from the French horn to the kettle drum. With the horn players, I shared that I'd given up the horn because it involved entirely too much spit. Tim and some of my team members later said that they were surprised to learn about my onetime musical prowess. It was another example of how there were so many more ways to connect with people, if I'd only had more time. On the way back to town we stopped at Sandfly BBQ, where we chatted with the owners and a group of teachers who happened to be dining there.

At 7:40 p.m., we reached the Savannah hotel where we would stay the night.

In my four years as VP, I can count on one hand the times I've walked through the front door of a hotel. I don't see the flower-bedecked foyers, the marble staircases. For security reasons, we go through loading docks, kitchens, the long, unadorned passageways walked by housekeepers and janitors. We take the service elevators, just like the people whose work allows for the comfortable stays of business travelers and tourists. We move through the spaces reserved for workers who are rarely seen, barely noticed.

I always made sure that the campaign booked us in hotels where the staff are union members, and very often those unfancy passageways and utility rooms were decked with posters praising the employees of the month or messages about leadership, or safety, or boosting morale. I would stop and read these messages. It allowed me to connect for a few moments with the people who did the work that would afford me a good night's sleep, a good breakfast.

Whenever I could, I shook their hands and let them know they were appreciated.

68 Days to the Election

First Interview

* * *

I left the campaign bus and stepped through a warm Savannah rain into the restaurant where my first major interview, with CNN's Dana Bash, was to take place.

Kim's Café is a family-owned soul food restaurant that supports causes such as literacy and young entrepreneurs. Famed for its generous portions of chitterlings and smothered shrimp, it would have been perfect for a drop-in visit with the owners and their community. It was not a good choice as background for a sit-down television interview.

As soon as I saw the setup, I felt uneasy. Emptied of customers, with blinds mostly drawn, it felt claustrophobic. Behind us in the shot was a distracting background, a table set with mugs and dishes.

Tim Walz and I were seated opposite Dana Bash at a small table probably designed for dinner for two. Our faces were so close I felt we should deploy breath mints. I'd done enough TV interviews to be aware of how the lighting is supposed to work: the three-point setup of key light, fill light, and back light that usually produces a flattering, even tone. But whatever *this* setup was, the lights cast dark shadows under my eyes and made me look worn out. The way the seats were arranged relative to the camera emphasized the difference in stature between Tim and me. I have a short body and long legs. Tim's a big man with a footballer's massive torso. Seated next to him, at that angle, I had to keep glancing up at him—not a good look.

We'd wanted to do the interview on the campaign bus, but the Secret Service had said no. There were too many security features on that bus that might be revealed in a camera shot. After Trump's close call, the agents were even more than usually cautious.

As a candidate, moving fast through the blur of the campaign, you can't micromanage every detail. Your team must feel that you trust them. If you're constantly second-guessing them, it's bad for morale. These kinds of details—the set, the lighting, the chairs, the angle—were the kinds of things my advance person should have noticed. But in the scramble to find an alternative venue in the agreed window of time when both Dana Bash and I would be in town, it hadn't happened.

This was my long-awaited first interview. In truth, it was far from the "first." I had done dozens of interviews *before* I became top of the ticket—mainstream outlets such as *60 Minutes, People* magazine, NPR's *Latino USA*—also numerous podcasts with large audiences, like *The Shade Room, PopSugar, Baby, This Is Keke Palmer*, and *Dear Asian Americans*.

There had been a lot of chatter about the timing of this first interview after becoming the candidate, that I should have done it sooner and followed quickly with several more. There was a feeling that we needed to feed the beast. But I knew that beast would eviscerate me if I wasn't properly prepared.

And I had to cram that prep time into all the other things that needed to be done in the thirty-nine days I'd had: crafting a comprehensive policy agenda distinct from Biden's, designing a convention, giving a convention speech, getting to swing states, vetting and picking a VP, *being* the VP.

I wanted to do the interview as soon as possible, but I couldn't get away with doing it badly. I'm not interested in doing jiujitsu with reporters, ducking questions or obfuscating. I want to be thoughtful and responsive in my answers, no matter what is asked. I needed to be sure I was ready.

As a former prosecutor, I know the importance of being prepared. Early in my courtroom career, when I was still a law clerk, I'd been prosecuting a case that required showing the jury elaborate maps. Explaining one of the maps, I'd become confused about north and south and had to keep correcting myself in front of the jury. After the trial (which I won) the judge had called me to his chambers and read me the riot act. "Don't you ever do that again," he chided. "You've got to know every detail of your case." Later, as attorney general going after irresponsible banks or a corrupt for-profit college, I was aware that what I said could move markets. I have been conditioned by my career to weigh my every word.

I wanted the interview to be flawless. I needed my A game. I didn't bring it, and that's on me.

Bash's first question: "If you are elected, what would you do on day one in the White House?"

It's a cliché question and I should have expected it and had a pat answer in my pocket about the executive orders I intended to sign. The truth: Day one is performative. That's not when the big problems are going to get solved.

So instead of a tidy, headline-making sound bite, I reeled off a slew of priorities such as extending the child tax credit—the most clearly proven way to quickly lift families out of poverty; the tax credit I wanted for first-time home buyers; my determination to end price gouging. I was setting out my agenda, and on day one I would absolutely begin working on these things. Unlike Trump, I didn't have a mouthful of lies about ending wars and lowering grocery prices on day one. I knew those kinds of things weren't possible, and I wasn't going to take the audience for fools.

I did slightly better on the follow-up. Bash asked me why I hadn't already accomplished the items on my agenda during my time in office. This gave me a chance to remind viewers of the chaos we'd inherited from Trump: the mismanaged Covid crisis, an economy in free fall. Our priority, I said, had been saving lives and saving jobs, and we'd brought the US economy back faster than any other wealthy nation.

But I didn't stop there. Joe was justifiably proud of that recovery and felt the statistics—inflation down below 3 percent from a high of over 9, wage increases outpacing inflation, millions of new jobs created—should be enough to convince people that he was a good manager of the economy. But I knew people didn't yet feel these metrics in their daily life. It wasn't what they experienced when they went to buy food or gas. I addressed that pain, acknowledging that prices were still too high. I said that's why now, with the Covid crisis behind us, the time was right to enact all the cost-of-living measures I proposed.

It was a good answer. But there was a better one. I should have simply said, *I haven't done those things because I am not president—yet.* It was a chance to offer a small civics class reminder: the vice president serves the president's agenda; she does not have the power to forge her own.

I could also have been sharper with my answer to her question on fracking.

It took me longer than it should have to clearly articulate the plain truth of my position. The climate crisis is an emergency. We urgently need to move off fossil fuels. But evidence had convinced me that we could do that without ending fracking. In 2020, I'd promised not to ban it, I hadn't banned it as vice president, and I would not ban it as president. I got there, but I could have gotten there quicker and cleaner.

I felt off my game for most of the interview. Having Tim there beside me, in hindsight, was an error. Bash asked him few questions, and none offered a moment that revealed his charismatic personality or convictions. My campaign felt we should do the interview in tandem because it was a thing that had been done by prior candidates and their running mates. But because we'd waited to do this interview, there was so much riding on it. And the plan to have him there fed a narrative that I wasn't willing or able to go it alone.

As we were beginning to wrap up, Bash asked me to comment on a photo from the convention that had gone viral: my baby niece Amara looking up at me as I stood behind the podium, flanked by American flags, accepting the nomination. It's a wonderful image. The picture is taken from behind her, so what you see is her upturned head bracketed by her two perky little braids.

I hadn't belabored the historic nature of my candidacy as a Black woman. I'd always felt that it was more important to stress that I was the most qualified person, regardless of race or gender. But that photo somehow spoke volumes about the past and the future. It reminded us how far we've come—that a woman and a person of color could be at that podium, accepting that nomination. It also spoke volumes about how far we can go, when children grow up knowing anything is possible for someone who looks just like them.

It was the one answer where I would not change a word.

67 Days to the Election

* * *

The signs went up overnight at the bus stops in Denver. Metal, official-looking, professionally affixed to the bus stop poles.

**BLACKS MUST SIT
AT THE BACK OF THE BUS
KAMALA'S MIGRANTS
SIT IN THE FRONT**

Similar signs showed up a thousand miles away, in Chicago.

Later in the campaign, a Nevada homeowner's yard sign supporting me was defaced with the N-word. The doorbell camera showed the vandal toting all the equipment he needed to do the job.

When I became top of the ticket, Republican lawmakers had a closed-door meeting, the message of which was a warning to lay off overt attacks on race and gender and restrict criticism to my record in the Biden–Harris administration. This came after several members attacked me as a "DEI hire." All of this did nothing to lower the volume of Trump's dog-whistling.

Sadly, racist, sexist attacks are not exclusive to Donald Trump. And someone had gone to a lot of trouble to make those bus signs.

As the first woman, or Black woman, in every office I have run for, except the Senate, where I was the second, racism and sexism have always been present.

They were not new to me: I would not let them throw me off my game.

62 Days to the Election

* * *

I'd planned to unveil my tax proposals to help small businesses at a picturesque brewery in North Hampton, New Hampshire, and then to visit a family-owned pretzel-making factory nearby. I was keen to share my plan to boost new businesses with a $50,000 tax credit and to help existing ones expand with low- and no-interest loans. I was looking forward to the day, with perfect late-summer weather predicted for our outdoor rally.

Because I am passionate about small business, when I became VP, the first meeting I scheduled outside of government departments was with small-business owners, and right after that with the CEOs of big banks to persuade them to do more small-business lending. It's the biggest engine of employment in our economy. But it is even more than that. Small businesses are the glue that holds communities together: the café where the barista knows you, the local pharmacist who asks after your kid's earache or sore throat.

When I was a child, before my mother saved enough for a down payment on our first home, we rented an apartment above Mrs. Shelton's nursey, and Mrs. Shelton looked after us while Mommy worked. She became a second mother to us. And she taught me early that the best business leaders are also civic leaders. Small businesses like Mrs. Shelton's represent the realization of millions of individual American dreams.

But at 9:42 a.m., just as I was getting ready to head to the landing zone for Marine Two, a fourteen-year-old in Barrow County, Georgia, texted his father: *I'm sorry, it's not ur fault.* And then, to his mother, a second text: *I'm sorry.*

By 10:30 a.m., he had shot eleven people at Apalachee High School, where he was a freshman. He had killed Mason Schermerhorn and Christian Angulo, both aged fourteen; a math teacher named Cristina Irimie; and a math teacher and assistant football coach, Richard Aspinwall. Aspinwall had stepped from his classroom to investigate the disturbance and was shot in the chest. His students pulled him back inside and tried to save his life, using their own shirts in a fruitless effort to stanch the bleeding.

Unless you live in Georgia, you've probably forgotten about that shooting, or maybe it's blurred into the details of the other eighty-three school shootings that happened in 2024. *Eighty-three.* And 2024 is not even our deadliest year.

Apalachee High School had just about every recommended security measure. Three armed officers on-site, self-locking classroom doors, smart boards programmed to flash an active shooter alert in every classroom, teachers whose high-tech ID badges included a panic button and real-time location software.

It wasn't enough.

You can buy a semiautomatic weapon in Georgia without a permit or any gun-safety training. Just weeks before the shooting, state lawmakers tried to pass a law offering a $300 tax credit for installing a gun safe. Even that modest proposal failed to pass.

We are the only country in the world where the leading cause of death for children is guns. Every day in America there are parents who drop their kids off at the bus stop or at the school gate and say a silent prayer that their children will return home that day.

As I set out for New Hampshire that morning, I'd only had a bare-bones briefing. I didn't yet have all the details on the shooting. I didn't yet know that the shooter's father had given his son a semi-automatic AR-15-style weapon as a Christmas gift, even though his boy had a picture of the Parkland school shooter on his bedroom wall and had been visited by police regarding threats he allegedly posted on Discord.

What I did know: It doesn't have to be this way. As VP I drove the creation of the White House Office of Gun Violence Prevention, which led to the first major gun-safety bill in nearly three decades, looking at gun trafficking and the training of fourteen thousand new mental health workers to work in schools like Apalachee and help avert such tragedies. But we need to do much more.

As a gun owner myself, I am not coming to take away anybody's guns. I am with the majority of Americans who want an assault weapons ban. I am with those who want universal background checks and red flag laws.

You just might want to know, before someone can buy a lethal weapon, if they've been convicted of a violent crime. You just might want to know if the person buying a gun is a danger to themselves or others. All of us certainly want to know our children can go to school, learn without fear, and come home safe.

As a prosecutor, I'd studied autopsy photographs in the aftermath of shootings. I know exactly what semiautomatic rifle fire does to the human body, especially to the tiny body of a child. This may sound harsh, but somebody needs to get lawmakers in a locked room and make them look at those images. Then they can go out on the floor of the chamber and vote their conscience.

In a statement that day, Donald Trump blamed the shooting on a "sick and deranged monster." He did not mention the gun.

Every country in the world has sick and deranged individuals. Only the United States had eighty-three school shootings in 2024.

61 Days to the Election

* * *

It was time to hunker down for debate camp. We left for Pittsburgh in the early afternoon. I would be mostly off the campaign trail for five days—no small thing. Trump mocked me for it. But I knew how vital it was.

We'd nailed the convention, and the debate was the next big test for my campaign. Most polls had us pulling ahead by more than 3 points. Since we had no firm commitment from Trump for another debate, I knew it might be my only choice to give voters a side-by-side comparison.

I suspected that Trump was still riding the ego boost of trampling Joe and would have high confidence. Indeed, J. D. Vance bragged to CNN: "We're not going to have some sort of formal debate prep session, because Donald Trump doesn't need it." I knew this was false and typical bluster. I was sure they would try to prepare him, and I was determined to put in the necessary work.

The team had tricked out the ballroom of the historic Omni William Penn Hotel in Pittsburgh. It was done up to exactly reproduce the actual debate set, including the same lighting. It was freezing in there, as studio sets often are. The value of duplicating the exact set proved itself right away. We'd had made-to-measure podiums built, and when I placed my notebook on it, it slid right off. There would be no way to take notes on a podium with that steep of a slope.

Brian Fallon called ABC and told them they needed to fix their design.

Philippe Reines was my sparring partner. He was a longtime political operative who had served Hillary in her Senate and presidential campaigns and worked for her in the State Department. He'd had various roles but was perhaps most well-known as her take-no-prisoners, highly combative press spokesman. He'd called a reporter's question "asinine" and told another to "fuck off." He was able to harness this natural aggression when channeling Donald Trump.

Reines had played Trump during Hillary's debate prep in 2016, and he approached the role with the dedication of a method actor. He had studied Trump's debates frame by frame, learning his every gesture. He'd memorized everything he'd said and exactly how he said it. Every night, he watched the video of Trump's latest rant to see if he'd updated any lines of attack. He wore makeup to give his skin an orange tinge, tortured his elegantly graying hair into a facsimile of Trump's cotton candy comb-over, and sported a long red tie dangling over his belt.

He was also a total jerk—but solely in pursuit of honing my performance. He lied, was confrontational, tried to rattle me one moment, distract me the next. It was a high-level hazing. Not even during our breaks did he step out of character.

The first day of debate camp, our method was to run through three or four questions, then stop to review how I'd done, refining my answers.

I had most of my team in Pittsburgh—Karen Dunn, Rohini Kosoglu, Minyon Moore, Cedric Richmond, David Plouffe, Sean Clegg (my longtime California political adviser and strategist), Ike Irby, Tony West, Brian Fallon, Lorraine Voles, and Sheila Nix, and later Jen O'Malley Dillon and Tony West—all there to tweak and tune my every phrase. Kirsten Allen and Colin Diersing role-played as ABC News moderators Linsey Davis and David Muir. James Singer was there as fact-checker, to go over every answer to make sure that on the night I had the facts straight.

Jake Sullivan, the national security adviser, and my own national security adviser, Phil Gordon, also flew in to help shape my answers on foreign policy. Of all the president's responsibilities, foreign policy is among the weightiest, and yet it is outside the experience of most Americans. The key is having advisers who understand the intersection of foreign and domestic policy and politics. Jake and Phil are gifted and helped me find words that would be immediately accessible to everyone, including those whose busy lives have little time to learn acronyms like AUKUS or JCPOA, but who want to know how these key agreements work to make our country more secure.

What had kept me up, long before I was the top of the ticket, was the sadness of realizing that many Americans don't fully understand how important they are to the rest of the world. Not the American government; the American people. We the people have for so long embodied ideals of equality, generosity, enterprise. In the eyes of many, we have been the reliable allies, the trusted friends, a source of aspiration and inspiration.

I knew Trump couldn't care less about the moral leadership of America in the rest of the world. His perverse notion of what strength looks like is, I believe, out of step with most Americans. I think the true strength of a leader is based not on who you beat down but who you lift up. His is a stunted, narrow definition of strength: the strength of the bully.

I hoped the debate would offer a moment to starkly reveal our difference. I wanted to show that he was very weak and entirely vulnerable, more interested in favor, grift, and flattery, and would yield to that, manipulated by leaders like Putin.

60 Days to the Election

* * *

By the second day I was working without my note cards, and we were going the full ninety minutes. Then doing it again. And again. It matters that you get your reps in.

You must get used to the cadence; you must get used to the clock. As for an athlete, a great shooter can't score if the shot comes after the buzzer.

Say the subject is the color green. You might have a bunch of incredible things to say on the subject of green, but the buzzer goes before you've landed your best point, and by the time you get to speak again, the subject's changed to orange. If you try to make your final great point about green, you won't have time left to spell out your position on orange.

Complex answers are often punished by the unforgiving clock.

After we ran through a full mock debate, I would leave the ballroom while the team deconstructed and analyzed my every answer. Because there were so many advisers, they didn't want ten or a dozen different voices bombarding me. While I was out of the room, they'd synthesize everyone's opinions: "She was visibly annoyed by that question—we've got to get her immune to that." "She needs to get to that answer faster." "She forgot to make that point."

Storm would make me a cup of tea. The team, if they were being kind, would bring me a small bag of Doritos, which felt like being handed a doggy treat. I'd come back in, and Karen or Rohini would deliver the critique. Then we'd do it all over again, going late into the evening so that I practiced how it felt to do the debate at the actual time it would take place.

I was on my feet the whole time. It's a test of endurance as much as anything. Keeping up the energy, staying focused. Questions I'd prepared for, new ones that I hadn't. And always, under the glare of the lights, the digital clock flashing.

59 Days to the Election

* * *

I wanted to get out of the hotel and out of my head for an hour, so we'd scheduled a lunchtime visit to a small business. Penzeys Spices is a Wisconsin-based company that has stores in more than twenty states. Bill Penzey, the founder of the thirty-year-old business, has long been an outspoken anti-racist and a critic of Donald Trump's politics of division. The company had a store not far from the hotel, so we headed over there.

Even though the visit hadn't been on my official schedule—none of these drop-ins could be, for security reasons—a big, enthusiastic crowd gathered in the narrow street as soon as the motorcade pulled up. They started chanting "We're not going back."

My mother bought her spices in bulk and stored them in used Taster's Choice coffee jars. I felt right at home in the store's delicious aromas of cardamom, clove, and nutmeg.

I chatted with the families browsing the store. One woman wept, saying she was afraid for the country if Trump was reelected. "We're going to be fine," I reassured her. "We are all in this together." Before I left, I loaded up on some of my favorite Penzeys mixes—Fox Point, Creamy Peppercorn, and Trinidad Lemon-Garlic Marinade—for Cole and his wife, Greenley, the rest for me. *One day,* I thought, *I'll get a chance to use them.*

A couple of the pool reporters had followed me into the store. One asked: "Best part of debate prep for you?"

"Being at this spice store," I replied.

They had no idea how much I meant it.

58 Days to the Election

* * *

"I hate my debate team!"

I was on the phone venting to my bestie, Chrisette. Of course I did not hate my debate team. I loved them. But they were killing me. By Sunday afternoon I was fried.

I needed to get away from that podium, from the stage lights, from my bullying nemesis in the droopy red tie. I needed some time alone with Doug, who'd arrived the day before. I needed fresh air. I needed a walk.

In my position, a spur-of-the-moment Sunday-afternoon stroll is no small undertaking. We conferred with my Secret Service detail. The only secure place possible at short notice, they said, was a National Guard air base about half an hour away.

Imagine the scene in *The Godfather* when Michael Corleone is on a stroll in the Sicilian hills with his fiancée, Apollonia. It is such an intimate moment. Then, as the couple walks on together, just about the entire village strolls into the frame, following behind them. Well, that's how our walk felt.

The air base was far from a scenic Sicilian hillside: Doug, me, a row of C-17 warplanes, and our many chaperones. The motorcade pulled in behind a building. My assistant Opal described our path.

She pointed out that as soon as we turned the corner, we'd be in view of the press pool for the rest of the walk. And, of course, my Secret Service detail would be right there with us.

It's impossible to get a moment when I don't have to be self-aware. If I leave the privacy of my room, someone is always observing me.

Doug and I navigated the perimeter of that treeless tarmac, laughing about how surreal our lives had become.

It was a mild, sunny Sunday afternoon. Like Michael and Apollonia, we made the most of our moment together.

57 Days to the Election

* * *

Was I the only one seeing the fly?

In the middle of the 2020 vice presidential debate, it landed on Mike Pence's head, during his answer to a question on race in America. And there it sat, a dark presence on his snow-white hair.

Should I motion to him to brush it away?

If I did, he—or the audience—might misinterpret the gesture. I thought about saying something, but I didn't want to embarrass him, or throw him off, or seem to be trivializing the debate.

All these thoughts, when I needed to be focusing on what he was saying.

You can prepare forever, but you can't know what will happen in a debate, live, in front of tens of millions of people.

In the late afternoon, we decamped from Pittsburgh and headed for Philly.

56 Days to the Election

Debate Day

* * *

That morning, I went for a walk-through of the actual set the studio had created for the debate. It's important to know every detail: what will be in your line of sight, whether the cameras will be on you when you're not speaking, even the length of the walk to the podium. The room was so much smaller than where we practiced. Network aides showed me where the moderators would sit, where the digital clock would be.

Then we headed back to the hotel for what I thought would be a practice of my closing statement. A final tune-up before the real thing.

Philippe Reines surprised me by entering the room dressed as himself, not Donald Trump. Unbeknownst to me, he and Karen Dunn had decided that the last thing I needed at that point was more intense work. They'd cooked up something different. Philippe rose to give what I thought would be a mock Trump closing statement.

Instead, it was a comic monologue. He started by making fun of me for what he called my un-politician-like punctuality. "What politician do you know who is ever on time? Sometimes she even gets there first!" Then he hunched his tall frame and pitched his naturally deep voice into a high register. "I may look big and strong, but I'm really a very small, very scared little man." And finally, dropping the Trump character entirely, he turned and looked at me directly for the first time in five days of prep sessions. He spoke about my strengths and ended with a twist on the "radical" label that his mock Trump had been hurling at me.

"You're radically ready. You've got this!"

It was exactly what I needed to hear in that moment, and I was so grateful.

It was followed by something that I didn't need to hear at all.

I was in my room at the hotel in Philadelphia, wrapped in a robe, fat rollers in my hair. The makeup artist had left. It was just Doug and me and my pre-debate butterflies.

I got a call that Joe Biden wanted to talk to me. I was pleased that the president had thought to give me a pre-debate pep talk.

"I'm calling to wish you good luck," Joe said, but there was little warmth in his voice. Still, he'd thought to call.

"I love you," I replied, smiling. "I'm about to go into the boxing ring."

"You're going to do fine." Then, with barely a pause: "By the way, are you going to be back in Philadelphia between now and the election?"

Why's he asking that? I wondered. It seemed, under the circumstances, a non sequitur. I told him I wasn't sure. I'd certainly be back in Pennsylvania, but I'd have to check my schedule to see which locations.

"My brother called. He's been talking to a group of real powerbrokers in Philly." He rattled off several names. "Do you know them?"

No, I replied, thinking he was maybe going to offer to introduce me to them or call them on my behalf. But I was confused as to why he was raising this right now, on this day.

Then he got to his point. His brother had told him that those guys were not going to support me because I'd been saying bad things about him. He wasn't inclined to believe it, he claimed, but he thought I should know in case my team had been encouraging me to put daylight between the two of us.

"Okay, well, have those guys talk to me directly," I said. "I'd like to meet them."

Joe then rattled on about his own former debate performances. "I beat him the other time; I wasn't feeling well in that last one." He continued to insist that his debate performance hadn't hurt him with the electorate. I was barely listening.

He knew what it was like to be in my seat, getting ready to face Trump one-on-one. Indeed, he and Hillary Rodham Clinton were the *only* humans who knew what it was like.

The pressure I was under before I would step onto that stage was immense. I'd just likened it to a fighter going into a boxing ring for the big prizefight. And that's what it felt like, only worse, because the outcome of my performance wasn't just a win or loss for me. It had grave consequences for the country, even for the world. My head had to be right. I had to be completely in the game. I just couldn't understand why he would call me, right now, and make it all about himself. Distracting me with worry about hostile powerbrokers in the biggest city of the most important swing state.

Doug could see how angry and disappointed I was. "Let it go," he said. He knew I had to redirect my focus. "Don't worry about him. You're dealing with Trump. Let it go."

Sixty-seven million people witnessed what happened next.

Donald Trump and I had never met. So when he walked right to his podium, I strode past mine over to him, extended my hand, and introduced myself. It wasn't a tactic. I always shake hands when I meet someone for the first time. I'd told my prep team I would do it, because it was the natural and polite thing to do. Trump's eyes widened; he hadn't expected this. He took my outstretched hand almost deferentially.

"Kamala Harris," I said. "Let's have a good debate."

In rehearsals, someone suggested saying, "It's pronounced *KA-mala*." But at the last minute I decided not to. It felt bitchy.

It was the last time he looked at me in the entire ninety minutes.

The small set was bathed in blue lights, with a graphic of the

Constitution behind the two podiums. It was lit so that from my podium I couldn't see anything except the impassive faces of the moderators and a massive screen featuring a countdown clock, which I
glanced at every now and then to make sure I had time to land my
points.

Donald Trump had won the toss and opted to give the first opening statement. He launched right into his lies about immigrants being
rapists and murderers, stealing "Black jobs." I figured viewers would
understand how demeaning and ludicrous that was, since I was right
there on the stage, enjoying my Black job as vice president. He bragged
about his economic plan—his tariffs—which gave me a golden opportunity to punch right back.

I was coursing with adrenaline. I'd studied this stuff for my entire career. I knew what those tariffs would do to the American people. Trump's tariffs, I said, were nothing but a national sales tax that
would send prices soaring and would plunge us into a recession by
the following summer. I quoted sixteen Nobel laureate economists
to back me up.

He responded with the absurd claim that I was a Marxist and disparaged my father. I decided not to go on his turf and hoped my smile
and raised eyebrow indicated how ridiculous it was. He has a skill
for going for the very personal and pulling people into a false reality,
forcing them to debate nonsense. Running after his crazy lies was a
trap I was determined to avoid.

When the question turned to abortion, Trump branded our policy as "extreme" and then repeated his lie about Democratic states al-
lowing newborns to be put to death. There hadn't been any real-time
fact-checking in Joe Biden's debate, but this time, to their credit, the
moderators cut in to say that there was no state in which such a practice was allowed.

No matter what question the moderators asked, Trump tried to
turn it back to his scaremongering of an immigrant "invasion." I pointed
out that he'd killed the bipartisan bill that would have strengthened the
border because he "would rather run on a problem than fix a problem,"

and I said that his rantings had become so rambling and tedious that people leave his rallies early out of exhaustion and boredom.

His obsession with his crowd sizes led him to take this bait. He had no good explanation as to why he had killed the bill, so he embarked on his "eating the pets" rant. I could not believe he was saying it. The cameras caught my look of incredulity.

I did have some clue that it might have been on his mind. Kirsten and Brian had noticed that when Trump deplaned in Philly, Laura Loomer, the conspiracy theorist who had been identified as a proponent of this garbage, was traveling with him. Apparently, as the last thing he heard, it had stuck in his head. It served to make my point about how unhinged he had become.

Once again, the moderators stepped in to say that this claim that Haitians had stolen and killed pets for food had been debunked by none other than the Springfield, Ohio, city manager.

"Talk about extreme," I interjected. It's his familiar tactic. Say the crazy. Everyone will dive on it. That will be the headline, the distraction. They will follow the heat instead of, for instance, his policy on tariffs.

When Trump tried to claim that crime was rising under our administration when it was actually falling, I answered that it was "rich" for someone who had been prosecuted and convicted of numerous felonies to be positioning himself as a champion of law and order. I heard him audibly gasp when I mentioned his convictions. He shot back that I had been in favor of defunding the police. Another lie. Even though my mic was off, I said, "That's not true."

He heard me and snapped, "I'm talking now."

"Don't lie," I countered. The camera was on me then and you didn't need to be a lip-reader to understand what I'd said.

We were not allowed to interact with anyone during the commercial breaks. Trump walked off the stage in one direction, I went the other. I took a moment in the wings and then went back to the podium, alone in my head, watching the seconds flash by on the massive clock until I could reengage.

There was little he said that night that I hadn't gamed out. But there were spontaneous moments where my adrenaline-flooded synapses fired off retorts I came up with on the spot.

When Trump tried to justify his bogus claim that the 2020 election had been stolen, I pointed out that this was a man who had been fired by eighty-one million Americans and "clearly he is having a very difficult time processing that."

Another moment came as he attacked us on a vulnerability: the withdrawal from Afghanistan. It was important that people understood the origins of that tragedy. It began with the disastrous deal he'd struck with the Taliban, committing us to an impossibly rapid exit date. It infuriated me that he had invited the Taliban—murderous terrorists, torturers, heinous oppressors of women—to Camp David, where true statesmen had worked to create real peace. I gestured toward him to reinforce the contrast. "And this . . ." I could feel the retort forming itself on my lips. I confess that sometimes I have a salty mouth. I keep it in check on most occasions. But the adrenaline was taking over. In a long pause, I just managed to stifle the name I so badly wanted to call him. "And this . . . former president, as president, invited them to Camp David."

Even though I hadn't actually said it, plenty of people filled in the blank. Later, the comedian Wanda Sykes would remark that I'd called the former president a "mutherfuckah" to his face, without using the word.

When the debate ended, I genuinely had no idea how I'd done. I felt like the survivor in the aftermath of a bomb blast, barely able to hear what was being said to me for the whooshing in my ears. I could see Doug's face, swimming in front of me as he came up on the stage. He was talking, but I couldn't take in what he said. I registered the fact that he was smiling.

Well then, I thought. *I must've done okay.*

55 Days to the Election

* * *

I'd had about two hours' sleep when the alarm on my phone went off in my New York hotel room.

The night before, Doug and I had gone from the debate stage to the holding room where the entire team was assembled. I grabbed Philippe and kissed him with gratitude. Over the heads in the group, I saw Lorraine crying. The tough taskmaster of my staff and daily agenda, she never cries. "You really do care about more than just my schedule!" I teased. Brian, usually dead serious, was grinning ear to ear. "I checked off all the numbers on my bingo card," he said. "You made every point."

Later, Opal started playing Taylor Swift songs on her phone. Swift had just posted her thoughtful endorsement: "I believe we can accomplish so much more in this country if we are led by calm and not chaos," she wrote, signing off her post "Childless Cat Lady."

The Harris–Walz campaign watch party at the Cherry Street Pier was thronged with celebrating supporters. I knew very well that this election would not be decided by a single event, a single debate victory. When I took the mic, I told everyone that it had been a good night, but tomorrow was back to work. Then I left for New York. By the time I collapsed on the bed in my hotel room, it was close to two a.m.

I was up just a couple of hours later to prepare for a somber day of three memorials: New York, Shanksville, the Pentagon. At 7:50 a.m., I was back in the motorcade, rolling to Ground Zero for the ceremony honoring the victims of 9/11. I'd been there as vice president every year except during Covid. Hundreds of people in black stood in silence, the memorial's waterfalls the only audible sound in the heart of that busy city. I stood next to the president. Michael Bloomberg was on his left, Donald Trump on the other side of the mayor. Trump and I shook hands. He said, "You were great last night." I didn't know what to say in return, except, "You, too."

It was a warm, clear, beautiful morning, just as it had been in 2001. The NYPD honor guard began a solemn drumbeat. At 8:46 a.m., the moment the first plane hit the North Tower, the drumbeat ceased. We all fell silent in memory of the dead.

Twenty-three years earlier, I was a young city attorney in San Francisco, getting an early start on the treadmill at my gym before heading to the office. There were three giant TVs in the gym, and as they played the moment when the first plane hit the tower, I turned off the treadmill and stepped down to follow the coverage. I remember the music in the gym stopped. Everyone stood side by side, watching in disbelief.

The reading of the names is a melancholy and moving tradition. The president and I departed as quietly and reverently as we could, about an hour into that litany of loss: we needed to leave for Shanksville, Pennsylvania, to commemorate the heroes of Flight 93.

The route from Johnstown–Cambria County Airport to the Shanksville memorial site runs through cornfields, wooded hills, and forests of Trump signs: TRUMP 2024. VOTE REPUBLICAN. AMERICA MUST END ABORTION.

It was a small crowd at Shanksville. About two hundred had gathered, many of them family or friends of those who perished on the flight. The president and I laid a wreath at the memorial and then walked out to the crash site.

I was taken aback that on that day, and in this place, I would see a man in the crowd wearing a bright red shirt emblazoned with messages insulting me in the most vulgar terms. KOMMY KAMALA SUCKS and ABORT HARRIS were the printable parts, interspersed with lewd sexual references.

This was such a solemn memorial service. It made me immensely sad for the heroes of Flight 93 and for the people who loved and honored them. They didn't need to be subjected to his indecent bile. *Surely,* I thought, *this cannot be who we are.*

Every year after the memorial service, Joe made it a point to stop at the Shanksville Volunteer Fire Department, where a cross made from the salvaged remains of the crashed plane stands outside the firehouse. That department was the first responder to the crash.

Inside, the volunteer firefighters and their families milled about or sat at tables. Many wore MAGA hats and Trump T-shirts. Some refused to shake my hand; others offered me their backs.

I had a lot of mixed feelings about being there. It was a solemn occasion, and I didn't want to intrude at such a moment upon people who saw me through the lens of Fox and right-wing media. I knew I would never get their vote. But I didn't want to write off the opportunity to connect with a fellow American, if there was any way I could reach across the divide and share a human moment.

Sometimes, as my motorcade moved through streets lined with supporters, I'd look out the window and see the one or two scowling people, arms outstretched, middle fingers raised. It pained me, especially if they had children standing alongside.

There are many good reasons that the Secret Service would have objected had I stopped the motorcade to speak with them. But I often wanted to. I wished I could ask every one of them, *What are you angry about? What about me makes you angry? Is it your health care, your grocery bills, a backbreaking job that doesn't pay what you're worth—and what can I do to help you?* An impossible wish, since I didn't even control the lock on my car door. And there were always people waiting for me—sometimes for hours—at the next destination.

One woman at the firehouse was willing to make eye contact and exchange a greeting, even though it was clear that her husband wanted nothing to do with me. I kept the conversation going, and I learned that the couple had suffered the loss of their child. There is no blue or red, no Democrat or Republican, in the experience of grief and bereavement. They spoke tenderly of their child, and I shared my own experience of loss, watching my mother undone by the ravages of cancer. That brief interaction is the kind of moment that sustains my belief that we share more than we realize. We just have to be willing to look for it and see it.

And then I glanced across to the far side of the room, where Joe was sharing a joke with some guys in MAGA hats. One of them took his hat off and offered it to Joe.

Don't take it.

He took it.

Don't put it on.

He put it on.

Cameras clicked. Within hours, the picture was all over: Joe Biden in a MAGA hat, with the caption "Biden endorses Trump over Harris."

I took the microphone that was offered to me and said, "We may vote for different people, but the people who attacked us on 9/11 couldn't care less who we voted for. We were all Americans that day. As we are today. And I hope we can remember that."

54 Days to the Election

* * *

I was back on the swing state trail the next day with an event in Charlotte. People in the audience shouted "Concepts!" and I knew they were referring to one of Trump's low moments in the debate. Moderators asked if he had a plan to replace the Affordable Care Act, which he'd tried and failed to destroy in his first term. It had been saved thanks to the vote of the late Senator John McCain.

"I have concepts of a plan," Trump had said.

Forty-five million Americans are insured under the ACA, and he wants to destroy it. For "concepts of a plan."

I told the rally we owed it to the voters to have another debate, "because this election and what's at stake could not be more important."

Our campaign had raised $47 million in the twenty-four hours that followed it.

Trump, meanwhile, was running hard in the opposite direction, telling a rally in Tucson that he was done debating. And, on his social media platform, even more emphatically: "THERE WILL BE NO THIRD DEBATE!"

David Plouffe answered with a post of his own: "At long last we discover his spirit animal. The Chicken."

53 Days to the Election

* * *

Laura Loomer had traveled on Trump's plane to the debate, to the 9/11 memorials, and to his rallies. It was clear that her special brand of vile crazy was getting in his head.

She'd suggested on social media that the earrings I'd worn on the debate stage were really earpieces through which I was being fed answers. Trump parroted that line in his next speech. I learned later that the sales of those Tiffany pearl-and-gold earrings I'd worn and of an earpiece that looked similar had both skyrocketed. I had to laugh.

Some of Loomer's racist bile was too much even for other extremists. Marjorie Taylor Greene, who'd blamed the California wildfires on Jewish space lasers, took exception to Loomer's post that if I was elected, the White House "will smell like curry & White House speeches will be facilitated via a call center." If you can offend Marjorie Taylor Greene, you're really at the deep end of the hate pool.

52 Days to the Election

* * *

They had to close the city hall in Springfield, evacuate schools, and lock down hospitals because of Trump's unfounded slander of the Ohio town's Haitian population.

Trump's baseless debate claims that Haitians were eating pets provoked a wave of bomb threats, even after the woman who started the rumor told a *Wall Street Journal* reporter that her cat had been found safe in her basement and that she had apologized to her Haitian neighbors. Another woman who had amplified the rumor on Facebook also apologized, saying she'd never had any evidence for her post.

None of that stopped Trump. His anti-immigrant rhetoric became even more intense in the days that followed. He appeared to revel in the chaos he could provoke. It reinforced my belief that it was a cunning strategy to distract from the fact that he had no plan to make things better for the American family.

51 Days to the Election

* * *

I was home at the vice president's residence, prepping remarks for a speech I planned to give on a subject of vital importance to me: the broken state of US childcare.

Too few places available for families; a labor-intensive profession with poverty-level pay; and razor-thin profit margins for the small-business owner. In short, a national disgrace and an issue where we lagged most wealthy nations. Our Build Back Better agenda had been designed to address this but had run up against a recalcitrant Republican Congress who, for all their talk of family values, refused to see either the social or the economic upside of fixing the problem.

Coming into office at the height of the pandemic, one of the first things I did as vice president was to call attention to the national emergency of women exiting the workforce en masse. Were women free to participate in the labor force at the same level as men, our national GDP would be 5 percent higher. Quality, affordable childcare, including universal pre-K, would massively improve both worker productivity and children's educational outcomes.

I was working on my remarks when staff called with the news of another attempt on Trump's life.

My initial reaction: How could this keep happening?

I was relieved he was okay.

I've had a protective detail since I became San Francisco district attorney. I have adapted to a life in which every move I make outside my own home must be coordinated with my protection detail. Death threats against me have been innumerable. I never talk about the threats or the people who have been prosecuted. Some elected officials speak of these things; I never have. I am not going to be *Oh, woe is me*. I never carry myself in a way that I feel vulnerable or act vulnerable. But I am acutely aware of it.

When you have been in the public eye as long as I have, people have long memories for things I have done that they didn't like and may have stewed over for years. I got some disapproval for saying that if somebody breaks into my house, they'll get shot. But it's the truth. I've never made a big deal of being a gun owner, but I have a reason to have a handgun. I store it securely. And I know how to use it.

Staff briefed me on what little was known of the attack. Trump had set out for an unscheduled Sunday-afternoon golf game at his West Palm Beach golf course. He was on the fifth fairway just after 1:30 p.m. when a member of his Secret Service detail saw the muzzle of a semiautomatic rifle poking through bushes at the very next hole. The agent opened fire; the would-be shooter fled. Trump, thankfully, had been whisked to safety. Very soon after, we learned to our relief that the man had been apprehended.

Trump was quick to blame our campaign rhetoric for calling him out as a threat to democracy. He should have been blaming the lax gun laws he championed, since the arrested man, who had a criminal record, had been flagged by the FBI as being illegally in possession of weapons, including a fully automatic machine gun. Despite numerous convictions, he'd obviously had no trouble obtaining a lethal weapon.

That night, Elon Musk posted his reckless tweet, musing as to why no one had tried to shoot me or Joe Biden.

50 Days to the Election

* * *

I walked into the International Brotherhood of Teamsters roundtable in Washington, DC, knowing I wasn't going to receive its endorsement.

Most major unions already had endorsed me, including the AFL-CIO, the United Steelworkers, and the United Auto Workers. But the 1.3-million-member Teamsters had yet to decide. When Biden was still in the race, we'd learned that the union was leaning toward remaining neutral for the first time since 1996.

Members were angry that Biden had signed a bill blocking a nationwide rail strike that would have devastated the economy and cost thousands of workers their paychecks. I knew very well that my candidacy wasn't likely to swing the needle in our favor, despite my lifelong support for the union cause.

Sean O'Brien, the union president, had spoken at the Republican National Convention. He'd asked for a speaking slot at ours as well, but why would I put someone on my stage who hadn't supported me? I'm not about to be punked. If you're flirting with my opponent, have at it.

I walked in there determined to speak the truth. I was not going to let them do what they were about to do without giving them a jolt to their conscience. I would make them weigh, in their own hearts and minds, the decision they were going to announce.

I laid out, chapter and verse, what unions would get from a Trump administration. I went down the list of Donald Trump's anti-union actions—and it's a very long list—from the beginning of his real estate career screwing over workers and busting unions, to his recent conversation with Elon Musk where he said it was okay to fire workers exercising their legal right to strike. I contrasted this with the equally long list of pro-labor stands that had marked my entire career.

"You know what I have done. You know who is going to be better for labor. If your endorsement is based on that, it is obvious you should endorse me."

I paused and looked directly at those longtime union guys.

"Regardless of whether you do or not, I will still be president for all your members."

I knew I had significant support in the rank and file of the union, and even some support in that room. And while the general executive board of the Teamsters elected to make no endorsement, many Teamsters locals wound up endorsing me. Before I left, I shook every hand.

From the look in their eyes, I could see that the majority knew exactly what I was saying. I'd spoken the truth, and they'd heard it.

49 Days to the Election

* * *

I'd flown to Philadelphia to be interviewed by the National Association of Black Journalists. They pressed me hard, especially on the Gaza issue.

I was explicit about our goals: "That there be no reoccupation of Gaza, that there be no changing of the territorial lines in Gaza, that there be an ability to have security in the region for all concerned in a way that creates stability . . .

"We need to get this deal done and we need to get it done immediately—and that is my position and that is my policy."

The day before, I had asked Sheila to call Donald Trump's chief of staff to set up a call. He and I had barely spoken since we'd left the debate stage, except for the briefest of exchanges on 9/11. But there are certain things that transcend politics. We are two human beings, both parents, both with family members who worry about us. And there are very few people who know what it is like to be in the position we were in.

I was backstage at the WHYY studios in Philly when it was the time agreed for the call. When we connected, his people said he'd be just one more moment. In the background, I heard him on another call. I couldn't believe they hadn't put me on mute. I could hear him, flacking his new book. "It's sold out at Barnes & Noble and just about everywhere . . . go out and get it . . . I hope you're gonna buy the book . . ."

When he finally got on the line with me, I said I was calling to check how he was.

"Well, I'm okay. And I hope it never happens to you. It's not a good feeling."

"I can only imagine for you, for your family. I'm so relieved you're safe, but I'm sorry you had to go through this. It's actually quite unbelievable that in our country this would happen. I pray for your safety."

He stressed how much he appreciated the call and stood up for "your Secret Service—they did a fantastic job"—despite the criticism he was hearing on television. He mused, "We're all in this very precarious position being president or vice president. It's dangerous, worse than race car drivers and bull riders."

Then he started to get surprisingly effusive.

"It's very nice that you called, and I appreciate it. You've done a great job, you really have. You've done a very, very good job . . . my only problem is it makes it very hard for me to be angry at you. It's like, what am I going to do? How do I say bad things about you now?"

"Well, then don't!" I said, laughing.

"I'm going to tone it down. I will. You're going to see. I said, 'I hate to speak to her because I can't be vicious.' "

I noted that it was important for us to be civil, especially at a moment like this. As I was wrapping up the call, he suddenly declared, "My daughter, you know, is your big fan. Okay?" And then after a few fulsome sentences about Ivanka's regard for me, he started gushing about Doug. "And say hello to your husband. He looks like a really good guy. He did a good job at the convention, by the way. I watched his speech. He really was good."

He was being amiable. This man who had called me dumb, lazy, crazy, and mentally impaired. Implied that I drank and took drugs. Said I was a Marxist, a fascist. People had told me that he had the capacity, one on one, to show a warmer side. That he could even be charming. I hadn't believed it. But now I was experiencing it. And then, a reality check: *He's a con man. He's really good at it.*

Jason Carter, eulogizing his grandfather, observed that Jimmy Carter "was the same person, no matter who he was with or where he was. And for me, that's the definition of integrity."

Trump epitomized the exact opposite.

I'd readied myself for a phone conversation with Mr. Hyde, but Dr. Jekyll had picked up the call.

48 Days to the Election

* * *

Before we left Philly the previous day, I'd made an unscheduled stop to say hi to young volunteers doing voter registration training at the city's community college.

There were about eighty kids who all jumped up, screaming, hooting, and whistling when I dropped in unannounced. They'd made signs for the walls: SHIRLEY RAN SO KAMALA CAN WIN and VOTE LIKE YOUR LIFE DEPENDS ON IT.

I told them we're all born potential leaders and that it inspired me that they'd kicked in to that role at such an early stage of life. "You're brilliant, you care, and you're impatient."

I thanked them for what they'd committed to do over the next forty-eight days. I'd been where they were. A young advocate, dedicated to change. "I know there are many other things you could be doing. Don't put aside your studies and, you know, shower from time to time. Eat some vegetables." They laughed in recognition.

Back in DC, I met with interns from the Congressional Hispanic Caucus Institute and had a call with the young leaders tasked with getting out the youth vote. I told each group they made me optimistic for the future of our country and that I knew what the stakes were for them. They were the first generation to grow up with our planet already in climate crisis. The first generation who went through school doing lockdown drills. I promised them I would take bold action "so that those here and yet to come have a livable planet" and safe streets and schools.

I advised the volunteers to use their interactions with potential voters as a way of building community, reminding young voters that they do have power.

"Your vote is your voice; your voice is your power. And we won't let anyone take our power from us."

Of course, in these meetings, in person and on Zoom, I was talking to the most politically engaged young people.

It was devastating to learn after the election that I lost some ground with voters under thirty, especially young men.

Pundits speak about the "bro vote," the "frat boy flank." I don't think of them in those reductive terms. Instead, I think about these young voters coming of age during Covid, unnaturally isolated, their lives lonely when they should have been at their most social. At the very moment their world should have been widening, it had contracted. For some, the voices that filled the void belonged to Andrew Tate, Myron Gaines, and others who grab attention with get-rich or fitness content, then deliver arguments that feminism is damaging to masculinity and women "need to know their place."

Polling revealed that many of these young voters didn't feel they knew me. And contrary to some predictions, they did not vote primarily on reproductive rights, or Gaza, or climate change. They voted on their perceived economic interests. In a postelection study conducted by Tufts University, 40 percent put the economy and jobs as their top issue. (The next priority was abortion, 13 percent. Climate change was a top issue for 8 percent; foreign policy, including Gaza, 4 percent.)

My policies, which would have helped young voters with protection for renters, a home down payment, or student debt relief, or elevating the opportunities of non–college graduates, or increasing access to capital, had not cut through the false notion that Trump was some kind of economic savant who would somehow be better for their personal financial position.

In 107 days, I didn't have enough time to show how much more I would do to help them than he ever would. And that makes me immensely sad.

Every night of those 107 days, my last prayer before sleep was to ask God, *Have I done everything I could do today?* I don't know if there was more that I could have done to help those young people know me better, to give me their vote.

I do know that I tried.

47 Days to the Election

* * *

If there was one event that best captured the diversity of the coalition that had come together to support me, it was the Unite for America town hall hosted by Oprah Winfrey in Farmington Hills, Michigan.

Before the town hall, I met with two families who would speak at the event. Fifteen-year-old Natalie Griffith had been shot twice at Apalachee High School. She was still wearing bandages on her arm and shoulder. Amber Thurman, twenty-eight, died of septic shock after doctors delayed her care for twenty hours because of Georgia's abortion ban. Her mother and sister had come to tell the story.

I had been scheduled to have fifteen minutes with each family. That may be a lot of time in a presidential candidate's schedule, but it is far from enough time for the conversations these families deserved.

I needed to hear their stories in their own words, to look at Amber's funeral service program, absorbing the pain and trauma they had endured. Was there any way I could help to get them access to the resources they still needed? I didn't want them to feel that they were just case studies to be wheeled onstage to make a political point. They were showing tremendous courage in sharing their stories, selflessly trying to help others. It was painful and draining to learn what they'd been through, and I was determined to take as much time as I could, even if it messed with the schedule.

Oprah was running this town hall and the mood in the auditorium was high-spirited. As I waited in the wings, listening to the queen of charisma excite the crowd, I took a moment to recenter myself.

There were just four hundred people in the hall, but more than two hundred thousand on the Zoom screens that rose in tiers, like stadium seating, on the walls on either side of us. There were some famous faces on those screens, supporters such as Meryl Streep, Ben Stiller, Jennifer Lopez, and Chris Rock, who joked he'd been a long-time fan of mine: "I remember writing her a check when she was like the district attorney for something, maybe it was to get out of a parking ticket." Now, he said, he wanted to bring his daughters "to the White House to meet this Black woman president."

But the power of the event wasn't so much the celebrities as the hundreds of thousands of other faces, not well-known, from every possible demographic that could vote.

In the front row was the driving force behind it: Jotaka Eaddy. She had been sitting on her parents' porch in South Carolina when she got a text saying that Joe Biden had dropped out and endorsed me. Not three hours later, she'd rallied forty-four thousand Black women to support me on a call that "broke" Zoom, which couldn't handle any more participants. The night raised $1.5 million.

She organized her group, Win with Black Women, in 2020 because of anger over how the Black women candidates in the running to be Biden's VP were being portrayed in the media. All the familiar tropes—the Jezebel who'd slept her way to the top, the Sapphire who emasculated and disparaged Black men—had been dusted off to smear us, and Jotaka, an activist and founder of a successful Silicon Valley consultancy, decided to mobilize Black women to fight back and rally behind Black women candidates.

After that first Zoom call, others contacted Jotaka to ask how to do the same thing. From her mentoring came: Win with Black Men, White Dudes for Harris, White Women: Answer the Call, Comics for

Kamala, Deadheads for Kamala, Cat Ladies for Kamala, Cooking for Kamala, Swifties for Kamala, Jewish Women for Kamala Harris, Caregivers for Harris, Republicans for Harris, and dozens more.

"I look around at these screens, I look at who's in the room, and this is America . . . ," I said. "This movement is about reminding each other that we have so much more in common than what separates us . . . Seeing in the face of a stranger, a neighbor."

43 Days to the Election

* * *

There are red lines and there are shades of gray. Many of our national security relationships exist in complicated tones. Very few are black and white.

We pursue common interests in some areas while managing major conflicting views in others. Where it is possible without compromising our principles, we strive for constructive engagement.

In September, as international heads of state converged on New York City for the UN General Assembly, I would generally schedule back-to-back meetings with world leaders, seizing the opportunity to renew ties and to talk frankly face-to-face. But in the midst of the campaign, I couldn't do that.

I scheduled just one meeting, with President Mohamed bin Zayed Al Nahyan, or MBZ, as he is known, ruler of the United Arab Emirates. The UAE is a key player in its roiling region. We have numerous economic and military ties, as well as areas of disagreement.

In May 2022, I led the US delegation, which included Tony Blinken, to the UAE capital, Abu Dhabi, to pay respects to the late ruler, Sheikh Khalifa, and to meet with his successor. It was a twenty-hour flight for three hours on the ground, which testifies to the significance the United States places on this relationship.

I had met with MBZ since then at the UN climate conference in Dubai. This time I would welcome him to my West Wing office, the first visit to the White House by a sitting UAE president.

MBZ realizes the importance of the relationship and works on it. He also understands his power and is no supplicant. He was born knowing he would very likely rule, and he now knows he will likely rule until he dies. In that time, he is undoubtedly aware that he will cycle through many elected leaders in the United States, just like his father and his brother, who preceded him as leaders.

In meetings like this, it is important to understand how the relationship has waxed and waned. I was aware that MBZ was not pleased when the Obama administration negotiated secretly with Iran in the neighboring state of Oman without informing him. I was also aware that despite the outward congeniality during Trump's first term, there had been concerns about the shallowness of Trump's grasp of the region's history and complexity.

The UAE is a major purchaser of advanced American weapons and, largely thanks to MBZ, has one of the most effective militaries in the region. He was twenty-nine years old when Iraq invaded Kuwait, and he shared his father's determination that such a thing would never happen to the UAE. The Emirates now has compulsory military service and highly trained special forces.

In many ways, he is a visionary, encouraging an outward-looking culture tolerant of non-Islamic religions, investing in education, supporting women's participation in the workforce and the military. He has streamlined his state's bureaucracy and diversified the economy away from oil, determined to make it a leader in artificial intelligence.

He has also created a surveillance state with zero tolerance for any hint of radical Islamism, which he sees as an existential threat. He has imprisoned his critics and stoked fighting in Yemen, Sudan, and Libya, with dire humanitarian consequences.

I have found him thoughtful, shrewd, and whether his priorities are aligned or in conflict with ours, I believe he is driven by conviction. He sees Hamas as an example of the radical Islamic movements that pose a threat to the stability of the Gulf regimes. He understands Israel's desire to crush it.

But he also wants an end to the Gaza war and innocent civilian suffering, and he wants to see a path toward a Palestinian state. Emirati investment will be critical in rebuilding Gaza, but he has made it clear that there will be no funding until there is a Palestinian state on the horizon. The thaw in his country's relations with Israel would not continue while the humanitarian catastrophe continued to unfold.

Sudan, meanwhile, has taken the UAE to the International Court of Justice, claiming the UAE has sent advanced weapons to the Rapid Support Forces, a paramilitary group accused of raping and slaughtering civilians. Our UN ambassador, Linda Thomas-Greenfield, had witnessed firsthand the civilian catastrophe it caused and had called on the UAE to support peace talks.

With my national security adviser Phil Gordon beside me, we discussed these two conflicts and what steps MBZ might be willing to take to de-escalate in Sudan and support humanitarian relief in Gaza. In both conflicts, I stressed that our priority was to get the warring parties to the table and allow unfettered humanitarian access.

MBZ had brought his brother Sheikh Tahnoun, who is leading the UAE's AI superpower campaign and is responsible for billions in investment. He has lived and breathed AI since discovering Google's AI chess program in 2017.

I expressed my concern that AI should be cultivated and used in the public interest, and that we need to establish international rules and norms for that. The sheikh's first priority was investing in innovation and securing the UAE's primacy as the tech leader in the Gulf.

He was, at least, receptive to the conversation.

42 Days to the Election

* * *

I t was a conversation of a very different kind the next day, with Stephen Jackson and Matt Barnes, two retired NBA stars.

Stephen and Matt reach a large audience of sports fans with their outspoken take on issues on and off the basketball court in their podcast, *All the Smoke*.

It's not a place you expect to find politicians, which is why I was eager to go there. You have to go where the voters are: you can't expect them to come to you.

We sat down in front of the fireplace at the vice president's residence and got to reminiscing about the season they'd spent together playing ball for my favorite team, the Golden State Warriors. It was the We Believe season of 2006–2007. I was San Francisco DA, and I was stuck in traffic on the way to the stadium. Thinking I was going to miss the game, I jumped from the car, causing consternation to my protection detail, and jumped on BART along with people from all around the Bay Area, from every walk of life.

Stephen, or Stak, as he is known, had a tough start in Port Arthur, Texas, where his older brother died of head injuries after a beating. Stak had carried a weight from that tragedy, always wishing he'd been by his brother's side to defend him in that fatal fight.

I recognized that protective impulse; it was so like the one that had always motivated me. For Stak, it was what made him a fantastic teammate, but it also got him into trouble as a young player for Indiana, when he leapt into the stands to back up another player in what turned into an ugly brawl with fans.

Don Nelson, then the Warriors' coach, had been the one who embraced him after that mess, without judgment, and helped him realize his potential.

Right from the start, our conversation was intimate and heartfelt, picking up shared threads of our experiences. We talked about things we had in common, like being stepparents, and our mutual concerns about mental health and childhood trauma.

Matt, who has an Italian mom and a Black dad, told of an incident in high school when someone called his little sister names, and he defended her. In response, the KKK vandalized his school. "And I knew at that point, although I was very proud to be Italian and Black, that the world looked at me as a Black man."

He spoke about his relationship with his stepsons, telling them, "I'm just an extra layer of support and protection. I'm not there to replace your dad." It was very much how I felt in my relationship with Ella and Cole.

I said that the particular blessing I had was a close and respectful relationship with Kerstin, their mother.

Matt made a face and indicated he had more work to do there: "You're giving me a hot flash!"

"You have to work at it," I told him. I'd learned that modeling healthy emotional relationships for our kids is just as important as anything else we do for them, like helping with homework or teaching them to drive. It's such a big piece of business that we don't think about nearly enough. We will be teaching them, one way or another, in what they observe of the emotional relationships we have.

As the three of us shared anecdotes from our lives, there was so much warmth and recognition. There was light banter in the conversation, the kind only possible between people who see each other, know each other, and can speak in a kind of shorthand. But we finished on a serious note.

Stak had been friends with fellow Texan George Floyd for years, ever since a mutual friend had pointed out how alike they looked. When they met in person, the first question each asked the other was "Who your daddy?" The only difference between them, Stak said, was that he had opportunities that George Floyd just did not get.

I said it was a failure of the system, to point to the exceptions, like Stak, who managed to transcend their experiences, as if that was an indication that there was some kind of level playing field. What about the kid who doesn't have a remarkable talent? That is not a system that is going to be productive for the greatest number of people. The system is not working if only the exceptional people are able to succeed.

The murder of Floyd had turned Stak into an activist. He became a powerful voice seeking justice, but also for seeking it by peaceful means. When Minneapolis burned, he called for restraint. Rioting, he said, was not the answer:

"I've never stood for that, and Floyd didn't stand for that."

George Floyd's daughter is only eleven years old. Stak has become close to her and spoke movingly of how they held each other up after her father's murder.

"A lot of days when I didn't know what I was doing, just hearing her call me uncle, and, you know, just telling me she loved me, those days picked me up a lot. She is definitely a special child."

As we wound up the recording and took off our mics, Matt, 6'7", and Stak, 6'8", unfolded their lanky frames from the formal chairs of the sitting room. As I stood between them for a photograph, I knew this disparity in our heights would be noticeable, to say the least.

But I was proud to stand with two giants of the court who were unafraid to speak openly of hurt and trauma, healing and love.

41 Days to the Election

* * *

With Mark Cuban in the audience, I addressed the Economic Club of Pittsburgh. Mark had been a big supporter throughout the campaign, doing numerous events in which he picked apart the dangerous flaws in Trump's tariff policy and warned of its consequences to both businesses and consumers.

He had credibility and was able to reach a variety of important constituencies: big business, small business, sports fans, and people who just liked his no-nonsense personality on *Shark Tank*. (At the end of long days, I loved to watch reruns of *Shark Tank*, and my habit was to then google and see how, years later, the various businesses that had won investment were doing.)

I needed voters to know the specifics of how I intended to put more money in their pockets today and to improve their prospects in the future. I started by acknowledging that the cost of living was still way too high: "You know it and I know it."

My proposal was for a new tax credit for investment and job creation in key industries like steel, biotech, AI, semiconductors, aerospace, autos, and farming.

I talked about the importance of retooling existing factories, the credits that would encourage local hiring, and protecting the right to organize.

I pledged to double the number of apprenticeships during my first term and increase skills-based hiring. As president, I said, I could eliminate the degree requirements for half a million federal jobs in favor of skills-based hiring and apprenticeships, and that I would then challenge the private sector to do the same. We could grow the nation's cybersecurity workforce in this way and provide a model that private enterprise could emulate.

My talk was of things I knew I could actually do as president and things that I knew would work. I warned that Trump's tariffs would raise costs and risk recession. I was confident about my analysis because I had a powerful team of economic advisers with different expertise. Brian Nelson had been my special assistant attorney general in California and understood my policy perspective. Brian Deese was a former director of the National Economic Council and had worked in the White House on the clean energy transition. Deanne Millison handled outreach to CEOs, small business, and private sector engagement in Africa and Central America for me at the White House.

But as much as I hammered my economic message, it didn't seem to be penetrating fast enough. Over the course of the campaign, my polling on the economy went up 15 to 20 points in battleground states, amplified by leaders like Mark and my Divine Nine brother Jimmy McMikle, head of Kappa Alpha Psi, along with the leadership of Iota Phi Theta. These fraternities are deeply committed to mentorship and economic empowerment, with powerful reach into the Black community. In a longer campaign, I might have had time to better bring the message home.

Later, I'd have a telling exchange with Charlamagne Tha God, the host of the popular radio show *The Breakfast Club*. I've been on his show many times. Charlamagne is a savvy interviewer with a missionary zeal for reaching Black men and a particular commitment to mental health issues. His show has a radio audience of eight million monthly.

When I appeared on his show, he lit right into me: "You come off very scripted. You stick to your talking points."

"That would be called 'discipline,'" I retorted.

When he pressed me, I explained that I needed to repeat my messages so that everyone could get to know what I stand for. It's not especially fun to give the same speech three times a day in three different cities four or five times a week, but it's necessary.

Trump stood up there and spouted unfiltered nonsense about Hannibal Lecter and electric sharks. He called it "the weave." I call it nonsense.

The double standard on our style of presentation was galling. If I hesitated or backtracked midsentence to try to clarify or better express a thought, it was "word salad." Meanwhile, Trump could describe Hurricane Florence as "one of the wettest we've ever seen, from the standpoint of water."

40 Days to the Election

* * *

A storm was heading toward Florida, Ukrainian President Volody-myr Zelenskyy was due for a meeting at my ceremonial office, and, as leader of the first White House Office of Gun Violence Prevention, I was scheduled to speak at the signing of an executive order creating a task force to combat ghost guns and improve safety drills in schools.

The low-pressure system that would become Hurricane Helene had begun forming on September 22 in the Caribbean and rapidly intensified as it moved across the warm waters of the Gulf of Mexico. It would reach Category 4 intensity before the end of the day and slam into the Florida coast before midnight, carving a path of awful destruction through five states. But all I could do that day was to urge people to heed warnings and follow the advice of their local officials.

The meeting with Zelenskyy would be my seventh. I'd first met him at the Munich Security Conference in February 2022. It was a tough meeting. I had to convince him of something he was reluctant to hear: that a Russian invasion was just days or maybe even hours away.

In my speech to the summit, I'd declared, "The foundation of

European security is under direct threat in Ukraine." I called out Putin's "playbook"—his spreading of lies, disinformation, propaganda.

After that speech, in a private room across the street from the conference venue, I sat down with Zelenskyy and laid out our intelligence, which differed from what the Ukrainians had gathered. I had to tell him bluntly that his numbers were wrong and invasion was imminent. Zelenskyy still believed that Putin was merely flexing and wouldn't mount a full-scale war against his country. It was my job to get him to face the urgent reality.

"What would you have me do?" he finally asked.

"Get your people ready," I replied. And he did.

Few of us know who we will be in a time of crisis until we are tested. I often think of the window cleaner, trapped in a stalled elevator the day the planes hit the World Trade Center. Refusing to give up, he used the sharp edge of his squeegee to gouge through the wall and led everyone in that elevator to safety. Did he know when he set out for work on that ordinary day that he would be the hero who saved lives?

Zelenskyy, who had been a comedian, has proved himself an exceptional wartime leader. He has stepped up to a task he never expected, inspiring his people with his personal courage, drawing support from the whole world, defending the sovereignty and territorial integrity of his country against the might of Russia.

Now, after almost a thousand days of conflict, we met in the midst of the bloodshed and destruction that his people were suffering to discuss how the United States could best continue to support Ukraine's resistance. Our conversation was candid; we had developed a relationship of trust.

It was the kind of day that reminded me why I was a public servant. What I said and did that day would have an impact on people affected by a natural disaster, a war, and the ongoing scourge of gun violence.

———

The executive order came in the wake of another dispiriting Supreme Court decision, striking down the federal ban on bump stocks. Sometimes I felt that improving our gun laws was a frustrating game of Whac-A-Mole. No sooner did we pass a law than the gun lobby filed suit and the conservative court overturned it. Meanwhile, the lawless found ways to get around the scant regulations still in place.

And so we live with the fact that one in five Americans has a relative who was killed by gun violence.

We gathered in the East Room of the White House. Sari Kaufman, who survived the 2018 mass shooting at Marjory Stoneman Douglas High School in Parkland, Florida, introduced me. Many other survivors and activists filled the room.

The new executive order was timed to mark the first anniversary of the White House Office of Gun Violence Prevention. It was aimed at deadly machine gun conversion devices, or MCDs, and 3D-printed ghost guns. Even though these devices are illegal, police had seen a staggering 570 percent rise in MCD seizures. The devices are cheap, easy to make, and deadly. One type, a "Glock switch," converts the pistol into a weapon capable of firing up to 1,200 rounds a minute. The new task force would come up with better ways to tackle the manufacture and distribution of these devices.

As Joe signed the executive order, he turned and handed me the pen, saying, "Keep it going, boss."

39 Days to the Election

* * *

As rain lashed the tarmac at Joint Base Andrews, a wet and miserable press pool huddled under the wing of Air Force Two, trying not to get soaked. Washington, DC, was experiencing the edge of Hurricane Helene.

Mark Kelly and I were headed to a drier climate in his home state of Arizona, where we would visit the border. Even though the devastation of the hurricane was beginning to be clear, I knew I wouldn't be able to visit the affected areas for several days. It was important to stay out of the way of the emergency efforts and not add to their logistical challenges. Search and rescue was underway, and first responders needed to focus all their efforts on relief and recovery without diverting their resources.

On my way to the border, I would get briefings from the Federal Emergency Management Agency (FEMA). I knew that a significant amount of my time would be dedicated to supporting the relief effort and ensuring that the people on the ground got everything they needed and deserved.

Although some of the most conservative Republicans had helped draft a bipartisan bill with the toughest set of border reforms in decades, Trump had intervened to kill it, calling it "a waste of paper."

So instead of a bipartisan agreement, which is so badly needed to properly address the border crisis after the lifting of Title 42, which curbed migration during the pandemic, we'd used executive action that had cut unlawful border crossings by half, to the lowest level in four years. We'd increased the number of border agents and provided fentanyl scanners, which had led to more fentanyl seizures in the past two years than the previous five.

Even so, Trump was slaying us in polls on this issue. He preferred to run on the problem, spouting incendiary language about an "invasion" by criminals and violent gangs, rather than fix the problem.

Never mind that immigrants are less likely to commit violent and property crime than American-born individuals, or that cities with more immigrants have similar or lower rates of violent and property crimes than areas with fewer.

Those statistics don't register like powerful visuals of migrant caravans or large groups of desperate people wading across the Rio Grande, especially when the visuals are accompanied by hysterical commentary by the likes of Fox News hosts, designed to whip up anxiety and anger.

There is a bleak and tragic history in this country of demonizing immigrants: the Jewish refugees who were denied entry when fleeing annihilation in Nazi Germany; the Chinese, Italians, and Irish who were hated, vilified, and slandered in almost the same terms as the Right uses about today's migrants; the Japanese who were interned, denied freedom and due process solely on the basis of their race.

Immigration *had* surged, and to some it *felt* like an invasion: we couldn't gaslight the people who felt that way by denying the problem.

We did not succeed in making a passionate case for a complete immigration overhaul that combined securing the border with a better legal mechanism for the people who arrive here with a dream of success and contribution. People who are no different from the parents, grandparents, or great-grandparents many of us love and revere who made a similar journey in search of an American dream.

I did not have time, in 107 days, to undo ten years of Trump's demonization of immigrants. All I could do was show that we had taken measures that were working, and that I took the issue seriously and would continue to press for the comprehensive reforms we needed.

The challenge was to make this visit more than a photo op.

Mark and I flew to Tucson and helicoptered to Douglas, in bright red Cochise County. The town of sixteen thousand people has close ties with its neighbor city in Mexico, Agua Prieta, as do many border towns, and the challenge is to facilitate efficient legal crossings, which are helpful for commerce, while cracking down on illegal ones.

It was a rough ride in the Osprey chopper, the rising desert air tossing us around as if we were in a spin dryer. The temperature was also like a dryer—106 degrees. At the busy port of entry, I listened as the border agents spoke of their challenges, and I thanked them for doing a tough job, covering about 260 miles of border. Then we took a walk along a line of fence built during the Obama administration. (Trump had once staged a photo op touting *his* "big, beautiful wall," but he'd done it in front of a section that Obama built—of the many things I was prepared to say at the debate, this was one observation I regretted not delivering.)

Trump had four years to increase the number of border agents, to boost the number of border judges. He did neither. All he did was fan flames of hate and division, highlighting rare, tragic cases of violent crime while smearing the overwhelming majority of hardworking immigrants.

I was the one who'd walked through tunnels that traffickers used to smuggle contraband and broken up a heroin trafficking ring connected to Mexican cartels. I'd done the hard work to bring criminals to justice and relief to the families of their victims.

38 Days to the Election

* * *

I was in San Francisco for a campaign fundraiser when I started to learn about the misinformation and conspiracy theories being spread about hurricane relief.

It was a demonstration, in real time, of the dangers posed to real people by an unmoderated social media swamp. Someone with the username MattWallace888, who had more than two million followers, wrote that "elites" had engaged in "weather modification" to target counties that voted for Trump in the last election. I thought the idea was too crazy even for the most gullible, but his tweet received more than eleven million views. In a second post, he overlaid the storm's path on a map of the 2020 election results, attempting to "prove" his crazy theory. The conspiracy took off on X and then TikTok, with videos there viewed more than a million times.

That night we flew to Los Angeles, where I had an event the following day. It was the only night I would sleep in my own home, in my own bed, during the campaign.

Being home was not necessarily a good thing. I knew as I opened my front door that everything would have deteriorated after such a long absence. I know this sounds crazy, but houses resent being unlived in, or mine seems to. Every time I come back from a significant time away, something goes wrong. If it's hot, the AC won't work; if it's cold, there will be no heat. One time, when I tried to use the oven, it literally exploded. The garden will look neglected, my herb garden yellowed. And I knew, arriving at 6:23 p.m. and leaving the next day, with a full binder of tasks and schedule of calls to accomplish, I wouldn't be there long enough to do anything about it.

I would keep my road warrior mentality. I would take a bath, get a good night's sleep, and pretend my own home was a hotel.

37 Days to the Election

* * *

Hair color. Manicure. Call, and call, and call.
14:01: VP rolling.
Fundraiser in LA.
Rally in Las Vegas.
21:23: Lid.

36 Days to the Election

* * *

I canceled my campaign swing through Nevada and rescheduled media interviews, including with Alex Cooper of the podcast *Call Her Daddy*. I needed to head back to FEMA headquarters in Washington, DC.

I had a lot of experience at this. As a senator I'd been on the committee that oversees FEMA, and I had an excellent relationship of trust with the agency's leadership. During the first Trump administration I'd seen how relief efforts had been shaped by a petty partisan agenda, and I was determined not to let anything like that happen on my watch.

And even as I was taking valuable time from my campaign to fulfill my responsibilities as vice president, Trump posted on his social media site that Joe and I were "going out of [our] way to not help people in Republican areas" hit by Hurricane Helene. In a second post, he said we had "left Americans to drown in North Carolina, Georgia, Tennessee, Alabama, and elsewhere in the South." He claimed that Georgia's Republican governor, Brian Kemp, had a "hard time" reaching Biden to discuss disaster relief, and that the president had been "very non-responsive."

All of it was, of course, lies.

Kemp quickly rebutted Trump's claim, saying the president had called him and asked, simply, "What do you need?"

More than 230 people had died in the worst hurricane since Katrina, but instead of consoling and helping, Trump was stoking rage with falsehoods and making it harder for FEMA workers to do their jobs. Some FEMA workers had guns pulled on them. At his rallies, he claimed that our administration had "spent all" of the disaster relief money "for housing illegal immigrants." As he knew, or should have known, the much smaller fund for migrant shelter is totally different from FEMA's disaster relief fund. It was Trump who, when president, took money from the disaster fund and directed it toward immigration enforcement. He tried to connect his bogus claims to his assertions about noncitizens voting. He said we'd given the FEMA money "to their illegal immigrants that they want to have vote for them this season."

Elon Musk would pick up the lies and amplify them in his own post: "Yes, they are literally using YOUR tax dollars to import voters and disenfranchise you!"

"Yes they can control the weather," Marjorie Taylor Greene would pile on.

On the plane I called and spoke with Governor Roy Cooper in North Carolina, Brian Kemp in Georgia, and mayors in the worst-hit communities in all the affected states. I tried repeatedly to reach Ron DeSantis, who remained unavailable. The list of what we were doing to help was extensive. FEMA trucks of food and water were arriving. Twenty-four search-and-rescue task forces had been deployed and already rescued and supported more than 1,400 people. The Coast Guard, the Army Corps of Engineers, the Environmental Protection Agency, the Department of Agriculture, the Small Business Administration, and the Department of Energy had all deployed personnel.

It was, in fact, a massive relief effort.

Sadly, in the aftermath, polls in the affected communities would show that whether people felt that the federal government had done a good job split exactly on party lines.

35 Days to the Election

* * *

The day leading up to Tim's debate with J. D. Vance had been filled with tension.

Though I'd come back to DC to get briefings on the hurricane catastrophe, it was a different crisis that put me in the Situation Room that day. The Iranian response we'd been concerned about had come in the shape of about 180 ballistic missiles. Sirens howled over Israel just before 7:30 p.m. local time, 12:30 p.m. in DC.

In the Situation Room, I monitored the attack. The Defense Department later shared publicly that our destroyers in the eastern Mediterranean were part of a coordinated response that downed most of the missiles. The limited damage and few casualties made it less likely that Netanyahu would mount a massive counterstrike and drag the region into full-blown war.

There was more riding on Tim's debate than there should have been. Trump's proposal, back in August, to debate me two more times had been withdrawn. We wanted another debate, badly. We needed it to shift our stuck polling numbers. We'd tried everything to goad or cajole Trump into it. He'd agree and then his team, who was more disciplined than he was, would pull him back.

So that meant Tim would have to be the closer.

It was not a comfortable role for him. He had fretted from the outset that he wasn't a good debater. I'd discounted his concerns. He was so quick and pithy in front of the crowds at our rallies, I thought he'd bring those qualities to the podium. He'd prepared with Pete Buttigieg, a consummate debater, and I thought his big heart and his good humor would counter J. D. Vance's malice and pessimism.

But J. D. Vance is a shape-shifter. And a shifty guy. He understood that his default meanness wouldn't play against Tim Walz's sunny disposition and patent decency. Throughout the debate, he toned the anger and the insults way down. As Van Jones later remarked, he sanewashed the crazy. There were no cat ladies, no pet-eating Haitians, no personal insults. Just a mild-mannered, aw-shucks Appalachian pretending he had a lot of common ground with that nice Midwestern coach.

When Tim fell for it and started nodding and smiling at J.D.'s fake bipartisanship, I moaned to Doug, "What is happening?"

I told the television screen: "You're not there to make friends with the guy who is attacking your running mate."

There was not supposed to be any on-air fact-checking in this debate, as there had been in mine. But the moderators did correct Vance twice, on the overwhelming scientific consensus on climate change and on the legal immigration status of Haitians in Springfield.

"The rules were you guys weren't going to fact-check," Vance complained petulantly, in a flash of his more familiar persona.

Tim fell into a pattern of defending his record as a governor. Then he fumbled his answer when the moderator, predictably, questioned why he had claimed to be in Hong Kong during the democracy protests in Tiananmen Square. Tim had been on his way to teach in China that summer but hadn't yet left the United States on the date of the massacre. Instead of simply stating that he'd gotten his dates mixed up, but that being in China during a period of human rights oppression had profoundly influenced him, he talked about biking in Nebraska.

The following weekend, *Saturday Night Live* did a sketch in which actors posed as Doug and me, sitting on our couch, watching the debate. While I did not in fact spit out wine, it was otherwise uncanny in its portrait of our evening.

Tim felt bad that he hadn't done better. I reassured him that the election would not be won or lost on account of that debate, and in fact it had a negligible effect on our polling.

In choosing Tim, I thought that as a second-term governor and twelve-year congressman he would know what he was getting into. In hindsight, how could anyone?

When they'd attacked his National Guard record, I had to talk to him about being resilient. It's a challenge when you have kids—Tim had a son still in high school and a young-adult daughter whom I'd come to know to be as bighearted as her dad. It's painful for them to hear their father unfairly attacked. For the candidate, the family that is your source of strength can become your weakness in a presidential campaign. Tim was outraged by the unfairness: "How dare they? This is BS." I had to tell him, "Don't let them get in your head."

When I was a newly elected DA, an elderly gentleman in Atlanta pulled me aside with a bit of advice: "Baby, you be sure and don't make it look too easy." He knew it was not. And the higher you rise in the political food chain, the harder it gets.

This is not a genteel profession. You must be ready to brawl.

34 Days to the Election

* * *

In the Augusta, Georgia, neighborhood of Meadowbrook, downed power lines looped over fallen trees. The once-tidy streets of low-slung ranch houses were strewn with debris.

A young woman wept as she recounted how her husband had been killed in the storm. She'd left her bedroom because her daughter needed something, and in the moment she was gone, a tree fell on that room where her husband lay in bed.

As I made my way through the wreckage of homes and lives, the first responders described their tireless efforts to bring help.

I was able to announce that the federal government would be reimbursing 100 percent of the cost of the recovery effort to local governments for the next three months, which doesn't always happen. I said that there was an immediate emergency grant of $750 available to anyone just by providing their address. This got wildly misconstrued. Misinformation spread that $750 was *all* the victims would receive, which was ridiculous, but caused much unnecessary pain and anger. Anger that Trump was glad to fan.

At the local senior center, I helped volunteers hand out meals to weary men and women facing the long labor of rebuilding their lives.

It was, as always, such a stark contrast of the way disaster calls forth the best and worst of human nature.

33 Days to the Election

* * *

COUNTRY OVER PARTY read the signs at the entrance to Ripon College. The Republican Party was founded before the Civil War in Ripon, Wisconsin, in 1854 with the aim of stopping the spread of slavery. Liz Cheney had come here today to help me stop Trump.

She had been the third-highest-ranking Republican in House leadership until her outspoken opposition to Trump and her revulsion at his role on January 6 cost her her leadership positions and then her seat in Congress.

There are many things Liz Cheney and I don't agree on. But we agree on many fundamental principles. High on that list: free and fair elections, the rule of law, and the First Amendment.

And you can have respect for someone with whom you disagree.

There had been a debate in the campaign about where to put our time and resources. Should we focus on turning out our base, or should we give equal priority to talking to our opponent's base?

At a strategy meeting in early August, Jen O'Malley Dillon advised that we really needed to bring Trump's numbers down, since the universe of undecided voters had contracted. The time for persuasion, she said, was earlier in the cycle and had passed. People were going home to their base.

Time is the most valuable commodity in any campaign, especially in one as brief as ours. I was glad to give some time to campaigning with Liz Cheney in the hope that we could reach those Republicans who believe, as we do, that fundamental principles of our democracy should never be partisan issues. The amount of that time, however, was exaggerated by the media's interest in our unlikely pairing. We campaigned together for only one and a half days.

She started her speech that day in Ripon by proclaiming that she had been a Republican "even before Donald Trump started spray tanning." She was frank about her conservative values: limited government, low taxes, strong defense, and that family, not government, is the most important structure in society. Fidelity to the Constitution, she said, is "the most conservative of our conservative values." She urged the audience "to reject the depraved cruelty of Donald Trump."

She said she had never voted for a Democrat, but that she would proudly vote for me.

"I know that she will be a president who will defend the rule of law. And I know that she will be a president who can inspire all of our children—and if I might say so, especially our little girls—to do great things," she said. "So help us right the ship of our democracy so that history will say of us, when our time of testing came, we did our duty and we prevailed because we loved our country more."

After the election, I invited her to come to the vice president's residence with her five children. I imagined her kids had the same fond feelings about the house where their grandfather lived for eight years as ours do.

Our security footprint was too big to go visiting, so family came to us, and the residence was the one place big enough for all of us to be together, casual and private. So casual that my baby nieces did not always appreciate that the art we had on loan from the Smithsonian was extremely valuable.

On a podium on the first floor, I had a large and gorgeous vase made by an acclaimed American artist. One day, to my complete dismay, I discovered Amara and Leela at the top of the stairs, bending over the banister, trying to see who could land a ball of socks in the vase the most times.

I imagine Liz Cheney's kids have memories of similar antics.

31 Days to the Election

* * *

In the hills and valleys of western North Carolina, the force of the flood-waters buckled roads, picked up tractor trailers, uprooted trees, and washed away homes. Eighty-six people in the state had been killed.

The damage was even worse than what I'd witnessed in Georgia. Usually, hurricane effects are most severe on the coast, but unexpectedly, inland mountain communities had been hardest hit. Before the storm, the area had experienced several days of heavy rain, saturating the soil and filling rivers. The Blue Ridge Mountains acted as a funnel, channeling the hurricane's massive rainfall through the valleys.

The North Carolina Air National Guard had been flying supplies into remote mountain communities and doing low-altitude sweeps of the hills and hollows, looking for people in need of rescue since roads and bridges had been washed away and communications were down.

As I shook hands and looked into tired young faces, I realized that some of them had also suffered loss in the storm, but were still showing up, helping others.

I told them, "You are doing God's work on the ground."

29 Days to the Election

* * *

I taped my interview with *60 Minutes* on the anniversary of the Hamas attack on Israel. Bill Whitaker's first several questions probed the state of Middle Eastern security and our relationship with Netanyahu, who had resisted our calls for a ceasefire and had gone into Lebanon despite US advice.

He wanted to know if, in pursuing our goal of ending the war, we had a reliable ally in Netanyahu. I answered that the question should be about the alliance between the American people and the Israeli people, which I maintained was strong.

He pivoted then to the US economy and other subjects.

It was a long interview, and it was of course edited down, as is usual. When a bit of the edited footage was used as a promo on *Face the Nation*, Trump sued CBS for $20 billion, baselessly claiming that *60 Minutes* edited the interview to make me look good.

It was a nonsense claim, a frivolous suit, and in normal times CBS management would have brushed it off. But CBS is owned by Paramount Global, which was in the midst of seeking a merger with Skydance Media and needed approval from the Federal Communications Commission. Paramount's controlling shareholder, Shari Redstone, stood to make hundreds of millions if the deal went through. Paramount ultimately settled the suit for $16 million in a move that veteran correspondent Dan Rather termed "a sellout to extortion by the President."

Bill Owens, the respected executive producer of *60 Minutes*, and Wendy McMahon, the chief of CBS News, both had earlier resigned from their jobs because of corporate pressure to shape the news to Trump's sensibilities.

The Fourth Estate is so called because it is a key pillar of democracy. When corporations take it over and put profit ahead of accurate, brave, and truthful reporting, the whole edifice trembles.

28 Days to the Election

* * *

Everything about my appearance on *The View* was going well. Until it wasn't.

I'd been on the show about five times before. Some of the hosts I knew from outside the studio. Whoopi Goldberg and I bonded over our shared ties to the Bay Area. Sunny Hostin I knew as a lawyer; she had been a prosecutor like me. Ana Navarro, a Republican, I'd debated on immigration during the Bush years, but we aligned on many other issues.

All the hosts are thoughtful women of different political stripes, but all had been outspoken about the dangers presented by Donald Trump. He'd refused to go on the show and face their questioning.

I had three interviews scheduled that day, one with Howard Stern and one with Stephen Colbert. Although this one—morning TV, a largely female audience—was friendly ground, my team and I had prepared, and I felt ready.

Whoopi Goldberg introduced me effusively: "We are thrilled that joining us right now for her very first talk show and live TV appearance since accepting the Democratic presidential nomination, please welcome back"—she paused for a long minute, emotional—"the next president of the United States!"

I walked on the stage to the pulsing rhythm of Beyoncé's "Free-dom," my campaign anthem; a standing ovation from the studio audience; and warm handshakes or hugs from the panelists.

Whoopi asked me about the day the president called me, so I related the story of the pancakes, the grandnieces, and the upheaval that followed. Then Sunny Hostin recalled Biden's appearance on the show, during which he'd said there wasn't a single thing that he did that I could not do.

"What do you think would be the biggest specific difference between your presidency and a Biden presidency?" she asked.

"Well, we're obviously two different people, and we have a lot of shared life experiences. For example, the way we feel about our family and our parents and so on, but we're also different people, and I will bring those sensibilities to how I lead. For example, one of the things I know we're going to talk about today is what we do around home health care. I have done a lot of work around violence toward women and children. I care a lot about that. I love our small businesses." I talked warmly about my "second mother," Mrs. Shelton, who ran a small daycare business. "So the influence of a personal experience will have its impact on a presidency."

If only we'd left it there. But Sunny asked a follow-up: "If anything, would you have done something differently than President Biden during the past four years?"

I had prepped for that question; I had notes on it. There was the answer I'd given in the debate: "I'm not Joe Biden and I'm certainly not Donald Trump." I had a note that I was a new and different generation. And I had this: *But to specifically answer your question, throughout my career I have worked with Democrats, independents, and Republicans, and I know that great ideas come from all places. If I'm president I would appoint a Republican to my cabinet.*

But I didn't say any of that. I said, "There is not a thing that comes to mind."

I went on to describe things in our record that I was proud of, such as capping the price of insulin, bringing drug prices down, investing in American manufacturing and creating eight hundred thousand new jobs in that sector.

I had no idea I'd just pulled the pin on a hand grenade. I wasn't braced for the explosion that was coming.

Stationed at various places around the set, my staff were beside themselves. Political operatives have an eye to see a moment, and I could kick myself for giving the other side that moment. During the commercial break, while I was having a bit of fun with some young students I'd noticed in the audience who were obviously playing hooky, offering to write notes to their teachers after the show, Opal passed me a note from our team, telling me to return to that question and mention that a big difference would be that I would put a Republican in my cabinet.

I made that point, but the damage was done. The earlier clip was a gift to the Trump campaign, and they used it in ad after ad to shackle me to an unpopular president.

Why. Didn't. I. Separate. Myself. From. Joe. Biden?

Over the course of the 107 days, I became increasingly aware that people wanted to know there was a separation and that it was a big issue for them. I just didn't realize how big.

The way I heard Sunny's question was that it was asking me to be critical of Joe. I've never believed you need to elevate yourself by pushing someone else down. To do so would have been to embrace the cruelty of my opponent. In the moment, I didn't see a way to answer the question without doing that.

Trial lawyers have a saying: There are always three closing arguments. The one you plan to give. The one you give. And the one you should have given. I lived the adage that afternoon.

To me, the difference was evident. Different background, different generation, different career. Obviously, a different person.

But I was still vice president to President Biden. We had three months left of our administration. Even after the lack of support from the White House, the debate night phone call, and the MAGA hat debacle, I felt I owed him my loyalty.

Had I, in that interview, come up with one area of policy difference, it would have limited the definition of the difference between us to that one thing, rather than my unique perspective on a variety of issues. And it wouldn't have ended there. It would have opened the door to a discussion that is backward-looking rather than forward-looking. There would be a slew of never-ending follow-up questions: *Well, apart from that one, how would you have made X or Y decision differently from Biden?*

Between the president and the vice president there needs to be a zone of trust: a place where the president can get advice, feedback, and criticism to make a good decision, and know that those discussions will remain confidential. Lawyer-client discussions are privileged; doctor-patient conversations are, too. And so, I believe, should be the discussions and arguments and, yes, differences of opinion between the president and vice president.

But my campaign team didn't see it that way. David Plouffe was the most outspoken. He felt that someone needed to do an intervention with me, that I needed to get it through my head that this was a real issue. That was when he told me bluntly, "People hate Joe Biden."

He also said this: "You're going to have bad days. You're going to have to keep moving."

Two of the three interviews I did that day went off well. Stephen Colbert met me backstage with his wife, and they presented me with their cookbook. He knew my days were long, and with a big smile he said, "Let's go out and have some fun."

Howard Stern was a great interlocutor. We covered very serious ground but also had a great time, bantering about music, Maya Rudolph's impression of me, and blind dates. Yet all I could think about that night was the one interview that hadn't gone well. I'm tougher on myself than anyone.

But Plouffe was right: I had to keep moving.

So that is what I did.

1 | Amara's handwritten contract for my wake-up time.

2 | One of the many notes Doug wrote and had propped on my pillow when we were apart those last days of the campaign.

3 | Day One at the vice president's residence. *From left:* Tony, Oliver Mittelstaedt, Josh Hsu, Brian Fallon, Nik, Meena, Leela, Amara, me, Sheila Nix, Lorraine Voles, Erin Wilson, Kirsten Allen, Steven Kelly, Opal Vadhan, Storm Horncastle, and Juan Dromgoole.

4 | Finally reunited with Doug in my cabin on Air Force Two after becoming top of the ticket. Tony West is smiling in the background and Doug's chief body person, Silas Woods III, is walking by.

5 | My first rally stop as the top of the ticket at West Allis Central High School outside Milwaukee.

6 | Bilateral meeting with Israeli Prime Minister Benjamin Netanyahu. To my right, my national security advisor, Dr. Philip Gordon, and deputy national security advisor Rebecca Lissner; and to my left, my chief of staff, Lorraine Voles.

7 | A typical vice-presidential vetting process takes at least a couple of months. We conducted ours in two weeks. *From left to right, back to front:* Lorraine Voles, Tony, Eric Holder, Dana Remus, Sheila Nix, and Jen O'Malley Dillon. *Onscreen:* Senator Catherine Cortez Masto, Cedric Richmond, and Marty Walsh.

8 | Inside an Eau Claire, Wisconsin, district event.

9 | Aboard Air Force Two on the way to Raleigh, North Carolina, with Erin Wilson, Andy Flick, Ernie Apreza, Ike Irby, Dean Lieberman, and Sheila Nix.

10 | Backstage at the convention with Doris Johnson and Stacey Johnson-Batiste.

11 | Doug and I join the Bidens onstage in Chicago after President Biden's speech. Joe and Jill Biden are incredible public servants.

12 | Tim Walz and I stood backstage at our rally in Milwaukee and watched the delegate roll call live from Chicago. This is the moment I officially became the Democratic presidential nominee.

13 | I loved watching the nation get to know my Dougie—our first Second Gentleman. I watched his convention speech on Air Force Two, coming back from our Milwaukee rally.

14 | Backstage at the convention, watching my sister give an amazing speech.

15 | Walking onto the stage for my acceptance speech as Democratic nominee for president of the United States.

16 | Backstage at the convention. Opal Vadhan placed framed photos of my mother at a protest and of my grandfather. I missed them so.

17 | CNN interview with Dana Bash at Kim's Café in Savannah, Georgia.

18 | First day of debate camp, in the tricked-out ballroom of the Omni William Penn Hotel in Pittsburgh. Greeting Philippe Reines, a.k.a. Donald Trump.

19 | Karen Dunn (*pictured with Brian Fallon*) led my debate prep and made sure we got every detail just right for our practice.

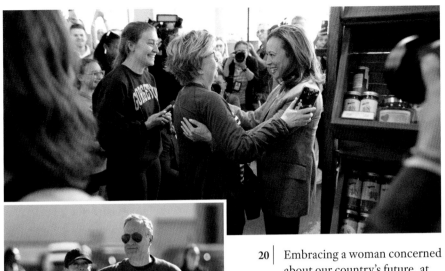

20 | Embracing a woman concerned about our country's future, at Penzeys Spices in Pittsburgh.

21 | Respite from debate camp. Romantic walk with Doug at the Air National Guard base, also known as 171st Air Refueling Wing.

22 | My debate prep team.

23 | Passing a cross made from the salvaged remains of the crashed plane on 9/11 as President Biden and I walked into the Shanksville, Pennsylvania, volunteer fire department.

24 | Holding the program to Amber Thurman's funeral. Amber was denied reproductive care in Georgia. Here with her sister and mother, who courageously told her story.

25 | Many days involved campaigning in multiple states. On this day, we were in both Georgia and Wisconsin.

26 | Meeting President Mohamed bin Zayed Al Nahyan of the United Arab Emirates in my West Wing office.

27 | At the VP residence with Stephen Jackson and Matt Barnes for their podcast, *All the Smoke*, where we talked about everything from family to sports to social justice.

28 | At the Economic Club of Pittsburgh, outlining my economic policies.

29 | Meeting President Volodymyr Zelenskyy for the seventh time in September 2024.

30 | Meeting with border patrol agents at the US-Mexico border in Douglas, Arizona.

31 | President Biden and I meet with national security advisors in the White House Situation Room to discuss Iranian plans to launch a missile attack against Israel.

32 | With Alex Cooper of the *Call Her Daddy* podcast, an example of an important alternative to mainstream media.

33 | Off-the-record conversation with the traveling press.

34 | Liz Cheney has courageously demonstrated her commitment to country over party.

35 | Members of the National Guard activated across the southeast in response to Hurricanes Helene and Milton. Here I am thanking Army National Guard members in Charlotte, with North Carolina governor Roy Cooper in the background.

36 | In the wake of Hurricane Helene, I spent time packing supplies with incredible volunteers in Charlotte, North Carolina. In the midst of crises, I have seen those who have the least give the most.

37 | Interview with Bill Whitaker for *60 Minutes*.

38 | In Las Vegas at a Univision town hall with undecided Latino voters.

39 | In Phoenix, Arizona, at the Gila River Indian community with young Native American leaders.

40 | Meeting with Bishop William Barber II and the incredible farmers of North Carolina who help power our domestic and global economy.

41 | The Sunday service at New Birth Baptist Church led by Dr. Jamal Bryant in Stonecrest, Georgia. Members of the congregation give me their blessings. *From left to right:* Jalisa, Adore Bryant, Karri Turner, and Chrisette. Over my right shoulder is Cedric Richmond and the mayor of Atlanta, Andre Dickens.

42 | A moment of calm before heading out to deliver my campaign's closing argument to 75,000 people on the Ellipse.

43 | Press gaggle at the Dane County airport in Wisconsin.

44 | At the IBEW local in Janesville, Wisconsin.

45 | Boarding Air Force Two in Atlanta the Saturday before the election. This was a five-state day: Wisconsin, Georgia, North Carolina, New York, and Michigan.

46 | Returning to DC in the early hours of November 5 after the Rocky Steps rally in Philadelphia.

47 | Practicing two sets of remarks for election night.

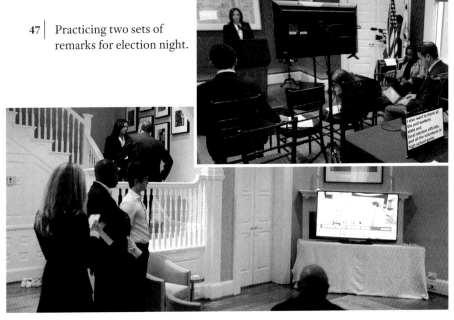

48 | Sharing the news with Doug that it appeared as if the election was not going our way. *Left to right:* Tony, Jasper, Lo, and Reggie, watching the returns.

49 | Calling voters with volunteer phone bankers on Election Day.

50 | Certifying the 2024 US presidential election.

26 Days to the Election

* * *

I was in Las Vegas to record "Los Latinos Preguntan . . . Kamala Harris Responde," a town hall with a hundred undecided Latino voters to be shown that night on Univision.

The questions—on prices, on immigration—were not particular to the Latino community. They were the same concerns that all Americans had.

But one woman became distressed as she spoke of her mother, who had died just six weeks earlier, unable to get US citizenship in her lifetime, even after years in America and having children who had grown up as citizens. As illness overtook her, she had been unable, as a noncitizen ineligible for Medicare, to afford proper medical attention.

It was an emotional moment for me. I thought of how painful it had been, watching my mother in the late stages of cancer, even with the benefit of access to good health care. I remembered trying to find soft sweaters that would not irritate her skin, trying to cook foods that she could still enjoy.

I felt for this loving daughter, who had probably done all those things for her mother and yet been unable to access the medical care that may have prolonged her life or eased her pain.

One of the first bills we tried to pass within hours of Joe Biden taking the oath of office was for comprehensive immigration reform that would have provided a pathway to citizenship for hardworking, longtime residents.

But it was not taken up by Congress.

Democrats, rather than Republicans, got the lion's share of the blame for failing to provide a pathway to citizenship. The Latino vote began to steadily drift away from us, starting in 2016.

The Latino vote is no monolith, and a variety of factors were at play. For anyone struggling to afford gas or eggs, inflation was certainly a factor. Though I had a jobs and investment agenda that would have benefited Latinos, it was rolled out October 22nd—too late to really resonate.

For the grieving woman in front of me, both parties had failed her mother, failed her.

In these settings, which are high stress and high stakes, it is important to stay focused and on message. But it is also important to respond as a human. I have said countless times that there is more that unites us than divides us, and sometimes you must feel it as well as say it.

It requires an enormous amount of emotional dexterity. It isn't easy.

And then there was the last question of the town hall: Could I name three virtues that Donald Trump possessed?

Really? Do I have to?

"I think Donald Trump loves his family, and I think that's very important . . ." I racked my brain for something else. "I don't really know him, to be honest with you. I only met him one time, on the debate stage. I'd never met him before.

"So I don't really have much more to offer you."

It was a tougher day than usual to be trying to enumerate Trump's virtues. We'd just learned, from Bob Woodward's reporting, that at the height of Covid, when Americans were scrambling to get their hands on scarce Covid tests, Trump had secretly sent tests to Vladimir Putin for his personal use.

I was heading from the town hall to a rally in Phoenix, where I would meet with young Native American leaders from a half dozen different tribes, including the Gila River tribe. I'd met many of the young people from that tribe a year earlier, when Doug and I had visited their tribal lands. They had been the first tribe to partner with the federal government to create a community school that was fully Native built, Native owned, and Native run.

I'd been inspired by those young leaders, especially their knowledge of and commitment to climate solutions based on traditional knowledge and stewardship. We have so much to learn from indigenous people about how to treat this fragile Earth. They were custodians of this land for thousands of years. Their long-term thinking, considering the ramifications of each decision on seven generations, makes a lot more sense than making decisions based on four-year political cycles or corporate quarterly earnings.

Native Americans serve in our military at the highest rate of any population in our country. I wondered how many Native veterans could have used the test kits Trump sent to Putin, as their communities were ravaged by the virus.

23 Days to the Election

* * *

I t was Doug's birthday.

He and I were born seven days apart. We joke that he dropped down to Earth to check out the situation a week before I arrived. We are both Libras, and friends who believe in astrology say it is totally unsurprising that we spend half an hour to an hour weighing the pros and cons of which TV show we will watch, and by the time we've settled it, it's time to go to bed.

Doug started his birthday campaigning in Pennsylvania. His team had cupcakes and balloons, but the real birthday gift was having our daughter, Ella, at his side that day, campaigning with him.

I was in church at Koinonia Christian Center in Greenville, North Carolina, telling the congregation how inspired I'd been by a man from Hope Springs, Eddie, who had jumped into floodwaters to pull a woman to safety during Hurricane Helene. He had told me he didn't feel he had a choice. I told the congregation, "Of course he had a choice . . . His choice was, in the words of Isaiah, to be 'a refuge for the needy in their distress.'"

After church I spoke at a rally and then had a meeting with Black farmers. When pundits talk about rural America, the picture they paint is white. But in the South especially, some rural counties are majority Black, including long-standing farming families who have persevered on the land for generations despite discrimination that began just after Reconstruction and continued right into this century.

Black farmers never got their forty acres and a mule, the promised reparation for their years of enslavement and the wealth their stolen labor had created for this country. Worse, they were systematically discriminated against by governments both local and federal. The US Department of Agriculture has only in recent years examined its shameful history of denying credit and subsidies to Black farmers while providing them to whites. This was especially damaging in the crucial years of early-twentieth-century agricultural industrialization, when white farmers received subsidies and credit to buy the new machinery that would increase efficiency and raise yields.

The Inflation Reduction Act, for which I was the tiebreaking vote, provided funds to begin to compensate any farmer who had been discriminated against by the USDA.

The farmers I spoke with that day were resilient elderly couples and also young farmers full of ideas on how to get their fresh produce where it was needed, into urban food deserts.

On the front lines of the climate crisis, farmers see more clearly than anyone the changes in the frost-free date, growing seasons, pests. They were using high-tech methods to make water and fertilizer use more efficient.

We talked about the potential of city farms and of giving urban youth a chance to experience work on the land and learn agricultural skills, while incorporating the tech these young people already understood with the traditions of farming. Our neighbor Mrs. Shelton had a sister who had a farm. Maya and I would go to Aunt Bea's to help pick up fallen plums in her orchard. I was lucky, as a city kid, to have that experience, to learn the labor that brings us our food.

These were programs I was intent to support as president.

I knew that Doug would arrive back to the residence before I could get there, so I had the staff drape the entrance with a banner saying HAPPY BIRTHDAY DOUGIE.

I have to confess that since I didn't get home till just after 7:00 p.m., I got a little help with the prep for his celebratory dinner. It was his favorite menu: chicken parm with spaghetti, followed by key lime pie.

I had bought his gift via FaceTime with his favorite menswear store in San Francisco. It was a sports coat, black and gray.

He looked great in it.

22 Days to the Election

* * *

The *Los Angeles Times*, my hometown newspaper, published its electoral endorsements.

The very first line of the article stated: "It's no exaggeration to say this may be the most consequential election in a generation." But there was no mention of the most consequential race of all.

The paper's owner, Patrick Soon-Shiong, had directed the editorials editor, Mariel Garza, to deep-six the endorsement of me that the editorial board had approved and she had already drafted.

She quit.

In her resignation letter, Garza said it mattered that the largest newspaper in California "declined to endorse in a race this important. And it matters that we won't even be straight with people about it. It makes us look craven and hypocritical, maybe even a bit sexist and racist," she wrote. "How could we spend eight years railing against Trump and the danger his leadership poses to the country and then fail to endorse the perfectly decent Democrat challenger—who we previously endorsed for the U.S. Senate?"

It hurt that my hometown paper hadn't endorsed me.

And then, eleven days later, my other hometown paper, *The Washington Post*, did the same thing. The endorsement of me that had been prepared by the editorial board was scrapped at the direction of Jeff Bezos.

The pre-capitulation of these powerful billionaires alarmed and dispirited me. As it turned out, they were early adopters of the feckless posture that would be embraced by a raft of business leaders and institutions once Trump was elected. They'd just been the first in line to grovel.

Marty Baron, the acclaimed former editor who led the *Post* during the first Trump presidency, was blunt: "This is cowardice, a moment of darkness that will leave democracy as a casualty. Donald Trump will celebrate this as an invitation to further intimidate The Post's owner, Jeff Bezos (and other media owners). History will mark a disturbing chapter of spinelessness at an institution famed for courage."

More than two hundred thousand *Post* readers canceled their subscriptions.

At least the *Post*'s political humor columnist, Alexandra Petri (now at *The Atlantic*), had a spine. She wrote:

> We as a newspaper suddenly remembered, less than two weeks before the election, that we had a robust tradition 50 years ago of not telling anyone what to do with their vote for president. It is time we got back to those "roots," I'm told!
>
> Roots are important, of course. As recently as the 1970s, The Post did not endorse a candidate for president. As recently as centuries ago, there *was* no Post and the country had a king! . . .
>
> But if I were the paper, I would be a little embarrassed that it has fallen to me, the humor columnist, to make our presidential endorsement. I will spare you the suspense: I am endorsing Kamala Harris for president, because I like elections and want to keep having them.

21 Days to the Election

* * *

I was in the back of the plane, doing one of my usual off-the-record question sessions with the traveling press. One of the reporters, whom I had come to know quite well, furrowed his brow and asked, "What do you think is going on?"

We locked eyes for a long moment. Then I answered with the simple truth:

"I don't know."

After drawing even with Trump in the polls in August and pulling ahead of him after the debate in September, by mid-October, we'd stalled out. The rallies were getting bigger, the crowds ever more diverse and enthusiastic. But the poll numbers were static. Three weeks out, we were stuck in margin-of-error territory and not budging.

And then, like most guys who watch a lot of sports, Doug started seeing the trans ads. No matter what he was watching—football, baseball—there they were. The Trump campaign would eventually spend as much as $40 million on those ads. They showed some version of it fifty-five thousand times in the seven swing states. They showed it in all fifty states during sport broadcasts.

Gabrielle Ludwig, the basketball player featured prominently in the ad, was at home in Nevada watching an Eagles game when she was astonished to see herself, in a photograph that had been taken twelve years earlier. She was fifty-two at the time of that photo. A registered Republican, she'd served eight years in the Navy and had gone to community college later in life, as many veterans do. She's a big woman, but she also looks strikingly different from her teammates because she's three decades older than they are, which hardly gave her the athletic advantage the ad implied.

Trump's team wasn't concerned with nuance. With the tagline "Kamala is for they/them. President Trump is for you," they thought they had landed on a winning message.

Unfortunately, they were right. Although not to the extent that has become conventional wisdom.

Why didn't I punch back harder?

There are two things to talk about: one is people, one is politics.

Let's start with people. Transgender people are Americans, with the same rights we all have, to liberty, equality, the pursuit of happiness, and equal protection under the law.

There aren't very many. A tiny minority of less than 1 percent of the population.

Of these, in 2024, less than ten played on women's college sports teams.

Less than ten.

The law says incarcerated people must be provided with medical care. Under that law, two federal prisoners have received court-ordered gender-affirmation surgery.

Two.

Very small numbers. But here are some bigger ones:

Three hundred and fifty transgender people were murdered in America in 2024. Fifteen of them were kids.

Trans people are over four times as likely as other Americans to be victims of a violent crime.

Almost half—42 percent—have attempted suicide.

I have been an ally of the LGBTQ+ community for my entire

career. As AG, I fought for their safety by outlawing the so-called gay panic defense in California. As DA and then as AG, I defended their right to marry the person they love.

I have joyful memories of performing some of the first gay marriage ceremonies in 2004, long before it was the law of the land and long before it was supported by most elected Democrats. In the 2004 presidential election, gay marriage was used as a wedge issue by Republicans, just as the trans issue was in 2024. And I'm sorry to say that in 2004, our candidate did not stand up.

In the Bay Area, I grew up at the epicenter of the fight for LGBTQ+ civil rights. One of my first political advisers, Jim Rivaldo, had worked for the assassinated gay leader Harvey Milk. When Jim was dying from AIDS, my mother helped take care of him.

This is a community with which I have a deep connection. I know transgender people. I know the parents of transgender kids. Beloved kids, just like any other. I know the pain and struggle that many families go through. I've heard so many personal stories. And I know the risks many of these children face from bullying and violence. Imagine being a parent, loving your child and worrying every day about the ugliness and attacks they might encounter. And for some families there are acute worries about depression, substance abuse, suicide. It's the height of hypocrisy for the party that has always championed the right of parents to make decisions for their children regarding homeschooling or opting out of sex ed to suddenly bring down the awesome power of the state on loving parents trying to figure out care for their children.

When Republicans lied about this tiny, vulnerable group with fear campaigns about schoolkids being taken away for gender surgery without parents' knowledge, I knew that Trump's increasingly hateful rhetoric was painting a bull's-eye on their backs and putting them in peril.

I've always been a protector. It's why I became a prosecutor. There was no way I was going to go against my very nature and turn on transgender people right when they were being so intensely and intentionally vilified. I was aware of the weight of my voice and had no intention of adding to their burden.

And then there is the politics.

When I was AG in 2015, a state prisoner sued to get gender-affirming surgery. My client was the California Department of Corrections and Rehabilitation, and, as its lawyer, I was required to support the case against that inmate, which we settled in the inmate's favor. In 2017 a transgender prisoner in California was the first to get gender-affirming surgery based on that case, and twenty-two others have followed in California. That's the law.

But because I'd been on the opposing side of the case, a cry went up: *Kamala doesn't care about trans people.*

That wasn't true. I wanted to rebut that claim.

When the ACLU, in 2019, asked me to fill out a questionnaire, and one of the questions was about gender health care for incarcerated adults, I said I supported whatever was medically necessary. (Which is what the law says and what Donald Trump upheld as president. During his term, trans people in federal prison received the hormone treatments they were seeking.) I reiterated that view when asked in an interview. And that was what the Trump team sliced and diced for their ad.

The ad also said that I supported "biological men competing against our girls in their sports." That's not my position. I agree with the concerns expressed by parents and players that we have to take into account biological factors such as muscle mass and unfair athletic advantage when we determine who plays on which teams, especially in contact sports. With goodwill and common sense, I believe we can come up with ways to do this, without vilifying and demonizing children.

The pundits proclaim as conventional wisdom that the ad was Trump's knockout punch, that this was the principal factor that stalled us out in mid-October. I believe that it is the conventional wisdom of middle-aged men who don't live in battleground states and were the target of those ads.

Men, like Doug, who watch a lot of sports. The first time he saw the ad, he wanted to yell at the TV screen. He told me, "It made me viscerally ill." He was hearing clamor for a rebuttal from Joe Scarborough, Bill Clinton, and Democrats who saw that ad during the World Series and didn't see any ads rebutting it from our side. Because we didn't run ads during baseball games in non-battleground states.

We did our best to rebut it *in battleground states.*

The approach that worked best in our testing was to say, *Trump says a lot of things about me, but I know the thing you care about is the economy,* and quickly pivot to our messages on price gouging, affordable housing, and small-business tax relief. And that was the ad we ran in rebuttal in the swing states.

I do not regret my decision to follow my protective instincts. I do regret not giving even more attention to how we might mitigate Trump's attacks.

Character matters, and voters respect it. When I was DA, I did not seek the death penalty in a case I successfully prosecuted for the murder of a police officer. There were demonstrations, death threats. The AG—a Democrat—and the US attorney tried to take the case away from me. I thought my career was over. Years later, an elderly man from a conservative part of town approached me. "You know, I didn't agree with your decision. But I respect the fact that you said who you were and what you were going to do. And you stuck with it."

I wish I could have gotten the message across that there isn't a distinction between "they/them" and "you." The pronoun that matters is "we."

We the people. And that's who I am for.

20 Days to the Election

* * *

Of course Bret Baier wanted to talk about the trans ad.

He wanted to talk, period. Especially while I was talking. He interrupted me thirty-eight times in the twenty-seven-minute interview.

I certainly wasn't expecting kid-glove treatment from Fox News. More like boxing gloves.

I knew exactly what I was getting into, being interviewed by Fox's chief political correspondent. After the Fox News Decision Desk correctly called Arizona for Biden in the 2020 election and faced a backlash from its MAGA audience, Baier had written an email that said: "I keep having to defend this on air . . . The sooner we pull it—even if it gives us major egg—and we put it back in his column, the better we are." I knew that Bret Baier was scared of the MAGA base and would go hard on me to placate them. But I wasn't about to write off his audience. I was running to be president for all Americans, including Fox viewers.

I was making a point just by being there. Trump had pulled out of a *60 Minutes* interview and a CNN town hall; he'd turned down CNBC. And I'm pretty sure Rachel Maddow didn't even bother to ask. It was clear he would only venture onto the friendliest of turf. My view was quite the opposite: if *any* Fox viewers were persuadable, then I was going to make the effort to get in front of them.

Baier might as well have been interviewing himself. He wouldn't let me finish a sentence before interjecting. We spent ten minutes of the twenty-seven talking over each other on immigration before moving to the transgender subject and then on to Joe Biden's age. It was the MAGA playlist.

But he made one major blunder. When I criticized Trump for his threats to use the military on US citizens and lock up his political opponents, calling the American people "the enemy within," Baier then tried to refute it with a clip from a town hall Fox had conducted with Trump earlier that day. The clip showed Trump saying, "I'm not threatening anybody."

I'd watched that town hall on the plane on the way to the interview. I immediately recognized that Baier had cherry-picked the most innocuous part of the quote. Because Trump had also said that the biggest threat to America isn't China or Russia. "It is the enemy from within and they're very dangerous. They're Marxists and communists and fascists and they're sick . . . the Pelosis, these people—they're so sick and they're so evil."

I challenged Baier on his deception and quoted the former chairman of the Joint Chiefs of Staff, General Mark Milley, who said Donald Trump is "the most dangerous person to this country." I was pretty sure it would be the first time many in the Fox audience would have heard that.

I had been advised, and I believed, that of all the Fox anchors, Baier was the most professional and the most reasonable. That he would be tough but fair. During the interview I had called him "a serious journalist." But I felt that the stunt with the video clip was the work of a propagandist.

I have a saying: Disappointment is a function of unreasonable expectations. At that point I was deeply disappointed and realized my expectations had been quite unrealistic.

There had been no small talk when I arrived for that interview and there was none when I left. I took off my mic, said thank you to his crew, and walked away.

19 Days to the Election

* * *

Democracy is complicated. And some days are more complicated than others.

That day, Mark Cuban was traveling with me to speak about entrepreneurship at the University of Wisconsin–Milwaukee. As we approached the campus, Gaza protesters held signs saying: KILLER KAMALA. Later, at the University of Wisconsin–La Crosse, it was: NO CEASEFIRE? NO VOTE. And then, in the middle of an upbeat rally in the university gym, there were two antiabortion protesters.

I was in the middle of my speech, laying out Trump's direct responsibility for the repeal of *Roe*, when I heard cries of "Liar! You're lying!" I smiled in the direction of the hecklers. "Oh, you guys are at the wrong rally," I said. "I think you meant to go to the smaller one down the street." The audience roared with laughter.

Later, the two juniors would go on *Fox & Friends* and claim that I had told them they were at the wrong rally after I heard them shout "Jesus is Lord. Christ is King."

That's just not true. The C-SPAN video of the moment clearly picks up the cries of "liar" right before I made the quip.

However, another video, made by a Fox reporter somewhere in the middle of the auditorium, does have the young men proclaiming their faith, although there's no way of telling at what point in my speech. Whenever it was, I never heard it, and I was certainly not responding to that. I would never make fun of anyone, or say they weren't welcome at my rally, for praising God.

On *Fox & Friends*, the hosts accepted the students' claims and showed an edited video, but not the C-SPAN footage where it's clear I'm responding to cries of "liar." One of the young men compared himself to Jesus, who also "was mocked." He said he believed they were sent by God.

Then, as the panel was wrapping up the segment, one student interjected. "If I could say something, before we go here?" The hosts told him to go ahead. "If I could ask my young Americans in this country, what do you want your future to look like in this country? Do you want to have to struggle to pay for gas, do you want to struggle to afford groceries on a daily basis? Do you want to even struggle to get your first mortgage on a house? Because that is the future you're going to get with Kamala Harris as president . . . a future where . . . people are stripped of the very power they have as citizens of the United States."

It seemed like the student was suddenly less interested in preaching the gospel of Jesus than the gospel of Trump.

In the first weeks of my campaign, the interjectors at my rallies had mainly been Gaza protesters, people deeply moved by the war. But as the election drew closer, Trump supporters began turning up to disrupt. Which is fine; they can say whatever they believe to be true. It's a democracy.

But it becomes a danger to democracy when powerful news organizations, who should be in the business of supplying facts, instead distort them for partisan reasons. Because of that *Fox & Friends* segment, it is now an internet "fact" that I ejected two young people from my rally for praising God.

The false rally narrative fed neatly into another line of attack Fox had been running that week: that I had dissed the Catholic Church by not attending the Al Smith Dinner. This annual white-tie event in New York in support of Catholic charities has traditionally been a good-humored affair where opposing politicians gently roast each other. Trump broke with that tradition when he delivered an unfunny and mean-spirited diatribe about Hillary Clinton, his fellow guest, in 2016. He was booed, a first in the history of the dinner.

His rude behavior didn't determine my decision not to attend in person. With just over two weeks to the election, I simply didn't want to be in a solidly Democratic state when I could be campaigning in a swing state. So my team had discussed with the dinner organizers that I would make a video instead, and they were agreeable. I did a comic bit with Molly Shannon playing Mary Katherine Gallagher, her dorky Catholic schoolgirl character from *Saturday Night Live*. I followed that up with remarks about my sincere respect for Catholic charities. I had worked closely with them in California on issues such as providing relief to unaccompanied immigrant children, victims of domestic violence, and, in my Back on Track initiative, formerly incarcerated young adults.

Fox & Friends didn't mention that: they made it sound as if I'd shunned the event entirely because of the same anti-Catholic, anti-Christian animus that they had falsely alleged.

Democracy is complicated. It's also easily compromised by blatant bias, downright lies, and the media organizations that enable them.

17 Days to the Election

* * *

A nd our democracy shouldn't belong to the world's richest man. I was holding a rally in Atlanta with Usher when I heard about Elon Musk's first $1 million giveaway.

According to campaign disclosures, Musk spent at least $288 million in support of Trump, maybe even more through indirect sources. It is entirely possible that those millions were the deciding factor in the swing states where the money was mostly spent and where Trump's margin of victory was wafer-thin. Elon certainly thinks so. "Without me, Trump would have lost the election," he tweeted in the midst of a snit with Trump over his massive spending bill. He clearly thought he had bought the presidency and should be able to dictate Trump's agenda—perhaps the most brazen admission of corruption in history.

In the Blue Wall states that could have made me president, Trump beat me by just 0.86 percent in Wisconsin, 1.44 percent in Michigan, and 1.73 percent in Pennsylvania. Ours was the third-closest presidential election in a century.

Musk hired paid door knockers—about four hundred in each swing state—far outpacing the Trump campaign's own listless efforts at mounting any kind of ground game. On my first day as top of the ticket, 28,000 volunteers signed up. By the end of the week, it was 170,000. For the battleground states, from that first day, we knocked on 19.5 million doors, and 13.4 million of these were done by volunteers.

Musk's notorious $1 million "random" sweepstakes, which his lawyers have since admitted in court was anything but random, drove traffic to X where he could praise Trump and denigrate me with insults and fake images, such as the ridiculous AI-generated picture where I am depicted wearing a cap with a hammer and sickle. He was Trump's one-man super PAC and campaign media arm all rolled into one.

The 2010 *Citizens United* Supreme Court decision gave corporations and the top 1 percent the ability to funnel unlimited money into our elections. In the Senate, I and my colleagues introduced a constitutional amendment designed to overturn it. It has been reintroduced, unsuccessfully, in each Congress. There were other efforts beyond the constitutional amendment, such as laws to disclose donor information, but none of those passed, either.

I have always been one of my party's most successful fundraisers, and I don't apologize for that. To do good work, you must get elected. And, unfortunately, until Congress has the courage to change the laws, it's ridiculously expensive. After Joe dropped out, I raised more money more quickly than any candidate, ever.

But it wasn't from a single billionaire with huge government contracts who essentially bought himself an unelected co-presidency.

Musk lied about his sweepstakes, saying names would be drawn at random and any registered voter in a swing state who signed a petition supporting the First and Second Amendments could be in the drawing. But when courts questioned the legality of that, his lawyers admitted that the winners were not random. They were vetted "spokespeople."

As for his paid door knockers, many were individuals who had to sign contracts before they knew whom they would be canvassing for. They included low-income Black people who were transported to their canvassing turf in the backs of U-Hauls with no seat belts—or even seats—forced to share rooms with strangers, and given impossible work quotas. Some who objected were fired without pay and without fares to return to their home states.

While Musk takes a chain saw to programs that help the poorest people in our own country and abroad, he is okay with government spending when it comes to his own companies, which have received about $38 *billion* in contracts, loans, subsidies, and tax credits. (Roughly $15 billion from NASA and about $7 billion from defense agencies. For some, like the spy satellite Starshield defense project, the amounts are not publicly documented.)

As the former head of the National Space Council, I am enthusiastic about space exploration. I support technological innovation and national security. But when you never talk about government spending on your own interests, no matter how laudable those interests, it's hypocritical to critique spending on equally valuable programs such as research at the Centers for Disease Control and Prevention and the National Institutes of Health.

His companies also stand to benefit from slashed regulations on environmental protection, and the lack of consumer protections for autonomous vehicles.

No good public policy can be made with a chain saw.

16 Days to the Election

* * *

When I was growing up, birthdays were a very big deal. My mother used to joke that my birthday was her birthday as well, since she was the one who'd done the birthing.

I think about my mother every day. But that morning she was especially on my mind, since my birthday fell on Pink Sunday, the day in Breast Cancer Awareness Month when churches pray for those who are suffering, or who have passed, from the disease.

My mother had two goals in her life: to raise Maya and me, and to cure breast cancer. When we were little, we knew that often "Mommy had to go to Bethesda." We didn't know that she went to that Maryland neighborhood as an adviser to the National Institutes of Health. As I pinned the pink awareness pin to my lapel, I thought of her and her uncompromising dedication to the cause of women's health. I made a silent promise never to let up and never to let her down in my commitment to that issue.

My senior adviser Jalisa Washington-Price had worked with me since 2019. And even though she has three small children, she put her life on hold for these 107 days, organizing in three key states and handling faith outreach. That Sunday she had selected two extraordinary faith communities for me to visit.

I was heading to New Birth Missionary Baptist Church that Sunday morning—a megachurch in Atlanta's suburbs. Chrisette, who had flown in to be with me on my birthday, was there, wide-eyed. Chrisette comes from a different faith tradition, what she describes as "a quiet little Presbyterian church." This was not that. The sanctuary seats over seven thousand souls.

We arrived as the choir was singing and made my way to my seat past throngs of women in pink, some in frothy tulle or sparkly pink sequined church hats. There were more than fifty elected officials at that service, as well as my friend Opal Lee, the grandmother of Juneteenth, and Reverend Amos Brown, who had flown in as a surprise. When the pastor, Jamal Bryant, called on me to speak, someone in the congregation called out, "Happy birthday!" which was the cue for the whole church to burst into song for me.

In my remarks, I talked about my mother's dedication to breast cancer research, and then I turned to one of my favorite Scriptures, Luke 10:29–37, the parable of the Good Samaritan. To me, it is the antithesis of the corrosive "otherizing" message, calling on us to look at a stranger and see a neighbor, and then to love that neighbor as ourselves.

Many years earlier, Pastor Bryant and I had been on a panel together, celebrating emerging Black leaders. The panel before ours was made up of senior leaders, notable men and women like Harry Belafonte and Sheila Jackson Lee. Jamal and I waited in the wings as they talked on. And on. Like a living metaphor, the old guard would not get off the stage. Jamal and I had shared a laugh about that.

In his sermon, he called on the men in the congregation, in particular, to vote for me. "It takes a real man to support a woman," he said. Men "who are not intimidated by an educated woman." Echoing the words of my own pastor when he had prayed with us two months earlier, he said I was born for a time such as this. Then he asked that vast congregation to move their right hand toward me and pray over me for strength in these last weeks of the campaign.

There is so much love in that tradition. The people in that congregation understood very well the forces working against me. I could feel the power of their prayer for my protection. Brimming with the emotion of the moment as I stood under those sheltering hands, I recalled the words of Isaiah: "No weapon formed against you shall prosper, And every tongue which rises against you in judgment You shall condemn."

The day before, Trump had called me "a shit vice president." It was the same speech at a rally in Latrobe, Pennsylvania, in which he'd lauded the penis size of Arnold Palmer, to the distress of the late golfer's daughter. His ravings were becoming increasingly unhinged. I wish he understood that in trying to demean me, he instead demeaned the office he sought to hold.

From New Birth Missionary Baptist we headed across town to a Souls to the Polls event being organized at a smaller church, Divine Faith Ministries. When I arrived, Stevie Wonder was singing and speaking to the congregation, warning of the perils so clearly set out in the Project 2025 plan. (Trump was still saying he had "nothing to do" with it, and yet as president he has moved to implement its agenda with stunning speed.)

An item I wouldn't have even imagined putting on my bucket list was having Stevie Wonder sing "Happy Birthday" to me, but it happened that afternoon. And then Reverend Raphael Warnock rose to address the congregation. He also spoke of the need for Black men to support me, saying he didn't believe the rumors that they'd be voting for the other guy. "The real enemy," he said, "is not Trump. It's not showing up." There was something in the way he looked at me, so caring and so knowledgeable. It was a look from a friend that expressed gratitude for all that he knew I was going through.

Extreme highs and extreme lows—I wouldn't allow myself to fully experience them. I refused to ride that roller coaster. I couldn't, for the sake of all those people turning up at my rallies, allow myself to dwell on my own emotions. There would be time later, I told myself, to reflect. I had to get on with the business.

And then Reverend Warnock led the crowd in a chant: "Real men vote."

I had one more stop in Atlanta, to tape an interview with Reverend Al Sharpton that would air on MSNBC that night. He had founded the National Action Network, one of the biggest civil rights organizations in the country and an effective advocate for voting rights.

I had known Reverend Sharpton for many years, working with him for criminal justice reform, praying with him at funerals for young Black men killed in police shootings. He was aware of my record as a prosecutor and how it had been mischaracterized. When I became a district attorney, this country was in an even worse place than it is now on criminal justice. I was one of the first elected progressive district attorneys, looking for ways to keep nonviolent offenders out of jail rather than put them in it. I didn't seek jail time for simple marijuana offenses. My Back on Track initiative, connecting offenders with services and jobs, and also taking care of their mental health by doing things like hooking them up with counseling and gym memberships, worked so well it became a model for other jurisdictions. It is true that prosecution rates for violent crime increased on my watch. If you rape a woman, molest a child, or take a life, consequences should be serious and swift. I don't apologize for that.

Although since becoming top of the ticket, we'd improved our standing with Black men by 20 points, some polls showed a slight drift. The trope that I'd been a punitive prosecutor was dusted off in explanation. Reporters seemed to love that narrative.

I was particularly grateful to the talented actor and comedian D. L. Hughley, a member of the Divine Nine fraternity Omega Psi Phi, for pushing back on it so strongly. He apologized in every forum he could, and eventually at the podium of the Democratic National Convention, for having formerly mischaracterized my record. "I feel repentant in the fact that I was so strident against a really amazing woman, and it doesn't matter how much you apologize or what forum you use . . . it's hard to pull your knife out of somebody," he told Don Lemon in one of the many interviews he did during the campaign. "Mostly I don't understand how it is I made those assertions without even looking" into it.

I certainly didn't think I was entitled to anyone's vote. In fact, I resented the assumption that Democrats, me in particular, would have certain votes in our back pocket. I knew very well that I had no more right to the vote of a Black man than to anyone else's vote. I knew I would have to argue my case and earn those votes. Every single one.

That afternoon, when I climbed the steps to the plane, I discovered it had been decorated in streamers. My team on board were wearing gold party hats and presented me with a deliciously rich German chocolate cake, my favorite birthday cake. They had red velvet cupcakes for the press. There was also a big helium balloon with fat numerals: 60. My team knew that I stopped counting birthdays a long time ago. So I looked at them with a big smile when I landed my stiletto heel in the middle of that balloon. Then I went to find my Uggs.

Throughout the flight, I was looking forward to a special evening with Doug. Though we were apart a lot those days, campaigning in different cities, for my birthday our staff conspired so that we'd meet up in Philadelphia. I was wondering what he'd planned for our evening.

The simple answer: Nothing. Not a thing.

Doug had been keeping to his own grueling schedule and had flown in from a campaign event in Michigan. He was tired and preoccupied. What I didn't realize: the attacks on me and the many personal assaults he'd been experiencing were finally taking a toll.

He hadn't put any thought into where we'd stay that night, so staff had picked a place for us that they thought would be a bit more special than the usual campaign hotel. It turned out to be a bland establishment whose red-and-black decor looked like it hadn't been redone since the '70s. The only distinguishing feature of the room was its larger size, but the curtains were broken.

Storm, knowing how much I love good food, had picked two possible restaurants from which to order dinner. She thought it would be nice if the meal was a bit of a surprise for me. So, on the plane, she knocked on Doug's door to ask him to choose the menu. He'd shrugged and told her to ask me. So she picked the menu herself. Ordered a cake. Dressed the table with candles. My girlfriends had sent flowers.

Doug at least had thought to get a gift for me. It was a necklace by a designer I admired from Ojai, California, Jes MaHarry, the same designer who'd made the piece he'd chosen for my anniversary gift. This one featured a set of baroque pearls nestled in a gold setting. When I turned it over, I saw that the pearls' backing had been engraved with the date. How thoughtful, to commemorate the milestone of my big birthday. But then I looked closer.

The date was *not* my birthday. It was the date of our wedding anniversary. He'd obviously intended to give me both pieces on our anniversary, until it occurred to him that by repurposing one piece, he could kill two birds with one stone. He could practice thrift and also save himself the bother of shopping for a birthday gift.

I went to take a bath. It's one of the things I did at the end of those long days to help me slow down enough to get to sleep. In the warm steam, I managed to relax and get over my disappointment. I was about to climb out of the tub when I noticed that all the bath towels were hanging on the far side of the room, unreachable. I called to Doug to ask him to bring me one. No answer. He was in the other room, watching the Dodgers eliminate the Mets in the playoffs. He couldn't hear me over the television. I called his phone.

His answer: a casual "What's up?"

Really?! It was a bridge too far.

And then we got into it. The stress had finally gotten to both of us. It was one of those fights that every married couple has had.

But we weren't every married couple.

Doug stopped the argument cold. As soon as his words were out, the truth of them landed on me like a bucket of ice water.

"*We* can't turn on each other."

With the hits coming from every direction, we had to stay united. Back-to-back, swords raised against all outside attacks. We had to protect each other, be each other's pillar of strength, givers and receivers of patience and unconditional love.

I noted earlier that Storm speaks bluntly but always with correct protocol. The next day she told Doug, "Mr. Second Gentleman, you have to fix this." She handed him a set of note cards. She'd numbered them one through five, for the nights we'd be apart through the end of the campaign. She instructed him to write a note on each one.

From then till the election, no matter what city each of us had landed in, at the end of the day I would find a note on my pillow, in Doug's chicken scratch, telling me how much he loved me.

14 Days to the Election

* * *

The Trump team announced that he would be on the *Joe Rogan Experience* podcast October 25.

That came as a surprise to us. I'd been told that Joe Rogan couldn't interview me on that date because he was "taking a personal day."

We'd been back and forth with Rogan since late September or early October. One of the young leaders on my digital team made the initial contact through Rogan's platform, Spotify.

Rogan's producers came back to us with a list of conditions. These included a one hour minimum, no topic limitations, only me and Secret Service in the studio. I had no problem with any of that, so we started to discuss recording the podcast while I was campaigning in Michigan.

The team was hearing all kinds of conflicting information from folks who knew Rogan: from one source, that he'd bragged he'd "rake me over the coals"; from another, that it would be great for me, because Rogan had said he didn't want Trump to win.

I wasn't in the weeds on any of it. I left that up to my staff. They'd suggested topics that might interest Rogan's audience, such as cannabis, social media censorship, and crypto. Rogan's team said they just wanted to discuss the economy, immigration, and abortion. Again, I was fine with that. They said they'd work with Spotify about securing a studio in Detroit. That sounded great.

But then they came back to say Rogan, having thought about it, wanted to record in Austin; that he never traveled and had only ever gone remote one time, to secure an interview with Edward Snowden. They wanted me to come to Austin. That was a big ask. I had to weigh spending time in Texas so close to the election, when every minute in a swing state mattered, and also the time lost traveling there and back.

Still, even though most of my team thought doing the interview at all was a gamble, and others bluntly argued it was a bad idea, I really wanted to do it. One podcast was not going to win or lose the election. But Rogan's audience was young and male. I wanted to reach those guys who might not otherwise hear from me.

We had a big rally on reproductive rights planned in Houston on October 25. So on October 18 my team called and told Rogan's people that we could come to Austin for the interview that day. My research and comms team started pulling together a prep sheet for me.

Then the word came back: "It's a personal day for Joe. He's not available. If you'd just called a day before, we could have done it." Then how about the following day? The morning after the Houston rally? They said they could do it at 8:30 a.m., not later, as Joe had "commitments." I had commitments as well, and it wasn't feasible to get from Houston to Austin by 8:30 a.m.

And then, on October 22, we learned that Rogan was spending his "personal day" interviewing Donald Trump. (Rogan kept Trump rambling so long he was three hours late to the outdoor rally he was meant to be addressing in Traverse City, Michigan, leaving a dwindling number of supporters standing in the cold.)

To be totally transparent, which sadly they were not, they offered us times on the 24th or the 27th or sometime after the rally on the 25th, which was set to conclude at 10:00 p.m. It wasn't realistic to go from Houston to Austin and do a podcast at midnight, nor was I about to hang around an extra day in Texas a week out from the election. I believe they knew that when they offered those times. We made one last pitch, offering an hour before my speech on the Ellipse, if Rogan would reconsider and come to DC. He declined.

On the eve of the election, Rogan endorsed Trump. Since then, he has lied on his show, claiming we pushed for tight topic restrictions. He even claimed that the very topics we had *suggested* were ones we'd refused to discuss.

His team says we "never committed," which is accurate, but misleading.

The plain truth: I wanted to go on Joe Rogan's podcast on October 25. He chose Trump instead.

13 Days to the Election

* * *

Anderson Cooper would make news out of the CNN town hall. He did it with the first question.

"You've quoted General Milley calling Donald Trump a fascist. You yourself have not used that word to describe him. Let me ask you tonight, do you think Donald Trump is a fascist?"

"Yes, I do. Yes, I do. And I also believe that the people who know him best on this subject should be trusted."

That became the headline. I was trying to make sure that the audience knew that John Kelly, Trump's former chief of staff, had said he thought the former president met the definition of the word and that Trump had often praised Hitler. I wanted voters to know that the men closest to him, members of his own administration, thought he was a fascist.

The stronger answer would have been: *Never mind what I think, listen to what his generals and top officials say. To have your own people who have worked with you say such a thing is far more damning than the opinion of your political opponent.*

The hall was full of undecided voters who had come ready to ask questions. Anderson was supposed to be the moderator and step in if he thought my answer needed follow-up or clarification. Instead, he asked the lion's share of the questions himself. In the eighty minutes on air, only about a dozen voters—probably less than half the audience—got to ask me something directly.

So when Anderson signed off, I walked off the stage to make myself available to any of these undecided Pennsylvania voters who hadn't had a chance to ask their question or maybe still had something on their mind.

Even though the broadcast was over, CNN's cameras were still running. As the broadcast went to a roundtable with commentators such as Dana Bash, David Axelrod, and Jake Tapper, they showed a split screen of me talking animatedly with one voter after another.

Kirsten, my media adviser, was bothered. She wasn't sure if I knew that the camera was still rolling. There's a long history of hot mics and B-roll footage making trouble for politicians.

"Go get her," she told Opal, my body person.

Meanwhile, the panel was nitpicking my performance.

About twenty minutes into the discussion, Tapper interrupted Kaitlan Collins midsentence.

"Let's listen in, because she's talking to—"

They cut to me just as I was asking a member of my staff to follow up with a voter with information on student loan debt relief.

Then I turned to an audience member, Joe Donahue, who had been introduced by Anderson as a registered Republican who disagreed with me on abortion but had doubts about Trump over January 6. His question to me on air hadn't been about either of those things, so I wanted to take a moment with him to talk about my position on reproductive rights.

I assured him I would not try to change his view. "My point is the government shouldn't be telling people what to do. It is not about ever disputing or criticizing anyone's faith, ever, never." And I told him I appreciated him asking his earlier question.

Then Opal reached me with word that we needed to go, so I thanked the audience as Jake turned back to his fellow panelists.

He pointed out that this was to have been the night of a debate between me and Trump. "She accepted. He did not. So, we said, okay, let's have two town halls. She accepted. He did not. The reason that we are not critiquing Donald Trump's performance at a town hall this evening is because Donald Trump did not agree to participate in a town hall here in Delaware County, and she did.

"So, yes, it's inherently unfair. That said, we're journalists, we're going to keep talking about what we saw tonight."

Van Jones said, "There were flashes of the Kamala I know. Who is really a true public servant, who really does work for people.

"Your job isn't to do town halls. Your job is to fight for people."

11 Days to the Election

* * *

I am the daughter of a woman who dedicated her life to women's health. Shyamala Gopalan could have had a very easy life in India, but she chose to come to America because it was the leader in breast cancer research. Finding a cure was her life's work, and by isolating and characterizing the progesterone receptor gene, she advanced understanding of breast oncology.

I had the words "mammary gland" and "uterus" in my vocabulary long before I could spell them. When I got my first period, I was at my best friend's house. My mom's reaction: "I wish you'd been home!" For her, it was a special moment, something to celebrate. If she saw a *Playboy* magazine on a newsstand, she'd note: "The female hip and breast exist to procreate our species."

Once, when we were living in Montreal, she came home visibly angry about something that had happened in the lab. A male scientist had been walking around with a breast, uncovered, on a petri dish. "Do you think he would have walked around with an uncovered penis on that plate?" she fumed.

As a prosecutor I worked with women and girls who were victims of rape and incest. To tell a victim of a violent crime, a violation of her body, that she has no say in what happens to her body next is immoral. You do not have to abandon your faith or deeply held beliefs to say that the government shouldn't be telling her what to do.

Some advisers told me not to put those words in my stump speech: "It will turn people off." But my mother's daughter was not going to leave these truthful words unsaid, no matter how uncomfortable some may feel.

Since Trump enabled the overthrow of *Roe*, the consequences have gone beyond denial of basic rights to the denial of care and the loss of health and life.

I had chosen to come to Texas to talk about this because the state's elected leaders had enacted the most restrictive and cruel laws in the country. There are no exceptions for rape, incest, or fatal fetal anomalies. The medical emergency language is so vague that doctors, fearing prosecution, have turned away women who needed lifesaving care. Because of confusion about what is and is not legal in Texas, women have unnecessarily lost fallopian tubes due to delayed treatment of ectopic pregnancies. Dozens have died of sepsis due to delays in treating miscarriages.

Although Trump, when he finally got to Michigan, derided me for being "at a dance party with Beyoncé," the superstar did not come to the rally as an entertainer. She came to speak from the heart about an issue that mattered to her and about the country she wants to see.

Months earlier, she had given me permission to use her song "Freedom" as my campaign anthem. No matter how many times I walked out onstage to those stirring lyrics and her powerful voice, it always lifted me. When Beyoncé let me know she would rather speak in support of my candidacy than merely perform, I was moved by her sincerity and her courage.

"I'm not here as a celebrity, I'm not here as a politician," she said. "I'm here as a mother. A mother who cares deeply about the world my children and all of our children live in. A world where we have the freedom to control our bodies. A world where we are not divided."

She told the crowd: "It's time for America to sing a new song."

9 Days to the Election

* * *

At Trump's Madison Square Garden rally, the so-called comedian Tony Hinchcliffe opened with a vulgar, racist set that the MAGA audience strained to laugh at. The lowest moment came when he announced, "There's literally a floating island of garbage in the middle of the ocean right now. I think it's called Puerto Rico."

In an extraordinary coincidence, earlier that same day I'd unveiled my plan for a Puerto Rico task force, aimed at bringing business and government resources together to create economic opportunity and fix the neglected energy grid that had been all but demolished by Hurricane Maria in 2017.

It wasn't a new area of focus for me. I'd been so moved by the devastation I'd witnessed there after the hurricane, and so appalled by Trump's callous paper-towel tossing and obstruction of aid, that I resolved, as United States senator, to represent the issues of the island, since the territory has no senator of its own.

I was doing a big swing through the diverse communities of West Philly that day. After church, I dropped in to speak to young Black men at a barbershop, chatted and watched practice with some middle schoolers at a youth basketball program, and bought books for

Amara and Leela at Hakim's Bookstore, which specializes in books on African American history and culture.

I'd also visited Freddy and Tony's Restaurant, a Puerto Rican–owned business. There are half a million Puerto Ricans in Pennsylvania, and I enjoyed talking to the crowd at the packed eatery about my ideas for uplifting the island, particularly its youth.

Later that evening, as word of the "joke" spread, we got calls from that warm group of Americans with whom I'd just spent the afternoon. They, and their beautiful island, didn't deserve to be denigrated in that way.

7 Days to the Election

* * *

They started lining up at sunrise. They arrived by car, by plane, and by train.

We had gone back and forth on where I should give my closing argument. Staff floated all kinds of ideas, from going back to my birthplace of Oakland, to New York City with the Statue of Liberty as my backdrop.

Since we'd failed to entice Trump back to the debate stage, we were brainstorming how to get another big moment, something that might shift the stalemate in the polls. When consensus emerged that the location should be Washington, DC, it was JOD who suggested the Ellipse.

On January 6, 2021, from that very spot, Trump had dispatched his angry mob to riot over the result of an election he knew he had lost. And now a different crowd was gathering, full of joy.

For our Park Service permit, we'd optimistically estimated a crowd of forty thousand. The official area extending back from the stage was designed to contain that number. But forty thousand had passed through the magnetometers and filled that space long before evening. Soon, the overflow area brimmed with a shoulder-to-shoulder crowd. By the time I spoke, there were people massed along the Mall all the way to the National Museum of African American History and Culture. Independent estimates put the total at seventy-five thousand.

Washington's soupy summer weather had ceded to the first brisk hints of fall. Red, white, and blue wristbands twinkled in the crisp evening air.

I had said to Adam Frankel that this speech was not an inaugural address. I was acutely aware that enthusiasm could distract us from the uncertainty of the result. We needed to hammer home not just what I would do as president, but also that we were not there yet and we still needed to make it happen.

I was polishing my speech right until the moment I walked onstage. The last piece I was determined to get right was the wording of what I wanted to say about being a leader who listens to experts, to people who would be impacted by decisions I made, and to people who disagree with me.

With Ike, my adviser, walking beside me, taking notes on the way to the stage, we landed on the line: "Unlike Donald Trump, I don't believe people who disagree with me are the enemy. He wants to put them in jail. I'll give them a seat at the table."

Ike took these last-minute revisions to the teleprompter operator, who fed them into the software as I moved to the beginning of the gangway, kissed Doug, took one step toward the stage, and turned back to Ike: "Did it make it into the prompter?"

As "Freedom" pulsed from the giant speakers, I walked out, down that long catwalk, carrying the weight of my belief that we had only seven days left, and everything rested on these last hours. Thousands of people: familiar, beloved faces—Maya, Tony, Doug—and all the faces that I did not know, full of fervor. The risers in front of me, packed. The cameras of every network I was familiar with and dozens of foreign networks with which I wasn't. Every monument brightly lit, standing testimony to who we are and what we believe, bearing witness to this moment.

"One week from today," I began, "you will have the chance to make a decision." I went on to outline the choice and the stakes in the election. Directly behind me, framed by tall American flags on the stage, the facade of the White House glowed in golden light.

I turned slightly to indicate that iconic building. "In less than ninety days, either Donald Trump or I will be in the Oval Office. On day one, if elected, Donald Trump would walk into that office with an enemies list. When elected, I will walk in with a to-do list full of priorities on what I will get done for the American people."

I wanted to infuse this moment with a heightened sense of urgency and contrast. It would reflect my vision of this country, the vision I'd started with, "the promise of America," the spirit of Normandy and Selma, Seneca Falls and Stonewall, of people fighting for freedom, for equality, for inclusion.

"In seven days we have the power—each of you has the power—to turn the page and start writing the next chapter in the most extraordinary story ever told."

6 Days to the Election

* * *

The night before, JOD had barely left the Ellipse after the rally when her phone rang. She was walking with her kids, making their way through the dispersing crowd. Instead of a minute to bask in the uplift of the evening, she learned that we were again about to go into crisis mode.

Ike and Kirsten, waiting for the crowd to thin, had found a table at a restaurant a few blocks from the White House. They were celebrating a sweet moment from right after the speech. In the front row of the audience, they'd spotted a woman they recognized from a TikTok post earlier that day. She had bused from New York City and posted about being the first person in line for my rally. Ike and Kirsten brought her backstage after the speech to meet me, and we'd both been delighted. They were thinking their work was done for the night when their phones blew up:

> *Joe Biden.*
> *Trump supporters.*
> *Garbage.*

Our campaign was going to have to clean it up.

Just as I had been stepping onto the stage at the Ellipse, Joe had been on a get-out-the-vote call to the group Voto Latino.

He was commenting on the Hinchcliffe "floating island of garbage" so-called joke at Trump's rally three days earlier. Joe said, "The only garbage I see floating out there is his supporter's"—meaning the comedian's hateful rhetoric.

But alas, on a Zoom call, no one can hear a possessive apostrophe.

What everyone heard was the president calling Trump's supporters garbage. It was covered as Hillary's "deplorables" on steroids. And this perception flew directly counter to the message of inclusion I had worked so hard to craft and communicate in my speech the night before.

Marco Rubio, informed about Biden's call right after it happened, ran onstage and interrupted Trump at a rally in Allentown, Pennsylvania, to breathlessly relate the gaffe. Rubio was there, no doubt, to shore up Hispanic support in Pennsylvania after Hinchcliffe's appalling remarks at Trump's rally.

The Trump campaign immediately sent out a fundraising email: "Moments ago, Kamala's boss crooked Joe Biden just called ALL my supporters GARBAGE - HE WAS TALKING TO YOU!"

So, before I got on Air Force Two at the beginning of a long day on the trail in North Carolina, Pennsylvania, and Wisconsin, I gathered the press pool. I told them that Joe had clarified what he meant to say. And then I added: "You heard my speech last night and continuously throughout my career. I believe that the work that I do is about representing all the people, whether they support me or not, and as president of the United States, I will be a president for all Americans, whether you vote for me or not."

What had been a big problem for the Trump campaign had been turned, instead, into a mess for us.

5 Days to the Election

* * *

I woke up on Halloween morning at the Edgewater hotel in Madison, Wisconsin, ready for my final swing west. Because I'd had to cut short my time in the battleground states of Arizona and Nevada to work on Hurricane Helene, I had ground to make up and precious little time to do it. This was going to be a big day: from Madison, we would fly to Phoenix, Reno, and then Las Vegas.

I did a short press conference in the hotel to comment on Trump's remarks that he was going to protect women "whether they like it or not."

To me, it was just one more revealing example of his demeaning view of women and his willingness to strip them of any agency. "He does not prioritize the freedom of women and the intelligence of women to make decisions about their own lives and bodies."

One of the reporters asked me if I thought it was an attempt to position himself in a hypermasculine way, like surrounding himself with UFC fighters. I said I thought his language was offensive to everyone, male and female.

Male voters were on my mind that day. Once we boarded Air Force Two, I got on the line with D. L. Hughley for his radio show. Ever since his appearance at the convention, he'd been using his microphone to argue my case in his own take-no-prisoners style. He had the most direct reply to the question of why I hadn't already done the things I now promised to do. "One of the things I'm gonna knock out of the way: Where was she for four years? Dumbass question, don't ask it. She wasn't the president."

Hughley was exceptionally good at decoding Trump's disparagement of cities such as Detroit, Aurora, and Springfield, all of which have large Black populations. He wanted to show his audience how Trump attempted to manipulate them by giving them somebody to blame and to look down on: immigrants—"Venezuelan gangs that do not exist, Haitians in Springfield."

He praised the way I came up with my plans for small businesses and for targeted health initiatives that would particularly help Black men. "You listened to Black men. It's the plan *we* wrote, and you co-authored it."

As soon as that interview was done, I had my daily check-in with Sheila, JOD, and Lorraine. Lorraine was anxious to work on transition planning, one of the matters that I had to find time for, even on the busiest campaign days. It would have been malpractice to neglect this in such a tight race, and I'd started back in September. I had memos to consider on key positions and forms to keep track of decisions I'd made and ones still pending. These would have a name suggested for the position and boxes for me to check: yes, no, maybe.

I'd selected the person I would want for White House chief of staff back in early October, and he had agreed to take the position if I were elected. Denis McDonough had been Barack Obama's chief of staff in his second term, chief of staff at the National Security Council before that, and had served as secretary of veterans affairs in our administration. I swore him in to that office.

One of the first public events I did as VP was with Denis. It was the height of Covid. He and his wife, Karin, and Doug and I took heart-shaped cookies to the nurses at the VA hospital on Valentine's Day. The son of Irish immigrants, one of eleven children, he taught school in Belize before coming to work in government. He is a deeply caring man who doesn't mince words. I knew he would run a productive and disciplined West Wing.

My Phoenix event had been facilitated by Sergio Gonzales, who had handled Latino outreach and immigration policy in my Senate office. At the Talking Stick Resort Amphitheatre, the pioneering band Los Tigres del Norte struck up one of their signature corridos, telling of the lives of immigrant workers, their battles with racism, and the struggles of daily life.

Chrisette, once again, had traveled from her home to campaign with me. On the plane from Phoenix to Reno, she looked at me, concerned. "Your shoulders are up by your ears," she said. She had brought treats she knew I loved, a goodie basket from her favorite cheese shop. She looked astonished when I scolded her: "You have to stop being nice to me!" At that point in the campaign, I was in fight mode, and I needed to stay there. I *couldn't* let down my guard, couldn't take off my armor. If I unclenched, if I remembered what it was like to be normal, I might not be in shape to handle the next blow. And there was too much at stake to risk that.

The last days of the campaign became increasingly kinetic. The team constantly watched the swing states' local data: Where are we gaining, losing? What assets can we move from here to there? Where would an ad spend move the needle most?

I was no longer in these meetings. My presence in front of voters, either at a giant rally or on a dozen small-market local radio shows, was the prime commodity of the campaign. If I could have been everywhere, I would have been. But I was determined to get in front of as many people as I could.

The last place I should be spending my time was at meetings with staff. I relied on them to make the calls and tell me what I needed to know.

So when my motorcade sped by the Las Vegas Sphere, the huge music venue east of the Strip, it was the first time I absorbed the fact that we'd just created the biggest election ad in history and put it on the largest screen in the world.

I'd surprised Doug and taken him to the Sphere just after it opened in September 2023. One of our favorite bands, U2, was performing. The band had been told of my ruse and had mistakenly conceived the idea that it was Doug's birthday, so they sang "Happy Birthday" to him from the stage.

I recall being impressed and a little overwhelmed by the magical, ever-changing visuals inside the Sphere, and thinking, *I hope the ticket warns people not to come in here on stimulants. They sure don't need them.*

Thirteen months later, I didn't have time for wonderment. My focus was on what I had to do: the meet and greets with Jennifer Lopez and the Mexican rock group Maná and with the elected officials; my speech; the rope line after. I needed to bring the same energy to the day's third rally as I'd brought to the first.

As we drove past the Sphere, I glimpsed my face—far bigger than I'd ever imagined—in the rearview mirror as we sped on.

4 Days to the Election

* * *

I knew it was going to be a long day. I just didn't know quite how long. We were rolling from our hotel in Las Vegas at 7:42 a.m. I'd already taped an interview for Univision Radio, and I'd been up for more than two hours before that.

There had been a lot of news from the Trump campaign that day. For several weeks, as well as my off-the-record sessions when I boarded Air Force Two, I'd been having a daily press gaggle, on the record, planeside, usually when we landed at our first stop. The press would deplane through the rear door and wait for me under the shade of the wing. When we arrived at Dane County Regional Airport in Wisconsin, I responded to Trump's comments that Robert F. Kennedy Jr. would have "a big role in health care."

I pushed back on how irresponsible it would be to give such a role to someone who had promoted junk science, opposed vaccines, embraced conspiracy theories, and vacillated on abortion rights.

Then I lit into Trump's remarks that Liz Cheney was a "war hawk" who should be fired upon "with nine barrels shooting at her." How a man who had been shot once and narrowly missed being fired upon a second time could be using such irresponsible rhetoric appalled me. He, of all people, knew the kind of violent undercurrents that could be so quickly roused by his words. I told the press it "must be disqualifying" as people considered their vote.

I also shared that what I was enjoying most in the last days of campaigning was that "in spite of how my opponent spends full time trying to divide the American people, what I am seeing is people coming together under one roof who seemingly have nothing in common and know they have everything in common."

My first stop in Wisconsin was a union hall in Janesville.

One of my favorite unions is the International Brotherhood of Electrical Workers. I've set myself a lofty goal to visit every IBEW local in the country. I'm not quite there yet, but I've made a big dent. The IBEW is a union that values workers as whole human beings and knows that their lives outside of work, with their families and their communities, also matter. Their apprenticeship program is a model of excellence that includes mentoring young people in and out of the workplace as they learn high-level skills and get paid to do it. They have encouraged and increased women's participation in the trades. And their members are increasingly the workers at the forefront of the clean energy transition. Without their skills and dedication, we will never come close to net zero.

The IBEW Hall in Janesville was packed. People stood shoulder to shoulder on the floor and filled an upper level, leaning over the railings. I talked about how we'd designed the Inflation Reduction Act to support good union jobs building the energy technologies of the future, such as batteries, solar panels, and wind turbines. I promised that we would retool existing factories, so that communities didn't get ripped apart by people having to move away to find work in manufacturing. In so many places, young people are forced to leave for lack of work. They shouldn't have to leave their hometown, their grandparents, the high school football team that they love to watch on Friday nights. It is much quicker and more efficient to retool an existing factory and keep the community intact than it is to break ground someplace else and build a new one.

From Janesville we made a quick flight to Green Bay for a community rally in the Little Chute High School gym, and then on to a big rally in Milwaukee.

As we rolled up to the Wisconsin State Fair Park Exposition Center, Flo Milli was performing to a high-energy crowd of more than twelve thousand people. Most of them were on their feet, dancing, screaming, cheering. Earlier they'd heard from actor-comedian Keegan-Michael Key, who'd likened the choice between me and Trump to a choice of how to get from Canada to the United States: "Take the train to get over the border, or you can take a barrel over Niagara Falls."

I was lucky to have on my team Kelsey Smith, who worked closely with my advance, media, and political teams to make sure the schedules they proposed for each day were actually something that was logistically—and humanly—possible.

On Kelsey's carefully constructed schedule it showed I would have a minute to myself to make some calls and read through important briefing papers before going onstage right after Grammy winner Cardi B. But Kirsten informed me that JOD had scheduled a last-minute interview with Doctor Mike, a podcaster. "Don't worry," Kirsten said. "Won't take long. It's just a brief thing on the RFK appointment."

The campaign in Wilmington tended to choose my interviewers on various subjects by asking, Who has the biggest audience, the widest reach? But it was up to my team, who knew I insisted on being well prepped, to inquire into the style of the show, the nature of the interviews the host did, the areas of likely questioning. Then they'd give me a briefing sheet so I could knock it out of the park. But that hadn't happened this time.

They ushered me into a room where the Zoom was set up on a laptop. Doctor Mike was all ready to go. He launched into his introduction. "Welcome to the *Checkup* podcast where today I have the pleasure of speaking to Vice President Kamala Harris. I was curious to know her plans surrounding health care costs. Anti-science rhetoric.

Barriers to primary care. Women's health. And the risks children face while eating overly processed foods for lunch."

WTF?! This is clearly NOT "a brief thing on RFK."

Doctor Mike was deeply knowledgeable, warmed up on all these issues, and raring to go. As I would have been, had I not just been ambushed by an unscheduled in-depth interview, with no notice, at the end of a nineteen-hour day. I slid a scribbled note across the table: *Where's my briefing?* The staff looked at each other. They had nothing.

When Doctor Mike asked, "Are you getting your seven to nine hours of sleep these days?" I didn't know whether to laugh or cry.

At the end of the interview, I sent the junior staffers out, leaving just Kirsten, Brian, Ike, and Sheila.

"What *the fuck* was that?" I said, my voice reaching a crescendo.

Brian, trying to channel JOD's thinking, launched into a detailed explanation about the rationale behind doing the podcast. I raised my hand and stopped him midsentence.

"Brian," I said through gritted teeth, "that was a *rhetorical* question."

Unbeknownst to me, for the next few days, any time any of those team members asked each other anything at all, "That was a *rhetorical* question" would be the lighthearted response.

Cardi B was delivering her speech by then. When a technical glitch caused her teleprompter to fail, she bravely called for her cell phone so she could read the heartfelt speech she'd written. "I took my time writing this speech, so I'm gonna make sure I deliver it right," she said, determined. She was so genuine and passionate as she spoke about being underestimated and, as a woman, having to have twice the talent and work twice as hard, only to be questioned when she got to the top as to what she'd done to get there. I know many women can relate to that.

She said she'd learned to stand up to bullies and took Trump to task for his creepy remark that he would protect women whether they liked it or not. "If his definition of protection is not the freedom of choice, if his definition of protection is making sure our daughters have fewer rights than our mothers, then I don't want it."

———

For security reasons, the hotels where we stay are never named on the schedule. It is referred to as the RON—short for "rest overnight." After the rally, I was very much looking forward to my overnight rest. That day had started for me in Vegas at the local time equivalent of three a.m.

We reached the RON at 10:11 p.m. Central Daylight Time. In the motorcade, I'd notice that my hands were scratched up from people enthusiastically grabbing them on rope lines. My feet ached. I couldn't wait to get out of my high heels, sink into a hot bath, and sip a cup of chamomile tea.

At 10:29 p.m. CDT, we finally had a lid.

3 Days to the Election

* * *

The *Des Moines Register* released a poll saying we were up, 47 to 44. Sheila, for one, didn't believe it. "We're *not* winning in Iowa," she said. But since the polling firm, Selzer & Company, was one of the most reputable, she suspected it *was* picking up something positive for us: perhaps a shift in the votes of suburban women, or perhaps Republican women moving to our corner. In Nevada, Jon Ralston, considered an election oracle in his state, predicted we would squeak to victory in that tight race.

Some supporters became unreasonably euphoric. They wanted to believe these predictions, thinking that a shift in a conservative state such as Iowa might signal the chance of a landslide elsewhere.

I was probably the most skeptical. In my first race for DA, I initially polled at 6 percent. If I'd listened to pollsters then, I never would have run for office.

Most polls showed us still stuck in a virtual dead heat. In six of the seven swing states, polls had Trump and me within a point of each other, me with the slightest of advantages in Pennsylvania, Wisconsin, and Michigan; Trump with a similar razor-thin margin in Nevada, Georgia, and North Carolina. He was up 3 points in Arizona.

The *New York Times'* chief political analyst, Nate Cohn, said it was "one of the tightest races in the history of American politics."

I wasn't leaving a thing to chance. I would visit five states in twenty-four hours. Meanwhile, in Oregon, ballot drop boxes had been set on fire and the National Guard put on standby, as it had been in Washington and Nevada, as a precaution against election unrest. In Washington, DC, police were on alert.

Trump did this to us. His baseless claims of voter fraud, claims that had been tested and found worthless in every court case—more than sixty of them—riled up people. It was no wonder states were nervous, given Trump's statement that there would be "a bloodbath" if I won.

Still, as I faced the press in Milwaukee that morning, I felt good about the race. When one of the reporters accidentally addressed me as "Madam President," I quipped, "Not for three days!"

I had events that day in two of the states where we were slightly lagging Trump: Georgia and North Carolina. Twelve thousand people had come to a big outdoor rally in the parking lot of the Atlanta Civic Center. Spike Lee had already addressed the crowd as we arrived. I had to keep interrupting my speech to call for medics as I saw people fainting from the heat.

Ike, my senior policy adviser, almost required a medic himself. Because I couldn't get all the way home to California to cast my ballot in person, like 71.5 million Americans, I planned to vote by mail. There were important initiatives on the California ballot, and I had snatched time here and there to study and consider them carefully. I'd finally made my decisions and marked the ballot, but I didn't want to take any chances on it not getting to the county clerk on time.

Ike located a FedEx office three blocks from the rally parking lot and said he would run it over there while I was giving my speech. They turned out to be three very long blocks. Poor Ike had twenty minutes to run a half mile there and a half mile back in Atlanta's soupy humidity. Aides live in fear of being left behind by the motorcade.

There's no way to catch up, especially on a five-state day. As I came off the stage, I saw Ike, breathless, sweaty, on his last legs.

"You don't look so good!" He probably didn't need me to tell him that.

We arrived in Charlotte to find ourselves sharing the tarmac with Trump's plane. That's how it is in battleground states the last few days of a campaign: you're always tripping over your opponent.

Trump's rally was in Greensboro. I'm not sure why it bothered him so much—it was futile to try to get inside his head—but for some reason, he hated the fact that I'd worked at McDonald's and repeatedly claimed I'd lied about it. When he made the claim again in Greensboro—"She never worked there"—someone in the crowd shouted, "She worked on a corner." Trump loved that. He laughed and pointed to the guy, encouraging the audience to cheer him. "This place is amazing!" Show him a gutter and he crawled right into it.

Meanwhile, I was onstage in Charlotte with a man who seeks to lift people up. The Jon Bon Jovi Soul Foundation has been building affordable housing and providing food in the rock star's Soul Kitchens since 2006. I was proud to have his support. As he performed his hits "The People's House" and "Livin' on a Prayer," it was a case of life imitating art. Bon Jovi appeared as himself in season seven of *The West Wing*, singing at a rally for the fictional Democratic candidate Matt Santos. In the series, Santos wins, so I took it as a good omen.

I was supposed to stay onstage after my speech. Jon would come back, and we'd acknowledge applause together. But at this point in the campaign, I was on autopilot. I finished talking and sprinted offstage to greet the crowd as I usually did, shaking hands. Halfway down the rope line I realized I'd left Jon to go onstage alone. *OMG*, I thought, *I just abandoned Bon Jovi.*

My schedule said we were heading directly from Charlotte to overnight in Detroit. We would still overnight in Detroit, but I had something to do first. The press had not been informed of the change in our itinerary and were surprised as the plane touched down at LaGuardia Airport.

They were waiting in their usual spot under the wing, and as I came down the plane's front steps, they yelled out to me, "Why are we in New York?"

It took everything I had to not shout back:

It's Saturday night!

By the time we rolled down Fifty-Third Street and turned south toward Rockefeller Center, they had worked it out.

I was doing the cold open with Maya Rudolph, who's played me on *Saturday Night Live* since 2019. In my interview with Howard Stern, he'd said, quite sweetly, that he couldn't stand to watch the *SNL* sketches, that it pained him to see me being made fun of. I don't feel that way. I think it's healthy to laugh, especially at yourself, and I think Maya is an incredibly talented artist who puts a lot of work into her impersonations.

I had just a couple of minutes to rehearse with Maya before they let the audience into that small, intimate studio.

Just offstage, a burly stagehand held up a large panel, positioned to hide me from the audience as I came onto the set. There was a tremendous cheer when I suddenly appeared in the "mirror" as Rudolph's reflection. (Lorne Michaels later told me it was some of the loudest applause he'd ever heard.)

At the close of the sketch, we stood up and hugged as Rudolph said, "I'm gonna vote for us."

"Great!" I replied. "Any chance you are registered in Pennsylvania?"

We'd been through a couple of script revisions in which, for secrecy's sake, I was identified only as "SPECIAL GUEST."

A gag that didn't make the final version:

Maya Rudolph: I will be a president for all Americans.

Special Guest: Even Donald Trump?

Maya Rudolph: Even Donald Trump—whether he likes it or not.

2 Days to the Election

* * *

When I woke up in Detroit that Sunday morning, I joined the worship at Greater Emmanuel Institutional Church of God in Christ, a congregation with a century-long history of social justice advocacy.

This Motown church has an extraordinary choir. My sister Maya and I used to sing in the children's choir at Twenty-Third Avenue Church of God in Oakland, but we never sounded like this. Except, maybe, in our own minds.

Honored to speak to that storied congregation, I spoke of our loving God who has called on us to defend the poor and the needy, to grow weary in doing good. After 105 days of nonstop campaigning, the word "weary" had a whole new meaning.

I talked about the message of God to the prophet Jeremiah: "I know the plans I have for you . . . not for disaster, to give you a future and a hope."

I urged the church to consider God's plans for healing and bringing us together as a nation, and to make them real in our works. "In these next two days, we will be tested. These days will demand everything we've got . . . In times of uncertainty, we are reminded, 'weeping may endure for a night, but joy cometh in the morning.'"

It is a beautiful Scripture. I believe in the truth of it, though anyone who has endured deep grief understands that it is a metaphor, that the night can be very long.

That Sunday, I still believed our campaign of joy would triumph in two days.

1 Day to the Election

* * *

The final day, and we would spend it barnstorming Pennsylvania. We took off from Detroit to our first stop in Scranton. As soon as we boarded, I headed down to the back for my usual off-the-record chat in the press cabin.

"What are you most proud of?" one reporter asked me.

"My team," I said without hesitation. They had put their lives on hold. For 106 days, they'd barely seen their families or slept in their own beds. They'd worked inhuman hours, living on this plane and in anonymous hotel rooms. They'd been positive and loyal and ready to laugh. No job had been too big, no job had been too small.

They were all of them accomplished people, top of their field in communications, politics, or policy. They had offered me their talents and their skills, but they'd also pitched in and done the unglamorous tasks, taking care of whatever was needed in the moment, whether it was in their job description or not. I loved them. And I was grateful.

In Scranton we met with campaign volunteers who would be canvassing through the election. In Allentown, rapper Fat Joe, who did so much campaigning for us, asked the heavily Hispanic crowd, "Where's the *orgullo*? Where's the pride?"

In Reading, Alexandria Ocasio-Cortez joined us at a tiny Puerto

Rican restaurant for delicious cassava and rice. AOC goes deep into policy but has a lightness with people, a joyful-warrior vibe, and the people in this restaurant clearly loved her. Her talent for deconstructing complex issues and her commitment to getting justice for working people make her an invaluable leader in this moment.

And then I got to go door knocking. Two doors. Of course, at this point, it was performative, with my advance and the Secret Service fully aware of who was behind those doors, but I love what it represented.

When I was first running for DA in 2004, I used an ironing board as a standing desk with a sign duct-taped to it saying KAMALA HARRIS—A VOICE FOR JUSTICE. I would set up at the entrance to the local supermarket and call out to shoppers: "I hope to have your support." That moment, the direct ask, from a candidate to a voter who has the right to decide, remains magical to me.

We invaded a quiet residential street trailed by a horde of reporters. At the first house, I met a young man with the same name as our son, Cole, and at the second, a woman who greeted me with a hug and the excellent news that she'd already voted for me.

In Pittsburgh, we rallied with fifteen thousand at Carrie Furnace, a national historic landmark and remnant of U.S. Steel's massive Homestead works. Even though steel production stopped in 1982, it has become a symbol of resilience: a place to learn about steelworkers and their culture, and to gain new skills in workshops that range from metal casting and blacksmithing to art and photography.

Everywhere we went, the events were vibrant. But the day was filled with unnecessary tensions for me, the staff, and the crowds. On this day, the number of magnetometers available was wildly insufficient for the size of the crowd waiting to be admitted. At one venue, we had to hold the motorcade because a suspicious drone was in the airspace. We had no way of knowing if these lapses were just unfortunate mistakes or partisan mischief.

We left as Katy Perry took the stage and arrived at our last rally in Philadelphia as Lady Gaga sat down at her piano to sing "God Bless

America." There were thirty thousand people—thousands of them clustered on the Rocky Steps of the Philadelphia Museum of Art, and several thousand more facing the stage. I told them that Pennsylvania would decide the outcome of the election.

In that moment, I was able to say with complete conviction:

"We finish as we started: with optimism, with energy, with joy."

Election Day

* * *

E lection Day began as I stepped into the motorcade in Philadelphia
at midnight.

At the airport, I climbed the stairs to Air Force Two with Amara
holding one hand and Leela the other. It was a very late night for two
little girls. But they had been there 107 days earlier when my race
started, and they'd be with me at the end. The vice president's residence would once again be full of family as it had been on that Sunday
afternoon. We'd come full circle.

Maya and Tony, Meena and Nik and the girls would spend the
night. Kerstin Emhoff, Cole and his wife, Greenley, would join us in
the morning, Ella in the afternoon. Chrisette Hudlin and her family
would also be there, along with Doug's brother, Andy, and his wife,
Judy, and their kids.

I got a couple of hours' sleep before Kirsten arrived at the crack of
dawn to help me wrangle numerous drive time radio call-ins.

Doug and Tony headed off to do Election Day campaigning in Michigan. In the afternoon I dropped in to the DNC to thank the volunteers
working the phone banks. I brought them a big box of my favorite Doritos. While I was there, I grabbed a phone and made a couple of calls:

"Hi, it's Kamala Harris, have you voted yet? You have? Thank you!"

To an eight-year-old kid who picked up: "Waiting for you to grow ten years more."

And then I returned to the residence to do the most difficult work of all: nothing. After running so hard, I'd almost forgotten how to stop.

Every morning during the campaign, Bishop Leah Daughtry, a pastor I've known for twenty years, would send me a meditation. That day, the meditation was titled, simply, "Stand." The reflections she'd prepared were perfect for me in that moment:

"There comes a point when you've done all you can do. When your work has been completed . . . That's when you just stand. Stand believing and knowing that you've done your part. Stand in the strength given to you by God."

We'd rearranged the residence, moving the table out of the entry foyer and pulling in sofas and a big TV. In the dining room we'd set up three round tables for a family dinner.

There were two other centers of gravity that night. JOD, David Plouffe, and Brian Fallon had set up a boiler room in a series of interconnecting ballrooms at the downtown Marriott. There, they had our staff of election analytics experts, tasked with comparing our voter modeling with the numbers actually coming in from polling booths.

At the Conrad hotel, a party was underway for our friends, big donors, and campaign luminaries such as Cedric Richmond. Later, they'd be bused over to Howard University for the speech I fully expected to give there. We expected one of two things: a victory speech in the early hours, or, if it was too close to call, an optimistic holding statement.

The residence was straining at the seams. Storm had wrangled staff to be on standby to drive family members to Howard. My core team—Adam, Ike, Lorraine, Kirsten, and Sheila—were crammed into office space meant for two people, polishing sets of remarks and adjusting them as required. They worked quietly as family members swirled around the house in high spirits.

When my family and friends sat down to dinner, Storm was strict: she would be the only staffer who would enter that room. She wanted to protect this time for me, a short period that night that was not public, not political, just a private respite.

While we consumed a supper of baba ghanoush, dolmas, hummus, and shish taouk, my team took the chance to head out to Cactus Cantina, a restaurant near the Washington National Cathedral. A family place, it had the advantage of being out of the way of the Capitol Hill–K Street crowd who'd know who they were and would be scrutinizing them on that suspenseful night.

Doug and Tony arrived back from their Election Day swing. They'd headed to the Detroit suburbs, dropping in on coffee shops and local diners, doing press interviews. Tony's account of their day sounded great to me. If Doug seemed distracted, I put it down to the heightened emotions of the evening.

It says a lot about how traumatized we both were by what happened that night that Doug and I never discussed it with each other until I sat down to write this book.

I had no idea that Doug was carrying a heavy weight when he walked back into the residence. He'd left that morning thinking we were going to win. Not *probably* going to win. That we *would* win. His confidence had only been reinforced during the day by the enthusiasm of the voters he encountered and intel he and Tony received from the teams running our ground game. They reported that turnout seemed to be flowing just as we hoped. On the flight back to DC, their spirits were high.

Then Tony received a text from a friend in the Fox News war room. It did not start well. *Being at Fox today is brutal.* The text went on to say that the decision desk was predicting a Trump sweep in North Carolina, Georgia, and Arizona, and that the poor early showing by my supporters in Pennsylvania had the state leaning toward Trump.

Fox has an exceptional election desk. They were, after all, the ones who accurately called Arizona for Biden long before anyone else had the data to do so.

Robert Wolf, former CEO of UBS in the United States, is a frequent contributor on Fox News and Fox Business. He's also a staunch Democrat who had advised Hillary and Barack. I'd met him years earlier at a Young Democrats of America event when I was elected DA. We're friends; he and Tony are close. He was tasked with being on camera after three p.m. that day and wanted to know if Tony had info from our side that countered the Fox desk's narrative.

Tony texted back that Detroit was overperforming and gave him the turnout figures, including higher Puerto Rican turnout than expected, and of that increased turnout, we were getting more of it than Trump was. The Georgia turnout also was running ahead of what we needed. He had been in North Carolina the day before and had positive reports from the campaign there as well.

Tony was unsettled but still confident. Doug, however, was dismayed.

At home, he went through the motions, mingling with our ebullient family, sitting down to dinner, raising a glass when I stood to thank everyone for all they'd done and all they'd sacrificed to get us to this night. He remembers none of it.

All he remembers is standing in the shower, freaking out, praying, hoping the Fox intel wasn't right.

At 9:15 p.m., I left the family, still enjoying a rowdy dinner, and went upstairs. I put on sweats to do my hair and makeup. The aubergine suit I planned to wear to Howard was pressed and ready on a hanger.

On my dresser was a handwritten note from Joe that he'd sent over the day before: *I could not have asked for a better partner and friend,* he wrote, *and can hardly wait to call you Madam President.* I smiled gratefully as I reread it.

The plan was to head to the university around 10:45 p.m. and be there when the last polls closed. If we couldn't yet claim victory, we would give a holding statement, an upbeat address saying, *Stay tuned, it looks good, we're still counting.*

Why were we feeling so confident in a race that had never shifted out of toss-up territory? We had been getting signals—objective information—from external sources. If we won in Nevada, as Ralston had predicted, that would be an indicator for other states where we were in an even better position. On the Friday before the election, the internal analytics team in the field had found we were winning by small margins in all the battlegrounds. And our final poll in Pennsylvania had us up 50 to 48—a big jump from the previous numbers.

We had plans for all kinds of contingencies—that Trump might win Pennsylvania and claim premature victory, that we might win narrowly and Trump's supporters would react with violent rejection of the result, that the count might drag on for days. We'd planned for everything, it seemed, except the actual result.

My team had come back from Cactus Cantina and were in constant touch with JOD's boiler room. They were getting snatches of info.

Turnout in Philly is better than expected.

Georgia not great.

Atlanta suburbs lagging.

Black votes are coming through in North Carolina. White votes are not.

North Carolina is gone.

Sherrod Brown has lost his Senate seat in Ohio.

Georgia is gone.

Okay, well, they were our toughest. It's going to have to be the Blue Wall.

Everyone was waiting for the word to go to Howard. When it looked like the family was getting ready, Kirsten went outside to get the waiting press pool into the van. Then the direction was contradicted: *Wait, we're not leaving yet.* She told the press to unload.

In the house, Chrisette shrugged off the jacket she'd just put on. *Oh well,* she thought, *it might not be decided tonight.* She poured more wine.

She had campaigned for me in four battleground states and had come to a certain conclusion: *America gets it, they love her, they understand who she is.*

Adam had worked up a holding statement and sent it over to the boiler room. They'd sent back an edited version. My team thought it was too bloodless. It didn't have a feel-good line. They wanted to pump it up a bit. The message was meant to be: *We expect to prevail, be patient, go home, rest up, but we've got this.*

Sheila sent that message and waited for what she thought would be a quick response. But minutes passed and nothing came back. She texted Brian: *What's taking so long?*

At the table in the boiler room, Brian read the draft aloud. Meg, the top analytics expert, grimaced.

Brian, surprised by her reaction, asked, "Is that line problematic?"

Meg replied that it could be contradicted within an hour of me saying it.

Brian recalls that it was the first time anyone had said, out loud, that it was more likely we would lose than we would win.

In the boiler room, the tone shifted.

If there was no likely path to victory, it didn't make sense for me to go out on the stage at Howard unless to concede, and it was too soon for that.

"If we can't insert this line she's asking for, we need to rethink."

Then JOD called Sheila.

"I'm recommending she not go to Howard."

They merged me in on the call to tell me. I was sitting on my bed, fighting off the first tendrils of alarm and apprehension. Some of my family had left for the party at the Conrad, to be my ambassadors there with donors and supporters. Kerstin, Ella, Cole and Greenley, Jasper and Arden, and the Hudlin kids—they had already left, anxious to join the celebratory crowd. The others were still downstairs, not yet grasping what was happening, still waiting for the word to depart for Howard.

Storm, who was the go-between, the only one moving from family to staff, had a sinking realization that things were going wrong. She'd ordered up champagne for the celebration, and specially decorated cupcakes. She quietly went to the kitchen and hid all signs of celebratory preparation. She painstakingly peeled icing that read "Madame President" off the top of each cupcake. Having converted them to innocuous comfort food, she sent them out, along with more wine, in case people needed it.

My team, desperately seeking privacy, decamped to Lorraine's car. Crammed into the small Audi hybrid, they took another call from JOD. Then JOD called me.

"I'm sorry, ma'am. I don't think you're going to get there."

"Oh my God. What's going to happen to our country?"

I could barely breathe.

"Should we fight this?"

"We're just not in the zone to ask."

I walked down the stairs in shock. Chrisette and Meena were the first people I saw, sitting together on the couch. I looked at them, slowly shook my head.

They had been with me in every campaign, and we had never experienced a loss. They both started to cry. Nik, sensing the tension, gathered up Amara and Leela and took them to their bedroom.

All I could do was repeat, over and over, "My God, my God, what will happen to our country?"

I found Tony and Maya. "JOD says we are going to lose. We need to concede."

"Let's wait," said Tony. "We need to know if there are concerns, complaints. If people were able to vote." He went off to call Karen Dunn and our election lawyer, Marc Elias. The answer: nothing actionable.

We would have to send the people at Howard home. But the person to do that could not be me. We decided on Cedric Richmond, the campaign cochair, and scrambled to find him.

Maya, stoic but exhausted, retreated to the pool house. Tony stayed by the TV, watching the count in disbelief.

At 12:45 a.m., Cedric Richmond walked out onto the stage that had been built for me at Howard. The stage stood on the Yard, the tree-lined, grassy expanse flanked by the Founders Library and Frederick Douglass Memorial Hall—storied places where strategies were formulated for *Brown v. Board of Education* and other landmarks in our nation's history. Cedric strode to the podium with head held high and addressed the crowd in a resonant voice that betrayed nothing of the abject disappointment and pain he was feeling.

"Thank you for believing in the promise of America," he said. "We still have votes to count. We still have states that have not been called yet. We will continue overnight to fight to make sure that every vote is counted, that every voice has spoken, so you won't hear from the vice president tonight." A groan, like a breaking wave, moved through the crowd. "But you will hear from her tomorrow. She will be back here tomorrow to address not only the HU family, not only to address her supporters, but to address the nation."

Although his tone was upbeat, everyone there understood what had happened. That beautiful crowd turned as if it were a single organism. They walked out of the brightness of the Yard and melted away into the darkness.

Dazed, I went back upstairs to my room. Through the wall, I could hear Amara and Leela crying.

My mind was doing crazy things.

We can still do something about this! It hasn't happened!

Tom Brady recounted an identical insanity after he and the Patriots lost the 2008 Super Bowl to the Giants in what would have been a perfect season: "I absolutely believed 100 percent that we were going to win and it was just devastating. I couldn't speak for the rest of the night. I just remember waking up the next morning and I thought, 'That's a nightmare. That's a nightmare. That game didn't happen.'"

This was no football game. This was our country. Our democracy. Our freedom. And my mind simply would not allow me to believe that we had lost.

The Day After the Election

* * *

I woke from a brief, fitful sleep, still unable to believe what had happened. My mind tumbled through impossible scenarios:

It's not true.

If it's true, how can we fix it?

What if we do this?

Could we do that?

I was ashamed to realize I was in the denial and bargaining stages of grief, a very long way from acceptance. I could objectively diagnose what I was experiencing. I had no cure for it.

But for our democracy, for my dignity, and for the more than seventy-five million who had supported and believed in our vision for the country, I had to get past my personal mental turmoil and do my job.

And part of that was restoring the norms of a peaceful transfer of power that Trump had flouted. I asked Sheila to set up the concession phone call—the call that Trump had never made to Joe Biden.

It was a fair election, I said, and I told him I planned to speak about that in the afternoon. I promised that the president and I would help on the transition, "and of course we will facilitate a peaceful transfer of power."

I thanked him for his call for unity. "I do hope you will be a president for all Americans. I think the country really needs their president to bring us together, and I hope you will do that." I knew, even as I was saying it, that it would turn out to be a vain hope.

Trump was effusive and magnanimous in the glow of his win. "I am going to be so nice and respectful," he said. "You are a tough, smart customer, and I say that with great respect. And you also have a beautiful name. I got use of that name, it's Kamala."

For once, he pronounced it correctly.

Adam Frankel had spent the night drafting a concession speech. I paged through it, barely able to focus on the words. I called Adam. It might be easier, I thought, to talk it through.

"How are you doing, ma'am?"

It wasn't the moment to wallow in my feelings. We could do that later. Right now, I told him, "We have to get through this speech."

In the early afternoon, the team gathered once again in the library. Pale, haggard faces. Tired eyes. I walked in and gave everyone a hug and thanked them. Then we got to work.

Crowds had already begun to gather at Howard. But the speech didn't feel right.

"Let's take a step back from this draft," I said. "What do we really want to say?" I hadn't watched or read the news. "How are people— how is the country—feeling?"

"Sad."

"Resigned."

Kirsten: "There's a range of feelings: sad, angry, disappointed, dismayed . . ."

Then, monotone, from JOD:

"Gutted."

Somehow, her one evocative, entirely apt word broke the desolate mood, and we all laughed.

"Well, we're not going to have a pity party. I'm not going to get up there and cry. I am proud of the race we ran and the way we ran it."

But this wasn't just any election. I had argued throughout the campaign that the stakes in this race were exceptionally high. I needed to find a way to motivate people—especially young people—to stay in this fight. I wanted to communicate that the stakes were still high. We did something, we had accomplished something, that we could not, just in one night, lose.

We had said it, chanted it, shouted it at every single rally:

When we fight, we win.

"There were all these families at those rallies, all those children. I can't just say *you win some, you lose some.* That's not what this has been about. We need to find a way to reconcile what they heard me say and what they chanted back with the reality we're facing today.

"Sometimes the fight takes a while. That doesn't mean that we won't win."

And there it was, the heart of my concession speech. While I would concede this election, while I would engage in the peaceful transfer of power that distinguishes democracy from monarchy or tyranny, I would *not* concede the fight that fueled my campaign.

Adam did a time check: the motorcade was set to depart in thirty minutes. I went upstairs and finally took that aubergine suit off its hanger. I ran through the draft of the speech in my head.

There was still something I needed to fix. Something not right.

On my way down to the cars, I saw Kirsten and Adam huddled over a laptop in the sunroom, putting in final edits.

"Take out the Trump language," I said. "It feels bitter."

There had been a section in the speech about the rollback of our rights and freedoms, but I'd said all that already. I'd prosecuted the case. The election was over. Going after Trump was not the work of this day. This day was about lifting our supporters.

Outside, the motorcade was loaded and waiting, but I needed to get this right. I told Adam the changes I needed. We sent half the speech to be loaded in the teleprompter and set up Adam with a secure hot spot so that he could work on the second half and send it from the car.

———

In the holding room at Howard, the immediate family had gathered. Then the Walz family arrived.

Tim said simply, "I'm sorry."

His daughter, Hope, was distraught. Sobbing. I put my arms around her. "We are not defeated," I said softly. "Our spirit is not defeated. There's so much in your future, so much to fight for."

At 4:24 p.m., to the percussive beat of the Howard marching band, I made the long walk down the blue-carpeted stage we had built out into the midst of that cheering, weeping crowd. Archbishop Óscar Romero once said, "There are many things that can only be seen through eyes that have cried."

In that sea of faces, four rows back, I recognized my auntie Lenore, my mother's best friend when they were students together at Berkeley, two young idealists, fighting for civil rights. She had navigated the big crowd, unannounced, not to sit in the VIP section, just to stand there, to smile at me, to say, *It's going to be okay, and I'm proud of you, and I'm here.*

On that day, my task was to show everyone, especially the young people, that as hurt and traumatized as we felt, we would not retreat from the fight.

It might take a while.

But the fight for our country is always worth it.

And we *will* win.

Certification Day

* * *

Half a foot of snow had fallen during the night. It was still drifting down as we drove through the gates of the Naval Observatory. The ride to the Capitol was slow through the icy streets.

During the campaign, I had become used to roadsides lined with waving crowds. This was not that kind of day. Today, as the wipers swished and thumped against the snowy windshield, I looked out onto deserted sidewalks.

With me in the car was Max, the head of my Secret Service detail. Four years earlier, this same veteran agent had hustled Mike Pence to safety when a mob threatening his life stormed the Capitol on January 6, 2021.

Sitting silently by myself in the back of the car, I recalled that day. I was a US senator and vice president–elect. I'd woken early in my DC apartment and headed to a SCIF for a Senate Intelligence Committee hearing on the current world hot spots. Then I'd gone to the DNC office to make some political calls thanking supporters. Just after 1:00 p.m., I was still there, working with an aide, when Secret Service agents burst in.

"We need to leave. Now."

I had been in this business long enough that when the agents say move, you do not ask questions. You go. I learned later that a pipe bomb had been found outside the DNC headquarters, mere feet from where I sat.

I spent the rest of that day in a secure location, following the news with disbelief, trying to reach my colleagues in the Senate and the House. Rioters bashed police, smashed windows, and carried a Confederate flag through the halls of the Capitol. They defecated and urinated in the offices.

At the White House, President Trump watched the violence on Fox News and did nothing to stop it.

Later that night, when the People's House had been cleared and secured at last, I walked through the vandalized halls to take my seat on the floor of the Senate. Mike Pence certified the election of Joe Biden as president at 3:40 a.m.

Now, as vice president and president of the Senate, it was my duty to preside over the certification of Donald Trump's election. I am one of only three vice presidents who have been in the position of certifying the victory of their opponent. The others were Richard Nixon to John F. Kennedy, and Al Gore to George W. Bush. Hubert Humphrey refused and left it to the Senate president pro tempore to certify his loss to Nixon.

Donald Trump had done everything he could to subvert an election, stand in the way of the peaceful transfer of power, and deny the will of the people.

I was there to keep my oath to protect and defend the Constitution. I would uphold the rule of law.

As I walked into that chamber, I knew that the eyes of the world were on me. I would have to muster the strength to override my internal emotional storm. As vice president *and* as Kamala Devi Harris, I had to call on every ounce of poise and self-discipline I possessed. I owed it to myself and to the nation to demonstrate what I believed: that this moment was bigger than any one individual.

I stood in front of the tall chair behind the dais, facing the full chamber of the Senate and the House. Each state read the number of electoral votes for Donald Trump and the number of votes for Kamala Harris. When they finished, I recited the necessary words.

"The state of the vote for the president of the United States as delivered to the president of the Senate is as follows: The whole number of the electors appointed to vote for president of the United States is 538. Within that whole number, the majority is 270. The votes for president of the United States are as follows. Donald J. Trump of the state of Florida has received 312 votes."

The Republican side of the room cheered. I waited, hands folded. When the applause subsided, I continued. "Kamala D. Harris of the state of California has received 226 votes."

It was one of the most difficult things I have ever done. I stood there and did my duty for democracy. And that day, democracy stood.

As I finished speaking, both sides of the aisle rose and applauded, as one.

Afterword

* * *

In the midst of half-filled packing boxes at the vice president's residence, Doug and I sat in silence in front of the television, watching LA burn.

I had seven more days as vice president of the United States, and I was spending them in FEMA briefings, making sure my home state had all the support we could give. Still, Doug and I felt powerless as we watched walls of flame, driven by searing hundred-mile-an-hour winds, incinerating familiar neighborhoods. A mandatory evacuation of our neighborhood had been called three days earlier. Kerstin Emhoff phoned me and offered to rush to our house to gather whatever few precious photographs and keepsakes I could describe to her.

As we sat three thousand miles away, a chyron crawled across the bottom of the screen: "Kamala Harris's house is now in the path of the fire."

In seven days, I was supposed to climb the steps for my final flight on Air Force Two. The plane was supposed to take me home. But now it looked like we might not have a home to go to.

We lived with that uncertainty until the day before we were to leave. The direction of the fire changed, sparing our immediate neighborhood, and on January 19 the evacuation order was finally lifted.

On the afternoon of January 20, Doug and I took off from Joint Base Andrews. As I was heading to the base, I learned that the Air Force had decided to give me an all-women crew, the first time in history for this type of plane.

We went straight from LAX to Altadena. World Central Kitchen had set up at Gordy's Garage, so we helped distribute meals alongside other volunteers, many of whom, as so often, had suffered losses themselves.

One woman looked at me sadly as I handed her a meal. "I really wish you weren't here," she said.

Almost a year before the election, Doug and I had planned to take a brief vacation to Hawaii. A crisis blew up, and I needed to stay in the West Wing. We'd paid the rent for the house and couldn't get a refund, but the owners said they'd give us till the end of the year to use it.

After election night, DC felt unbearable. Numb and grieving, we were in no condition to organize a trip, but then we remembered that house near Mauna Kea.

"Let's go now," Doug said. "Let's get out of here."

Lorraine and my other team members made it happen. This was not like going on vacation. It was reaching for the oxygen mask that had dropped from the ceiling. In that house, at that distance, we started a process that is still continuing.

Two of the trending searches after the election:
What is a tariff?
Can I change my vote?

Gore Vidal called them "the four most beautiful words in our common language":
"I told you so."

I disagree, I don't think they're beautiful, and I wish I had no cause to say them.

Tariffs *are* a tax on everyday Americans. We *are* at risk of a recession.

The marines, war-fighting warriors, have been deployed in our streets against civilians.

The authoritarian, nationalist Project 2025 *is* the blueprint for the Trump administration's second term. As of this writing, of its 316 objectives, 114 have been fully realized and 64 more are already in progress.

The Justice Department is going after Trump's enemies list, while Trump supporters have been pardoned and released: January 6 rioters who attacked police, the fentanyl dealer Ross Ulbricht, numerous tax cheats.

Foreign leaders *have* played him with flattery, grift, and favor. A luxury jet, or a Trojan horse?

He has lined his own pockets and enriched billionaires while doing nothing for the middle class and worsening the condition of the poor.

The destruction of scientific research aimed at fighting our worst diseases and the climate crisis, the targeting of SNAP, Medicaid, and programs for our veterans, the deterioration of our global friendships, the terrorizing of our immigrant communities, the starvation and sickening of millions around the world for lack of foreign aid, the reckless abandonment of clean energy, the rollback of environmental protections, the attack on intellectual freedom in our universities, the bullying of law firms, the breathtaking corruption. I could go on.

Trump says he has a mandate for these things. He does not.

His victory was whisker-thin. He beat me by 1.5 percentage points in one of the closest elections in a century. A third of the electorate voted for me. But a third of the electorate stayed home. That means two-thirds of our country did not elect Donald Trump.

Two-thirds of us did not choose this man or his agenda.

That's why I have no patience for anyone saying, *I'm giving up on America because America wanted this.* We did not. Of the third that voted for Trump, a good part of them voted for him on promises unkept.

He did not "immediately bring prices down starting day one." Instead, the opposite. He did not "cut energy prices in half within twelve months." He could not bring peace to Ukraine "before I even become president." Instead, he has acted as enabler to the aggressor and shamefully attacked a brave leader defending democracy.

I predicted all that. I warned of it. What I did not predict: the capitulation.

The billionaires lining up to grovel. The big media companies, the universities, and so many major law firms, all bending to blackmail and outrageous demands.

So what do we do?

The answer will not come out of Washington, DC. Their immediate task is to win the midterms and restore some checks and balances on this unchecked and unbalanced president.

What we the people must understand is that the dismantling of our democracy did not start with the 2024 election.

The right-wing and religious nationalists have played the long game, working for decades to take over state houses, gerrymander districts, and dominate local government boards. Their think tanks like the Federalist Society created the blueprint for stacking the Supreme Court, while the Heritage Foundation created Project 2025.

Their plans have been amplified by the rise of a right-wing media ecosystem built to operationalize their agenda through massive propaganda, misinformation, and disinformation. Trump was their vehicle, his road paved for him, years earlier, by a hot and pungent brew: Ronald Reagan's celebrity, Newt Gingrich's belligerent discourse, and Pat Buchanan's nativism.

Don't be duped into thinking it's all chaos. It may *feel* like chaos, but what we are witnessing is a high-velocity event, the swift implementation of an agenda that was written many decades ago.

"This is how fascism begins," warned Françoise Giroud, a journalist who served in the French Resistance. "It never says its name. It creeps, it floats. When it reaches the tips of people's noses, they say: 'Is this it? You think? Don't exaggerate!' And then one day it smacks them in the mouth, and it is too late to get rid of it."

It is not too late for us, but we need to think both strategically and tactically.

When we go to the streets, as we will, we must not give them the spectacle they are craving. We will go out of love of our country and belief in its promise. We cannot let them lie about that.

We need to come up with our own blueprint that sets out our alternative vision for our country. A blueprint on how we will lead a government that truly works for the American people.

There will have been so much damage done.

Perhaps so much damage that we will have to re-create our government. And that doesn't mean nostalgically reproducing what has been before, but something leaner, swifter, and much more efficient.

At the heart of my vision for the future is Gen Z. The youngest member of that cohort is thirteen now, the oldest is twenty-eight. In five years, the younger members will be about to vote, the oldest might be having kids.

They have lived through the pandemic, the resulting economic upheaval, the accelerating climate crisis, the increasingly toxic dominance of social media. And now they are living through Donald Trump's global tariff chaos, isolationism, and slashed safety net, including health coverage and food assistance.

Their generation is larger in number than the Boomers'. We need to invest in them. I'm talking about something on the scale of the investment that we made in the Greatest Generation. Initiatives such as the GI Bill allowed people to harness their potential, to realize their greatness. Since Ronald Reagan, we've systematically gutted Pell Grants, which once covered much of the cost of college for talented but low-income kids. These grants now cover less than a third, making them useless to the kids most in need.

The education we fund shouldn't focus only on college degrees but should equally value and uplift the trades and skills that build our homes, modernize our electric grid, improve our infrastructure, realize the clean energy transition.

As they enter the workforce, Gen Z is feeling the greatest impact as AI and robotics revolutionize industries. We will need to govern with vision so that the opportunities of the new era fall equally. It is a challenge of massive complexity. Gen Z needs access to an education that is supple enough to adapt to rapid change and that helps them move nimbly through those innovations.

This generation is the destiny of our country and the world.

These days, unemployed for the first time, I have literally been unpacking my life.

Folders of letters and emails sent to me, some by voters, some from people in distant countries, expressing gratitude for the campaign we ran and despair over the aftermath. Boxes of awards I received in elected office and before. Each engraved plaque or lead glass tchotchke reminds me of the work I have done, the people helped by it.

That's consoling. But it also brings up a swell of regret for all the work that I wanted to do.

By now, maybe, young people would be applying for their $25,000 housing down payment assistance. An increased child tax credit would be lifting thousands more families out of poverty. Medicare would be helping thousands of families and people in the sandwich generation to provide home care for their elderly loved ones. People in Africa would still have access to their AIDS medications. Our global friendships and our national reputation wouldn't be in tatters.

I can't help having these thoughts, when the daily barrage of bad news becomes overwhelming. But I'm not looking back.

Of all the advice and consolation I have received since the election, Minyon Moore's words have moved me: "God gave you a beautiful 107 days to reclaim who you are. You have been able to push back against the caricatures, all the vile and ugly things, and be yourself. You gave America your heart and soul. You gave it your all."

I did. And I'm not done.

When I decided to become a prosecutor, I had to defend that decision to my family, like a student defending a thesis. I asked why, when we seek change, must it either be by breaking down doors or crawling on bended knee? I wanted a seat at the table. I wanted to make change from inside the system.

Today I'm no longer sure about that. Because the system is failing us. At every level—executive, judicial, legislative, corporate, institutional, media—every single guardrail that is supposed to protect our democracy is buckling. I thought those guardrails would be stronger. I was wrong.

To keep people safe and help them thrive. That's what I've always worked for, and that work has never been more needed—when the government sends armed, masked men into churches and courthouses, when children are washed away in known flood zones starved of resources for adequate warning systems, when the Department of Education is torn apart and the hungry and sick are denied their basic needs.

In this critical moment, working within the system, by itself, is not proving to be enough.

I'll no longer sit in DC in the grandeur of the ceremonial office. I will be with the people, in towns and communities where I can listen to their ideas on how we rebuild trust, empathy, and a government worthy of the ideals of this country.

One hundred and seven days were not, in the end, long enough to accomplish the task of winning the presidency.

But we accomplished other things, as I learn every day.

This spring, Doug was winding up a business dinner when one of the restaurant staff, Myshay Causey, shyly handed him a menu, on the back of which she had written a note to me:

While I hope this message doesn't cross the line of professionalism (considering our meeting place) I couldn't pass up the opportunity to speak on the class act and inspiration you've been, especially to young Black girls like myself . . . handling adversity with a smile, a laugh, and levelheadedness. I hope to develop into someone similar one day and be someone of benefit to my community.

Three weeks later, I attended Myshay's graduation from Compton High. In the fall, she will be going to Cornell to study public policy, with an emphasis on education. She has already served as the student representative on the school board for the Compton Unified School District. A good start.

Sitting among the faculty, I looked out on the bright faces of the graduates, filling their new football stadium. Their proud parents, packing the stands. As Myshay walked across the stage and accepted her diploma, I felt real optimism for our country.

She had written that I inspired her.

That morning, she returned the gift.

Acknowledgments

I tend to be task-oriented and rarely allow myself enough space or time to reflect, and a marathon campaign run at a sprinter's pace leaves little time for reflection. This book is my effort to capture what I saw, experienced, and learned on the campaign. This experience was almost like living the campaign in reverse, which has not been easy.

Writing this book would have been a solitary effort if not for many crucial collaborators. Adam Frankel, who with skill, care, and grace helped me express my thoughts through many years and throughout the campaign was an early Sherpa on this book; and one of the greatest blessings of this book was that in the process of working with the amazing Geraldine Brooks, a new friendship developed. Her ferocious and brilliant artistic insights were indispensable. She has seen and lost so much, but despite her tough exterior still believes in the light.

It is nearly impossible to capture the thousands of people who poured their hearts and souls into this campaign—so many that they'd barely fit between the covers of this book. But I must start with those joyful and dedicated warriors who, on an early Sunday afternoon in July, dropped everything to arrive at my dining room, and for the following 106 days—every day—worked around the clock and by my side. Tony, Nik, Meena, Kirsten Allen, Juan Dromgoole, Brian Fallon, Storm Horncastle, Josh Hsu, Steven Kelly, Oliver Mittelstaedt, Sheila Nix, Opal Vadhan, Lorraine Voles, and Erin Wilson. You and your loved ones sacrificed so much, and I am forever grateful. I am especially grateful for the gift of photographer Lawrence Jackson, who could always be trusted to see my family and me in our most private and important moments, including that day. His artistic eye leaves a treasured account of this experience.

To our entire campaign team—the campaign chairs and advisory board, everyone in the Wilmington headquarters, the advance teams, the OVP team, state directors and staff, volunteers, interns, Air Force Two crew, military aides, NEAs, DNC staff, consultants, and vendors; and thank you always to the men and women of the United States Secret Service. To the Democratic members of the Senate and House, to the governors and mayors, thank you for your tireless campaigning wherever you were needed. Thank you also to members of the president's cabinet and many senior White House staff. Behind the scenes, I'm deeply grateful to Leslie Fremar, Jen Atkin, Nia Page, Marquia James, Dayna Fields, and Erika Vasquez. To all my friends and supporters, both long-standing and most recent, thank you for your prayers, for traveling, for volunteering, and for being wherever and whenever you were needed. And for always bringing me a hug or smile as our paths would cross.

To Tim Walz, thank you for joining me on this journey.

To Joe Biden, thank you for the honor to serve as your vice president.

This book would not have been possible without the support of a few particular folks who were not only integral to our campaign but who, while still recovering, in the writing of this book helped me recreate those hectic, joyful, and difficult 107 days. Sheila Nix, a road warrior with me on the trail for long days and nights, and now helping me navigate and figure out the afterward, always with a belief in what's possible. Kirsten Allen, wise beyond years, always with a sharp recall and invaluable strategic perspective. And Ike Irby, a brilliant thought partner who objectively offers me cherished advice. Thank you to Tony West, Meena Harris, Brian Fallon, Lorraine Voles, Minyon Moore, Erin Wilson, Storm Horncastle, Chrisette Hudlin, and Jen O'Malley Dillon for taking the time to share your personal memories of these 107 days. Maggie Murphy and Alexia Lewis for making the trains run (and stop!). Juan Dromgoole for, among everything else, acting as my tech savior, and Morgan Burke. From my core traveling team, first and foremost thank you Opal for predicting everything I needed and doing everything with special care. Thanks to campaign speechwriters Adam Frankel and Megan Rooney, to core traveling staff including Azza Cohen, Chris Evans, Andy Flick, Storm Horncastle, Lawrence Jackson, Steven Kelly, Alexia Lewis, Dean Lieberman, Rebecca Lissner, Jason Low, Oliver Mittelstaedt, Juan Ortega, Josh Orton, Josh Simmons, Erica Songer, Opal Vadhan, Saige Wenik, and Erin Wilson; to campaign leadership including Liz Allen, Nasrina Bargzie, Maca Casado, Stephanie Cutter, Jen O'Malley Dillon, Adrienne Elrod, Rob Flaherty, Quentin Fulks, Rufus Gifford, Ilan Goldenberg, Jasmine Harris, David Plouffe, Julie Chávez Rodriguez, Ian Sams, Michael Tyler, and Stephanie Young; to members of my debate prep team, including Sean Clegg, Colin Diersing, Karen Dunn, Phil Gordon, Rohini Kosoglu, Minyon Moore, Philippe Reines, Cedric Richmond, James Singer, and Jake Sullivan; to pollsters and media consultants, including Matt Barreto, David Binder, Geoff Garin, Ann Liston, Molly Murphy, Jefrey Pollock, Adrian Saenz, and Terrance Woodbury; to my core team in Washington, including Katie Prisco-Buxbaum, Andrea Colmenero, Kristin Bertolina Faust, Sergio Gonzales, Megan Jones, Rhyan Lake, John Monahan, Brian Nelson, Jalisa Washington-Price, and Stephanie Daily Smith; to campaign digital and photography, including Eric Elofson, Bexx Francois, Neeharika Simha, and Ilana Wurman; to amazing supporters of my campaign, including Yohannes Abraham, Brian Deese, Marcia Fudge, Greta Gerwig, Maya Harris, Eric Holder, Josh Hsu, Jeffrey Katzenberg, Dan Koh, Kristine Lucius, Jennifer Liu, Senator Catherine Cortez Masto, Carla Meyer, Deanne Millison, Dana Remus, Kelsey Smith, Marty Walsh, and Tony West; to the DNC, including Mary Beth Cahill, Colleen Coffey, Shelby Cole, Sam Cornale, Jaime Harrison, and Michael Pratt; to the SG Team, including Liza Acevedo, Alethea Harney, Jessica Killin, Kendall Krupkin, Jen Palmieri, and Veer Sawhney;

for great company on the plane, including Jobie Crawford, Isabel Keller, and Silas Woods III; to my current transition team, including Ana Patchin and Lauren Dent.

I'll be forever grateful and owe a special debt of gratitude to my dear friend Bryan Lourd, who from the beginning—and then on the morning of Day 108—believed in, convinced me of, and pointed out the importance of telling my story and writing this book. To all the others of the CAA crew: Thank you for shepherding me through the hard work of publishing this book, especially Craig Gering and Sloan Harris, and of course, David Larabell, Mollie Glick, Kate Childs-Jones, Zascha Fox, Khalil Roberts, and Jamie Stockton.

Thank you, Simon & Schuster. This book you hold came to pass because Jonathan Karp and Dawn Davis believed in its potential. I thank you two for that clandestine meeting and your encouragement that late winter afternoon in New York, and more important for your extraordinary acumen and care in handling this project throughout. Enormous thanks to all the folks at Simon & Schuster, including Jonathan Evans, Lewelin Polanco, Beth Maglione, Lauren Gomez, Olivia Perrault, Amanda Mulholland, Jackie Seow, Irene Kheradi, Julia Prosser, Stephen Bedford, Elisa Shokoff, Nancy Tan, Nurah Lambert, and Julie Tate.

Deep gratitude to Andrew Strelka and Jonathan West, and to my team at Latham & Watkins, who supported this undertaking from the beginning.

To my family, I know how much you each gave, and I know it wasn't easy. Thank you for always believing. And to my darling husband, Doug, even in the hardest times you helped me locate the gravity, priorities, and humor with bighearted support. Always.

And a deepest thank-you to the Americans who voted for me. Thank you for your enthusiasm in believing in what is possible, and please don't give up. Let us not throw up our hands; let's roll up our sleeves.

About the Author

Kamala D. Harris served as the forty-ninth vice president of the United States from 2021 to 2025—the first woman in American history to hold the office. She began her career in the Alameda County District Attorney's Office before being elected district attorney of San Francisco, where her Back on Track program became a national model for reducing recidivism. As California's attorney general, Harris prosecuted transnational gangs, big banks that defrauded homeowners, and for-profit colleges that targeted students and veterans. She defended the Affordable Care Act, fought for marriage equality, and pioneered the nation's first open-data initiative in the criminal justice system. In the United States Senate, Harris fought for civil, immigrant, and voting rights, and gained national recognition for her incisive questioning in committee hearings. As vice president, she led efforts to strengthen global alliances and address child poverty, gun violence, student debt, maternal health, economic opportunity, and reproductive rights—casting more tiebreaking votes than any vice president in history, including for pandemic relief and the largest climate investment ever. Throughout her career, she has always fought for the only client she has ever had: the people.

Closing argument at the Ellipse.